Chevrolet Inline-6 Engine
1929-1962
HOW TO REBUILD

Deve Krehbiel

CarTech®

CarTech®

CarTech®, Inc.
6118 Main Street
North Branch MN 55056
Phone: 651-277-1200 or 800-551-4754
Fax: 651-277-1203
www.cartechbooks.com

© 2018 by Deve Krehbiel

All rights reserved. No part of this publication may be reproduced or utilized in any form or by any means, electronic or mechanical, including photocopying, recording, or by any information storage and retrieval sys-tem, without prior permission from the Publisher. All text, photographs, and artwork are the property of the Author unless otherwise noted or credited.

The information in this work is true and complete to the best of our knowledge. However, all information is presented without any guaran-tee on the part of the Author or Publisher, who also disclaim any liability incurred in connection with the use of the information and any implied warranties of merchantability or fitness for a particular purpose. Readers are responsible for taking suitable and appropriate safety measures when performing any of the operations or activities described in this work.

All trademarks, trade names, model names and numbers, and other product designations referred to herein are the property of their respec-tive owners and are used solely for identification purposes. This work is a publication of CarTech, Inc., and has not been licensed, approved, sponsored, or endorsed by any other person or entity. The Publisher is not associated with any product, service, or vendor mentioned in this book, and does not endorse the products or services of any vendor men-tioned in this book.

Edit by Wes Eisenschenk
Layout by Hailey Samples
Cover Art Courtesy Mecum Auctions

ISBN 978-1-61325-839-2
Item No. SA455P

CarTech books may be purchased at a discounted rate in bulk for resale, events, corporate gifts, or educational purposes. Special editions may also be created to specification.
For details, contact Special Sales at 6118 Main Street, North Branch MN 55056 or by email at sales@cartechbooks.com.

CONTENTS

Dedication 4
Preface 5
Acknowledgments 6
Introduction 7

Chapter 1: Engine Identification 9
  Casting Numbers 9
  Serial Numbers 11
  Head Casting Numbers 11
  Visual Differences 11
  Engine Condition 13
  Is It a Rebuild Candidate? 15
  Organization Is Key 15

Chapter 2: Tools and Engine Cleaning 16
  Tools List 17
  General Cleaning Procedures 19

Chapter 3: The Head and Associated Parts 21
  Lifters 21
  Pushrods 22
  Rocker Assembly 23
  Head Machining Prep 25

Chapter 4: Engine and Sheet Metal Parts Preparation 27
  Bellhousing Disassembly 30
  Oil Pan 30
  Valve Cover 32
  Side Cover 32

Chapter 5: Engine Teardown 33
  Harmonic Balancer and Oil Pump Removal 33
  Dipstick Tube 34
  Timing Gear Cover 37
  Camshaft 38
  Crankshaft and Pistons 41
  Water Jacket 46

Chapter 6: Choosing a Machine Shop 47
  Preparing for Machine Shop Work 47
  Standard Shop Procedures 49

Chapter 7: While the Engine Is at the Shop 51

Chapter 8: Distributor 54
  Distributor Rebuild 54
  Vacuum Advance 57
  Ignition System 58
  Reluctor 59
  Wiring and Details 63
  High-Energy Ignition System 64

Chapter 9: Carburetor 70
  New-Style Carb to Old-Style Filter 70
  Rochester B Carb Disassembly 73
  Rochester B Carb Reassembly 76
  Fuel Delivery System 80

Chapter 10: Miscellaneous Important Details 89
  Intake/Exhaust Manifold Assembly 89
  Engine Sheet Metal Prep and Painting 91
  Flywheel Tips 91
  Starter Engagement 92
  Clutch Choices 93
  Water Pump Adapter 93
  Positive Crankcase Ventilation System 93
  Spin-On Oil Filter Adapter 94
  High-Energy Ignition 96
  Thermostat and Housing 96

Chapter 11: Post–Engine Shop Preparation 103
  Building an Inline-6 Engine Stand Adapter 103
  Cleaning and Prepping for Paint 106
  Final Machining Prior to Assembly 107

Chapter 12: Engine Assembly 108
  Crankshaft 108
  Timing Plate 110
  Camshaft 111
  Oil Seal 112
  Timing Cover and Harmonic Balancer 112
  Oil Pump and Pickup 113
  Pistons and Piston Rods 113
  Rings 115
  Pistons 115
  Oil Pan 117
  Head 117
  Intake and Exhaust Assembly 120
  Water Pump 120
  Carburetor 121
  Miscellaneous Attention to Detail 122
  Fuel Pump 122
  Valves 122
  Hard Lines 126
  Spark Plugs and Plug Wires 129
  Water and Oil 130
  Engine Break-In 131

Appendix 135
Resources 144

DEDICATION

The most memorable year for me was 1991 when I was honored to marry the woman of my dreams. My wife, Vietta, is a quiet, reserved wonder who has always supported me in every way, including stopping me from doing stupid things, helping me run a printing business for 28 years, and being there through it all. I am sure there are many of you who feel similarly about your spouse; however, my Vietta takes the prize. This woman helped me put the pieces of my life back together after divorce and helped raise my three children, now in their 30s, Kelly, Jesse, and Kasey. To my family, I love you.

ABOUT THE AUTHOR

Deve Krehbiel is a vintage Chevy pickup enthusiast who spends his free time writing how-to articles and designing add-on kits for vintage Chevy engines. Deve's Technical Network (DTN) was created to help bring other enthusiasts together to brainstorm ideas and solutions and to help everyone obtain a better understanding of this wonderful pastime. For every kit Deve creates, he makes sure to document how you can make that same kit yourself without any money changing hands. This honest approach has proven to work out better in the long run, providing for a happier clientele whom he refers to as his friends. Deve realizes the satisfaction of accomplishment and the feeling of pride when anyone tackles something that is hard and actually pulls it off! Check out www.devestechnet.com and let him know what you think.

PREFACE

The year was 1978. I was driving down a two-lane road near Waco, Texas, and I saw an old pickup with a tree growing through it. The farmer who owned it let me have it for $75. After much ado, I hitched it behind my 1973 Gremlin X and hauled it back home to Hesston, Kansas. I had no idea of the engine's condition, but the truck was in relatively good shape, considering. It was a 1954 Chevrolet 3100 pickup. The only remaining picture of it is with me in front of Airman Housing at Keesler Air Force Base, Mississippi, during my Air Force Technical School days.

I will never forget that truck. After a few parts changes, the engine started right up. The entire truck was mostly serviceable, and I used it all over the country. I drove that truck during Christmas break from Biloxi, Mississippi, to see my new wife at Kirtland Air Force Base in Albuquerque, New Mexico, 1,200 miles! No engine overhaul, no maintenance other than the usual (after removing the tree).

Even at the age of 20, I knew that Chevrolet made an outstanding product in the 6-cylinder Stovebolt engine. They are the most resilient engines that I have ever had the pleasure to work with. To this day, if you can find them, you can take a 1950s farm truck that hasn't been started in more than 40 years, free it up, start it, and run it most of the time without much trouble. Although my marriage didn't last, the old truck just kept right on!

That truck was my first foray into vehicle restoration, and I didn't do much with it, but years later I began new frame-up restorations focusing on 1950 Chevy pickups. I decided to write down every aspect of these restorations in careful detail and create a website so my experiences were documented for others. It is a labor of love, and it documents all the mistakes I made along the way and, more important, how to fix what is broken. One system after another, careful documentation, lots of pictures, and a deep desire to succeed drove my work.

As you use this book with your own project, be sure that you follow accepted safety procedures and clearly understand the dangers of machinery, equipment, etc., as well as how to mitigate the dangers by being cognizant and diligent while operating machinery. Please use your common sense. And don't forget to have fun!

The 1954 235 was a combination of old style and new styles. With slits in the valve cover and older bottom-end engine parts, it was a unique year for the 235. It was the first truck engine to have insert bearings and full-pressure oiling.

This 1954 235 has the oil bath air filter, bypass oil filter cannister, and mounted horn. After this year, General Motors stopped drilling the intake manifold for mounting the horn but left the boss in that location.

A young and inexperienced Deve in Biloxi, Mississippi, in 1978. Sir. Yes, sir!

CHEVROLET INLINE-6 ENGINE 1929–1962: HOW TO REBUILD

ACKNOWLEDGMENTS

Even though I did the writing and all the physical labor, the component that makes this book a guaranteed success is the people who gave their time and knowledge to help keep each procedure exacting and precise.

This was my strategy: I asked at least three professionals the same question. If all three agreed and it made common sense, it went in the document. If two agreed, I solicited a fourth person's perspective, always keeping the odds well in the favor of precision. This was done at every step using Chevy documentation, outside sources, and tapping the expertise of some of the best engine rebuilders from all over the world. Some of these people were notable because of their giving attitude and the fact that they were always just a phone call away.

You do not get where you are going without the influence of others, and this journey was no different. I was lucky enough to find Dave Folsom, a respected mechanic and shop owner, who specialized in this vintage of Chevrolet. His father taught him the business, and his knowledge is impeccable. There is nothing this man doesn't know and no problem he hasn't run across. Although this is true for a lot of people in a lot of professions, the thing that sets Dave apart is his willingness to share everything he knows.

Along with my long-distance friends, a few local people were of major influence. My dad taught me to "always have common sense in your back pocket"; he was invaluable to me and is sorely missed. The late John Erb was known around these parts as the expert on this vintage, and I was honored to have spent many hours in salvage yards all over Kansas helping him salvage parts for vendors. This was an amazing learning experience that I will never forget. Another great man, Gene Swartzendruber, taught me how to weld, how to view things as a mechanical engineer, and how to work with metal. His influence can be seen all over my shop. I am so grateful for the influence of these great men: Nathan Hall, Jeff Pohlar, Jeff Nelson, Allen Jones, and the list goes on and on, you know who you are. Thank you all!

Left to Right: My dad, me, John Erb, and Gene Swartzendruber solving all the world's problems.

INTRODUCTION

Chevrolet introduced the first overhead valve 6-cylinder engine, affectionately called the Stovebolt, in 1929. There is speculation on where this nickname came from; some think it is because the hardware used on the engine looks like the hardware used in old stoves. Others have said that it has to do with Ford owners needing something insulting to call their competition. No matter where the name came from, it stuck over the years and refers to Chevrolet 6-cylinder engines from 1929 to 1962.

The Stovebolt is an amazing engine in its simplicity, yet it has very strong torque specifications and an ability to handle the heavy abuse of the American Industrial Age hauling steel, wood, and all the products of an emerging economy. In Kansas, it was used for agriculture and was significant in the effort to feed the entire world.

Although the Stovebolt was a strong runner with very good statistics, the 1929–1953 engines had one weak spot. This does not diminish its heritage, mainly because the engine used the technology of its day. I am referring to the babbit used in making the engine's bearings. In engines after 1953, Chevrolet used insert bearings. The company still uses the same technology today. But prior to 1953, engine rebuilders had to learn the art of repouring babbit into the bearings forms. They then had to shave off this babbit and shape the "bearings" into proper form. This was time-consuming, expensive, and less accurate than the next technology.

As time went by, these babbit professionals grew older and retired. Now, you are lucky to find a babbit professional. This is the main reason that most 1929–1953 Chevrolet cars and trucks have

This 1964 261 has a replacement block (no numbers on the distributor deck). The 261 of that era is called Jobmaster.

the newer 1954–1962 Stovebolts in them. It was not cost effective or, in many cases, even possible to salvage an older 216/235 engine. That heritage lives on, however, because you can use some of the parts from the older engines on newer ones.

It is easy to see the evolution of these engines year by year. The big transition year was late 1953. The 1954–1955 235 engines used some bottom-end parts from the older 216/235 series.

For the reasons stated above, I concentrate on the newer vintage 1954–1962 235 and 261 engines. In this book, I perform a complete rebuild of a 1959 235 engine. This is the tail end of the Stovebolt era and a good example of how to do a proper rebuild. If you have a 261 engine, a good article to read is found at devestechnet.com/Home/TheVenerable261.

With a little patience and the ability to read instructions carefully, it is a very rewarding experience to rebuild one of these engines. I also use the principles of restoration, which means that you stop and evaluate every step of the process and take no shortcuts; no matter what.

I hope you enjoy the journey!

You can tell this is a 1954 or early 1955 by the slits in the more modern valve cover. The 235 of that era is called the Thriftmaster.

What is a Workbench® Book?

This *Workbench®* Series book is the only book of its kind on the market. No other book offers the same combination of detailed hands-on information and revealing color photographs to illustrate engine rebuilding. Rest assured, you have purchased an indispensable companion that will expertly guide you, one step at a time, through each important stage of the rebuilding process. This book is packed with real world techniques and practical tips for expertly performing rebuild procedures, not vague instructions or unnecessary processes. At-home mechanics or enthusiast builders strive for professional results, and the instruction in our *Workbench®* Series books help you realize pro-caliber results. Hundreds of photos guide you through the entire process from start to finish, with informative captions containing comprehensive instructions for every step of the process.

The step-by-step photo procedures also contain many additional photos that show how to install high-performance components, modify stock components for special applications, or even call attention to assembly steps that are critical to proper operation or safety. These are labeled with unique icons. These symbols represent an idea, and photos marked with the icons contain important, specialized information.

Here are some of the icons found in *Workbench®* books:

Important!—
Calls special attention to a step or procedure, so that the procedure is correctly performed. This prevents damage to a vehicle, system, or component.

Save Money—
Illustrates a method or alternate method of performing a rebuild step that will save money but still give acceptable results.

Torque Fasteners—
Illustrates a fastener that must be properly tightened with a torque wrench at this point in the rebuild. The torque specs are usually provided in the step.

Special Tool—
Illustrates the use of a special tool that may be required or can make the job easier (caption with photo explains further).

Performance Tip—
Indicates a procedure or modification that can improve performance. Step most often applies to high-performance or racing engines.

Critical Inspection—
Indicates that a component must be inspected to ensure proper operation of the engine.

Precision Measurement—
Illustrates a precision measurement or adjustment that is required at this point in the rebuild.

Professional Mechanic Tip—
Illustrates a step in the rebuild that non-professionals may not know. It may illustrate a shortcut, or a trick to improve reliability, prevent component damage, etc.

Documentation Required—
Illustrates a point in the rebuild where the reader should write down a particular measurement, size, part number, etc. for later reference or photograph a part, area or system of the vehicle for future reference.

Tech Tip—
Tech Tips provide brief coverage of important subject matter that doesn't naturally fall into the text or step-by-step procedures of a chapter. Tech Tips contain valuable hints, important info, or outstanding products that professionals have discovered after years of work. These will add to your understanding of the process, and help you get the most power, economy, and reliability from your engine.

CHAPTER 1

ENGINE IDENTIFICATION

Whether you are looking to purchase a Stovebolt for your project or already have one, the most important first step is identifying everything you can about the engine. This will serve you well when ordering parts and perusing parts at swap meets. Again, the desirable years are 1954–1962 with the 1958–1962 being the most desirable because of all the lessons learned by Chevrolet through the years. I encourage you to hold out for those years and purchase the newer engines wherever possible; however, there is more to an engine than its birth date.

Casting Numbers

The first place to start when researching information on an engine is a list of GM casting numbers in the appendix. It is an accumulation of data that has been updated over the years, so you should have no problem finding your Stovebolt in the list.

On the distributor side of the engine there is a treasure trove of information about the engine. Casting numbers appear just below and to the right of the distributor on the passenger's side. They are notoriously

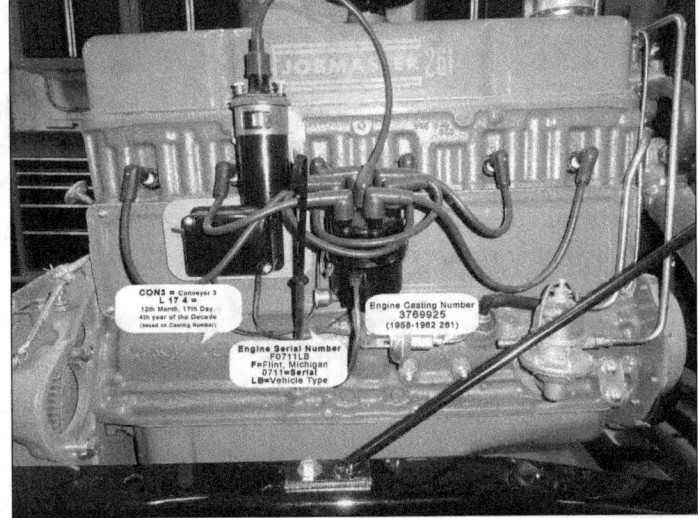

You may find road grime and buildup that fills in the numbers. You can use a good engine degreaser on a shop towel to clean around these numbers. It's worth the trouble. Be sure to write down these numbers. Later, when you need parts, you will be glad you did.

Under the hood, the distributor's vacuum advance can often obstruct the view. It's easier to confirm this number from underneath the vehicle. This is the engine's main casting number.

CHEVROLET INLINE-6 ENGINE 1929–1962: HOW TO REBUILD

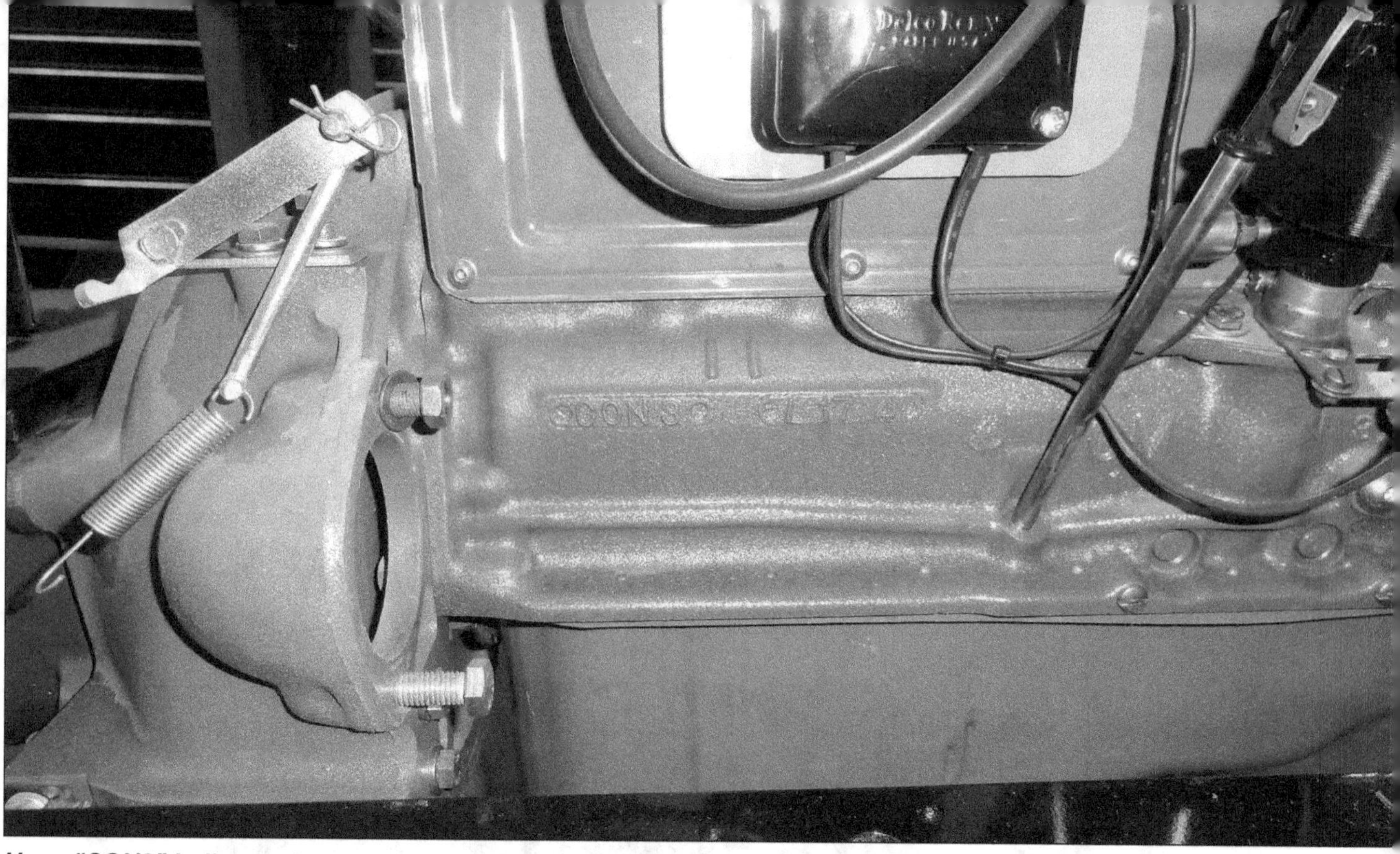

Here, "CON3" indicates the conveyor number that the engine came from. The numbers beside it are important for the exact date that the engine was manufactured. Also, of interest here are the captains bars above the starter. Most of the time, with few exceptions, this indicates that the engine is a 261.

hard to read, and people sometimes mistake a 3 for an 8. Clean the area thoroughly and use a bright flashlight. This is usually a seven-digit number and each letter/number is about 1/2 inch tall. A little engine degreaser and a wire brush often makes reading the casting number easier.

The next numbers you need are the ones just below the starter on the passenger's side: the conveyor number. Beside that is a usually four-digit letter/number combination separated with spaces like this: X XX X. For example, the first X is a letter from A through L (A for January through L for December). The center two digits represent the day of the month. The final digit represents the year that the engine was made within the years represented by the casting numbers below and to the right of the distributor.

The next set of helpful numbers are on the flat part of the distributor deck. This machined area has serial numbers stamped into it. If you have looked very carefully and found no numbers, chances are that your

The flat part where the distributor is mounted is the deck; it was used to stamp the particulars concerning the original vehicle where this engine was originally installed. This information makes a difference in obtaining parts because most cars had hydraulic lifters and trucks had solids.

ENGINE IDENTIFICATION

block is classified as a replacement block and has no numbers stamped on that deck.

The characters you are looking for are stamped (about 1/4 inch high) and usually have a letter followed by three numbers and ending with another letter (or two). The first letter is almost always F because most GM engines were made in Flint, Michigan. The following numbers represent the month followed by the day of the month. The final letters denote the vehicle in which the engine was originally installed.

Without removing the valve cover, the head's casting number is clearly stamped just before the carburetor. The rest of the head's information can be obtained by removing the cover. This is one of those infamous high-compression 848s.

Serial Numbers

A stamped serial number appears on the flat part of the distributor deck. The first letter is either F for Flint, Michigan, or T for Tonawanda, New York. These were the two locations where engines were manufactured at the time. The numbers following the F or T designate the calendar month and the date the engine was produced. The remaining letters are in accordance with the type and series of the vehicle. This helps to tie the vehicle together with the engine. Regular production orders (RPOs) were standard orders that could include many variables, and Chevrolet had several of them that were popular with dealers. (The appendix includes the car and truck listings for 1954–1962.)

Head Casting Numbers

The head also has important casting numbers. In my research, I found very little information for heads manufactured between 1954 and 1962, but I found the three most popular. The head casting number is located outside the valve cover in plain sight on the driver's side. If you have heard that the new-style 235 gets better compression numbers with an "848" head and that's important to you, look for those as the last three numbers of that casting number.

Here are the head casting numbers that I can verify, so this is a short list:

- 3835913   1954–1955   235 engine
- 3836848   1956–1962   235 engine
- 3836850   1956–1962   261 engine

With the casting information, you should be able to decipher everything General Motors recorded about your engine. This is invaluable in determining what engine parts you need for your rebuild.

Visual Differences

You see a few telltale differences when perusing listings of engines during the purchase or selection process. These differences help you determine the correct Stovebolt era in which the engine was made.

The acorn nuts have a rubber grommet under them with a metal washer. Notice the slits in the valve cover that allowed underhood road grime into the engine. It's best to close those up and use a vented cap.

CHAPTER 1

Deciphering Engine Numbers for This Project

Below the distributor is the casting number, 3764476. This engine was built between 1959 and 1962. Just above the starter is CON3 (the third conveyor at the factory) and B 28 9. The first letter corresponds to its month, A through L (A for January, L for December). B is February, 28 is the day of the month, and 9 is the year. We now know this engine was built on February 28, 1959.

Now let's look at the serial number that is stamped on the flat part of the distributor deck. That number is F302B. The "F" means that the engine was made in Flint, Michigan. The "3" indicates the third month, March. The "02" signifies the day of month. The "B" stands for the model/series of the car engine with Powerglide (hydraulic lifters).

So, March 2, 1959, is the date! When you stop to think about it, the line must have been busy at the time because the serial number only lagged the casting of the engine by two to three days.

The head follows a similar numbering scheme. On the driver's side on the outside, not covered by the valve cover, is the casting number; in this case 3836848. It indicates that the head was made between 1955 and 1962 and was used on cars and trucks. Just inside the valve cover in almost the same location is another clue: CON9 (the ninth conveyor at the factory), and about four springs to the right of that is another number H 3 0, which is the date that the head was made, August 3, 1960.

So, this probably isn't the head that originally came with the engine, unless the engine sat on a shelf for about 18 months. When you see a casting number ending in 848, you know you have the highest-compression head Chevrolet made for that engine. ■

 Important Tip

The year 1953 was a transition for Chevrolet. In early 1953, cars were equipped with the older-style engine; in the latter part of the year, some were equipped with the newer style as the factory ran out of old parts. The factory did not start everything new at the beginning of a year. So, some 1953 cars had the new engine, some did not. As far as I can tell, all 1953 trucks came with the old-style engine. This is why I use pre- and post-1953 to describe these engines. ■

The coil was mounted in the center of the engine until late 1953. At that time, Chevrolet located the coil between cylinders number-4 and number-5. This is a 1950 216. You know it's an earlier engine by the long side cover, short cap distributor, and acorn nuts holding down the valve cover from the top.

ENGINE IDENTIFICATION

Notice the space between the center of the harmonic balancer and the center of the fan. It is considerably more than the post-1953 engines. Prior to 1953 all the engines had 5/8-inch-wide belt pulleys.

The short cap distributor cannot use a tall cap because the internal shaft is too short. This prohibits installing HEI, but other than that, the distributors are interchangeable.

Post-1953 intake manifolds have the knob sticking out for mounting the horn, just no holes drilled.

Pre-1954 216/235 Engines with Babbit Bearings

- Two acorn nuts on the top of the valve cover holding on the valve cover
- A side cover that extends from above the spark plugs, all the way down to the oil pan
- A water pump arrangement that centers the fan on the radiator (this is on the vehicles that the engine came with due to a taller radiator)
- A short cap distributor
- A horn mount on the intake manifold

It is easy to put an older-style valve cover on a new-style engine because the rocker assembly bolts are in the same place. It is not recommended, however, because they tended to leak more. If you want to preserve the shape of the holes, be sure to add reinforcements.

1954–1962 Engines with Modern Insert Bearings

- Four screws at the base of the valve cover to hold it down
- A short side cover
- A lower-set water pump
- A tall-cap distributor

There are other much-less-noticeable differences, such as carb style, generator, and starter differences, but these are the best identifiers of the era of the engine.

Engine Condition

The project engine for this book was completely unknown to me. It was sitting in a garage, all taken apart in boxes. I had no idea where each specific lifter was located when it was running nor the condition of the engine. This was good for documenting because you can't take anything for granted.

In your case, you might have a good reason for rebuilding it. One good indication that an engine needs a rebuild is excessive blow-by. This is obvious by the amount of visible smoke that comes out of the valve cover cap. There shouldn't be any. This could be valve adjustment, worn piston rings, or worn cylinders. Another obvious sign of wear is low oil pressure at idle.

Compression Testing

If you have a desire to know the overall health of your engine, a good

CHAPTER 1

The side cover is much shorter, starting below the spark plugs, than in previous years. This is a better design. Chevrolet made many subtle changes between 1938 and 1962.

The tall-cap distributor has a taller cap and a taller internal shaft. Also, the rotor is taller, so those parts are not interchangeable with the pre-1953 distributors.

place to start is with checking the compression. A few things contribute to low compression, such as piston ring wear and valve issues. Purchase a compression gauge kit. It will come with all the connectors and fittings that you need. The following is a quick procedure that works well.

With the ignition switch off, remove all the spark plugs and the distributor cap. Prop the throttle wide open to get the most accurate reading. Screw the fitting into the number-1 spark plug hole until the rubber O-ring squashes just a bit. Turn the engine over (with the starter) long enough for the compression gauge to register the compression number of the cylinder. Keep cranking until the gauge needle stops rising. This is important. Record the number, release the gauge's pressure (small pushbutton on the gauge), and do it again to make sure it's reading very close. Do this on every cylinder, one at a time.

They need to be within 5 percent of one another. Any numbers above 95 psi means that the engine is okay and will run well. Compression as low as 65 psi should be okay but may smoke and idle poorly. With a new engine, they are in the 130 range.

On the 261 engine I recently worked on, the measurements were number-1, 140; number-2, 137; number-3, 138; number-4, 137; number-5, 137; and number-6, 138.

Flywheel Identification

The flywheel is something you don't automatically think of as a big deal; however, these engines are in the transition years, so be careful. Chevrolet introduced the 12-volt system in 1955. Prior to 1955, everything was 6 volts. Why this matters is because the 6-volt starter had a different gear pattern, and the flywheel had 134 teeth on the 6-volt starter version while the 12-volt version of the same flywheel has 168 teeth.

To add to the confusion, the starter gears both have the same

The flywheel's ring gear is the issue here. It is relatively easy with heat to remove a ring gear, but finding a replacement is the problem. Most of us just replace the entire flywheel when necessary. Don't skip over the fact that you can turn the ring gear around to get fresh gear meat for the starter.

ENGINE IDENTIFICATION

Safety Note

Due to the concern of unwanted combustion, make sure the ignition is off or the distributor cap is removed before attempting anything that requires removal of a spark plug. Safety first always!

number of teeth, but the pitch is different. I am really talking about the flywheels' ring gear; however, unless you want to remove and replace a ring gear, the difference is insignificant. Be sure to count the teeth on the flywheel so you know which starter to purchase.

Even if someone has upgraded your vehicle to 12 volts, it may still use a 6-volt starter. I prefer the 6-volt starter because to carry double the current of 12 volts, the windings are beefier. You won't hurt a 6-volt starter if you use it for the normal short periods of time it was designed for.

Is It a Rebuild Candidate?

Here I am talking about the quality of the engine candidate. Is it worth the considerable expense to rebuild? Do you see visible cracks in the water jacket or anywhere else? Do you have any documentation that would lead you to understand the cylinder bore size that was done at the last rebuild?

Sometimes the piston has a number stamped on the top face of it. You discover something very important when you remove the head of an unknown engine. You should wire brush away the carbon and dirt from the center of the top of the piston. A number such as .010, .020, .030, etc., stamped on the piston, tells you the last cylinder bore size. If it reads .060, you are getting very close to the last bore size that is available for these cylinders. This may be a prohibitive factor for you because it costs just as much to do the first overbore as it does to do the last.

Organization Is Key

The engine for this specific rebuild has hydraulic lifters. I like that, even knowing that an argument could be made that they cost horsepower because the engine is very quiet and runs very smoothly without much adjustment. In the box of engine parts, I found the 12 lifters for this project. Three of them are missing the retainer springs and

A compression tester costs about $25 at your local tool store, and it is well worth it so you know you have good compression. In the United States, the inside scale is used because you are reading PSI.

the caps, and there is stuff all over the bottom of the box.

Because hydraulic lifters are expensive, I'd like to save them. After a little research, I learned that I could take them to a machine shop and have them surfaced so that they run against the cam as good as new. I will not use them if the machine shop expert recommends that I buy new ones.

Since I am doing a complete rebuild and do not care about the current timing of the engine, I removed the head, distributor, plug wires, spark plugs, coil, road tube, starter, generator or alternator, water pump, carburetor, intake and exhaust manifold, valve cover, and lifter side cover. I organized these subsystems carefully, keeping the hardware separate. I separated the hardware, putting things in labeled bags. And the fun soon begins!

Stovebolt Tips

The best years for Stovebolts are 1958–1962. Think of Chevrolet as a company with technology that is constantly evolving. The Holy Grail of Stovebolts is the 1958–1962 261 engine. It is the same physical size as the 235 with about 40 more horsepower due to its larger displacement. It also has native full-flow oil filtering. Keep in mind that any Stovebolt after 1953 is considered the best 6-cylinder engine for that vintage. Another major factor is engine wear. You do not want to purchase an engine that is bored .060 over because it is reaching the end of its life. You also do not want to purchase an engine with cracks or casting issues.

CHAPTER 2

TOOLS AND ENGINE CLEANING

You don't need anything this fancy, but the roll-cart on the right contains a battery, a set of gauges, a fuel delivery system, and a safety switch for rolling up to any project and providing the necessary power. See devestechnet.com/Home/StartKartPlans for the plans to make your own version.

> **Special Tool**
>
> A shop manual is the authority on tolerances, procedures, and methods. However, it is outdated and many of the tools represented in it are either hard or impossible to find. I use modern equivalents. ■
>
>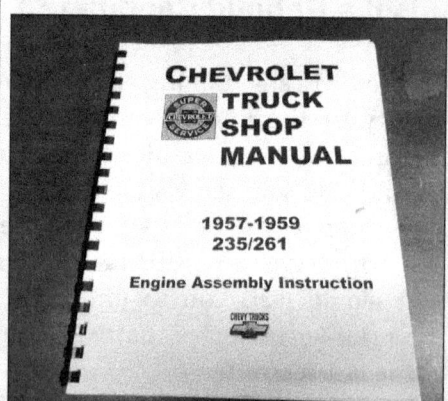
>
> The shop manual for the correct year of your engine will contain all the important specifications and tolerances for your engine. It is a must-have item for the rebuild. Be sure to get the shop manual for the year of your engine, not the year of your vehicle if they are different.

There are many tools required for this job. As I address each system, I will add to it. One important tool for this job is the shop manual for the year of your engine. Remember, the shop manual for your vehicle may be different from the one for the engine if the engine has been replaced. You can purchase a copy of the shop manual from many sources.

TOOLS AND ENGINE CLEANING

Tools List

- Three-gallon parts washer (or equivalent)
- Miscellaneous scrapers, brushes, Scotch-Brite pads, etc.
- 3/8- and 1/2-inch socket and open-end wrenches to 3/4 inch
- Harmonic balancer puller
- Miscellaneous screwdrivers and pliers
- Cylinder ridge reamer
- Piston ring pliers
- Shop press (for cam gear removal)
- Valve spring compressor
- Vernier calipers
- Steel number/letter stamping set
- Piston ring compressor
- 3/8-inch-drive torque wrench
- 1/2-inch-drive torque wrench
- Foldable engine hoist
- Foldable engine stand
- Feeler gauge set
- Flare tool kit
- Tube straightener
- Adjustable tube bender
- Tube cutter
- Spark plug stripper/crimper
- Electric hoist (optional)
- Electric/fuel provision

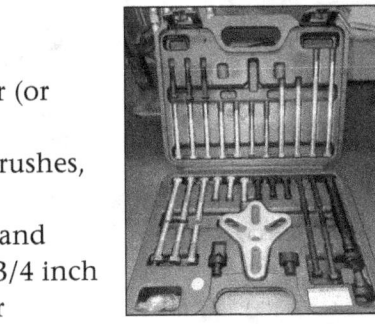

This is the correct tool for removal of the harmonic balancer on a Stovebolt. You attach this puller to two threaded holes on the balancer.

This tool is designed to remove the carbon buildup or ridge that is present on top of the cylinder walls that restrict the ability to remove the pistons.

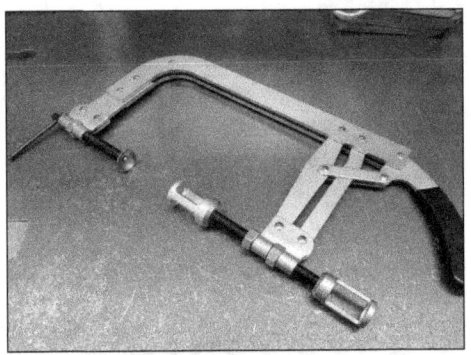

This model is barely long enough to reach, but it gets the job done. Be sure to center the shaft so the tool does not slip.

This simple tool allows you to control the spread of the piston rings during installation. I use it because it helps prevent scratches on the piston and its action evenly spreads the stress.

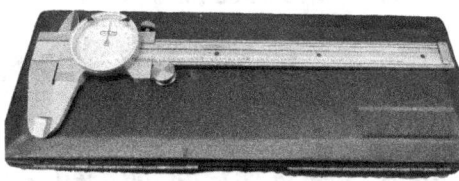

This is a handy tool to have around the shop for measuring pushrod diameters, bolt sizes, etc. It is as old as I am. The ones you get these days have digital readouts and can measure in standard or metric.

Be sure the pump is rated for petroleum-based caustic chemicals, such as kerosene, if that is what you have planned for cleaning. Most are not. I have found it necessary to replace my pump with one that is properly rated.

I prefer the 20-ton model because it can be used for removal of the cam gear, U-joints, and other press-fit items. A Swag Offroad attachment works great for bending metal, too.

This is the proper 1/8-inch letter size that is good for marking piston rods, etc. As with most tools that I use intermittently, it comes from Harbor Freight.

CHEVROLET INLINE-6 ENGINE 1929–1962: HOW TO REBUILD

CHAPTER 2

This ring compressor wraps around the piston and serves as a guide and compresses the rings in place for proper piston replacement. Don't forget to spread oil inside the compressor prior to starting.

A good feeler gauge set that has at least .005 through .045 gauges is a must for this sort of work.

Your shop wouldn't be complete without a tubing cutter. Cutting stainless steel is hard on the blade. This BrakeQuip version does a good job.

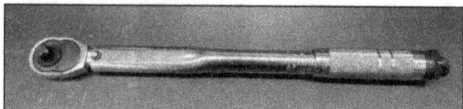
It is not necessary to purchase an expensive set of torque wrenches. These are obtainable for around $20 each. You need 3/8- and 1/2-inch-drive sizes for this job.

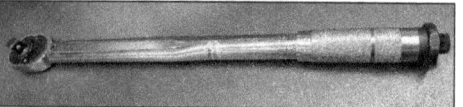
The 1/2-inch drive is for the head bolts and heavier-duty items on the engine. Be sure to set it properly so you don't break bolts off by accident.

BrakeQuip makes a robust kit for flaring stainless steel or any other grade fuel/brake/vacuum lines that eliminate slippage.

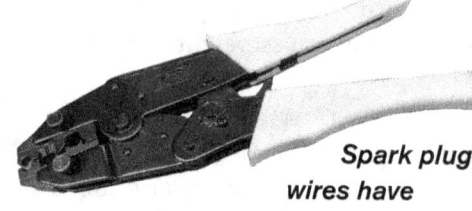
Spark plug wires have changed over the years, and I have become a believer in purchasing wire kits and cutting them to length with a stripper/crimper such as this Accel version. The new low-ohm wires require a special crimping tool. This is the ticket.

The foldable engine hoist, commonly referred to as a cherry picker, is a great way to move your engine in and out of the vehicle and around the shop.

A tubing straightener is a must if you purchase the lines in 20-foot rolls. This BrakeQuip version does a more-than-adequate job.

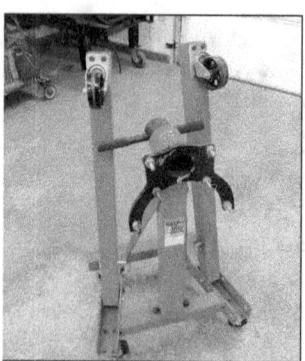
It is imperative to have a strong and stable engine stand for this extra-long 6-cylinder engine. The one I recommend is a 2,000-pound model. If you primarily work on 6-cylinders, make yourself a head like this one.

This BrakeQuip fully adjustable tubing bender has an intuitive design. It has a tab for clamping it in a vise.

This electric hoist is rated at 880 pounds. With the engine block weighing about half of that, you are good to use it to move the engine from the engine shop to the engine stand.

I use this to raise the engine to a cleaning height, or to place it on a cart, or to install it on the engine stand. Mounted in the right place, you can use it for installing the engine if you choose.

Selecting Modern Tools

Some of these tools are optional and can be rented from your local auto parts store or tool rental store. For example, the BrakeQuip listings are for making high-quality fuel lines, vacuum advance lines, and positive crankcase ventilation (PCV) lines. As expensive as they are, it may not pay to purchase them for onetime use. The harmonic balancer removal tool should be the one listed in the shop manual or equivalent. Common sense and perusing the shop manual will come into play here. Quality tools pay great dividends in the long run. Purchasing cheap tools may mean having to purchase them again. On the other hand, if there is a solution that works and is safe, you can use what you have.

General Cleaning Procedures

Still in inspection mode, the next step is to clean the block, head, and small parts thoroughly. You are looking for cracks in the cast iron, wear points, broken studs, etc. This requires removal of the transmission, bellhousing, flywheel, head, and all attached parts.

Once you spray brake cleaner or engine degreaser on the block, for example, most cracks become apparent. If you find cracks in the engine block, stop. It is time for a new engine block. Due to the expense of engine shop work, it is not a good idea to

A spray can of engine degreaser, toothbrush, scraper, and large wire brush go a long way toward a clean engine. Be sure to chase the threads on all areas of the block and head while you are at it.

 **Documentation Required**

The cardinal rule of vehicle/engine restoration is to label everything! Get a bunch of resealable bags, such as from Ziploc, and a Sharpie and be very meticulous about labeling. This is crucial! You need to know exactly where a bolt came from, what position it was in, etc. It's not as necessary for valve cover screws and that sort of thing, but it's crucial for head bolts or anything having to do with the engine, such as lifters and pushrods.

start with a cracked block. The same is true for the head. Replace and forget about it.

On the bellhousing, you may be able to get away with an expert cast-iron repair, but not on the head or engine. This is because of the deep heat cycles that the engine and head are exposed to. Later in this process, you will have the engine shop do a Magnaflux test on the head and block to ensure there are no cracks prior to machine work.

Cleaning Small Parts

Back in the day, you just filled a coffee can with gasoline, used a small wire brush, and called it a day. These days there are safer and more environmentally friendly chemicals. Options range from lacquer thinner, white vinegar, kerosene, and water with baking soda to parts washer solvent. Soak parts overnight for best results.

In addition, an important discovery concerns air nozzles for your compressor. You have regular, everyday air nozzles used to get rid of unwanted residue. These are generally safety nozzles. They have a center opening for discharge, but they also have two holes on each side of the nozzle. This is to prevent injury to you from too much pressure against the skin. It also prevents the nozzle from working at 100 percent. The closer you get to the work, the more air is vented off to the outside holes.

You can purchase nonventing air nozzles that nearly double the performance characteristics of the nozzle. This is for removing all the sand, residue, or whatever out of your work.

Always wear appropriate safety gear and never point any nozzle at your skin. You need to be careful with this new option, but it's worth mentioning because it is the difference between clean engine parts and *clean* engine parts.

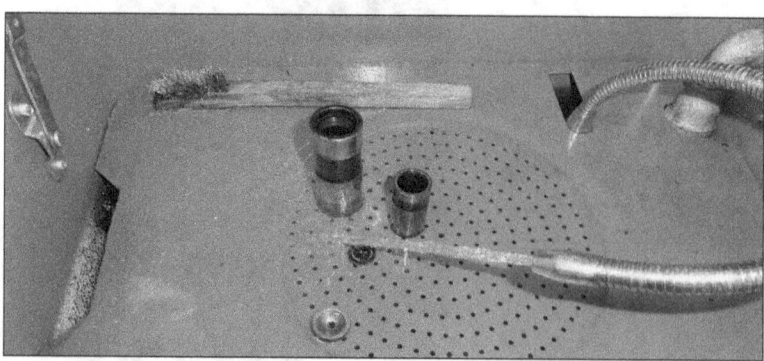

The 3½ Gallon Benchtop Small Parts Washer is a handy tool to have around. I retrofitted a Little Giant 1-YS submersible pump for this system that handles kerosene without damage to the pump. It wasn't a difficult conversion, and it has lasted several years so far.

For this build, I used a small parts washer with kerosene as the washing agent. Kerosene, a little pump pressure, and a wire brush can really do the job. To get into hard-to-reach places, a spray can of engine degreaser (with a straw) helps break everything free.

Finally, I like to blow off everything with compressed air to ensure there is nothing hiding.

Cleaning Large Parts

If you have access to a pressure washer, clean the engine block, head, oil pan, etc., thoroughly. Or, you can do it the old-fashioned way with a scraper, a wire brush, and some engine degreaser.

You want to knock off most of the dirt before taking these parts to the engine shop because their procedure takes care of most of the final cleaning. Remember, the nicer you clean the engine, the better the paint will look, and you can sleep at night knowing your engine was done right.

Metal Blasting

Bead blast at 40 psi for the sheet metal parts. This includes the oil pan, valve cover, timing gear cover, etc. I have found through several rebuilds that doing this reveals cracks and poorly done fixes so you can address those parts. The oil pan is particularly subject to this phenomenon.

People have been known to braze holes shut or put excessive Bondo over holes, etc. I want to see exactly what is happening. Any way you can get down to the bare metal is good. If using the blasting method, be sure to clean all residue out of every orifice prior to reassembly. A good document on media blasting can be found at devestechnet.com/Home/Sandblasting.

The engine block can be grimy with caked-on dirt that is difficult to remove. Use a pressure washer if you have one, or do what I do and use an old-fashioned garden hose and a lot of elbow grease.

CHAPTER 3

THE HEAD AND ASSOCIATED PARTS

The lifters on this specific engine are hydraulic. Hydraulic lifters get their name by filling with engine oil on engine startup and then compressing/decompressing as they move up and down over the camshaft. This makes for a much quieter and smooth-running engine. A retainer clip on the top of a hydraulic lifter holds in the internal parts.

Solid lifters are as named: solid. They have a cone on the top to accept the pushrod but no internal parts, thus no retaining clip.

You can learn if your engine has solid or hydraulic lifters by shining a flashlight down the pushrod hole. If there is a retaining clip on the top of the lifter, they are hydraulic.

This is not needed if you did your homework on the identification because the block's numbers tell you which type you have. Cars usually had hydraulics and trucks always had solids.

Lifters

Load each lifter one at a time into the small parts cleaner, making sure to keep the parts together and not mix them with any of the others. My first three didn't have retainer clips, so I substituted a 3/4-inch snap-ring retainer from one of my boxes. The edge of the retainer may need to be carefully ground down, so it is away from the pushrod, but it's a very solid fix.

The head assembly after cleaning the rockers. Once cleaned, it's important to refit to make sure you have all rockers and shims in the exact spot they were in before disassembly. Spray all that pretty, clean metal with WD-40 for safe keeping.

These hydraulic lifters may have been the originals; you can see the wear patterns. With a thorough cleaning, they could be reused without problems.

CHAPTER 3

The cleaning product Simple Green can be your friend in the shop. This stuff even cuts through the pitch left on saw blades when woodworking. It works great for removing residual kerosene.

From left to right: tension spring, ball bearing cover, pushrod cap, inner lifter barrel, ball bearing, and lifter housing. Not shown is the 3/4-inch snap-ring retainer. After a thorough cleaning, the parts look practically new.

Once the parts are cleaned using kerosene and a soft brush, soak them overnight in Simple Green cleanser. This removes all the petroleum-based contaminants so you start off with fresh metal. Use a soft, green Scotch-Brite pad for cleaning, rinsing each part carefully and applying some engine oil to all the surfaces.

Lifter Reassembly

With oil all over everything, including inside the lifter housing, turn the inner lifter barrel upside down and place the ball bearing over the hole, then place the ball bearing cover over the top of it. I like to drip a little oil over this assembly to sort of make everything stick together.

Next, place the tension spring on top of the ball bearing cover. Everything should go together perfectly. If it doesn't, you are doing something wrong.

Now, while balancing the inner housing, ball bearing, ball bearing cap, and tension spring in one hand, turn the lifter housing upside down and gently twist it down over the assembly. It should be smooth until you feel some hydraulic resistance.

Most of the resistance is from air being trapped between the two barrels. With a very small, thin tool (I used the plastic straw from a WD-40 can), push on the ball bearing just a little until you feel the resistance burp away.

Keeping a little downward pressure on the assembly, place it on a flat surface and fill the inner lifter barrel to the top with engine oil. Place the pushrod cap over the top. This cap pushes down below the surface of the lifter housing. Place the snap ring in the pliers and hold it over the pushrod cap, push down on the assembly using a pushrod so that the cap is sufficiently below the surface of the lifter housing to get the snap ring to engage. (Keep in mind that most lifters have their own retaining spring that is much easier to install, but I am telling you this just in case you run into what I did.)

You should have one fully loaded, fully burped, serviceable hydraulic lifter. Now do that 11 more times. When finished, find a nice container that you can use to hold all 12 of them and be able to fill it with engine oil over the top of the lifters.

These lifters are fully assembled and ready for reinstallation, it's a good idea to soak the parts in oil for safe keeping. This keeps them filled with oil, which is a good way to start the first engine runup.

For this build, the machine shop decided that it would cost the same amount to purchase new hydraulic lifters as it would cost to resurface the old ones ($7.50 each). With that in mind, I just had the shop order new ones. The effort was not wasted, I learned something new!

Pushrods

You need to test the pushrods (mine were also in the box) to be sure they are perfectly straight and that

THE HEAD AND ASSOCIATED PARTS

The machine shop advised that these be replaced due to very small pits in the metal. These rods get a lot of abuse and the worry of failure is too likely.

The lifter end of the pushrod is shiny due to its metal-to-metal contact. The hole in the center is to allow for a small amount of oil.

The 1954–1962 235/261 engines used 11¼ x 5/16-inch pushrods. Never try to straighten a bent rod. The metal has memory, and it won't be long before it fails again. New ones cost about $7, and it is cheap insurance to replace those that are pitted, bent, or cracked.

The design of the rocker end of the pushrod captures the rocker assembly so everything stays straight and true. The indention allows for a small amount of oil.

each end is in the proper condition to be used. To do this, you find a perfectly flat surface (glass is good) and roll them across your work table or bench, watching for any wandering or out-of-straight condition. If they are not straight, do not try to bend them back; just get new ones.

Next, carefully inspect each end to make sure the little hole in the center is pronounced and clean. If there is any residue in the center, clean it thoroughly so that its surface is shiny and smooth. You can go the extra mile and clean the entire length with Scotch-Brite or similar pads. Test for straightness one last time.

In this rebuild, I was not happy with the condition of five of the pushrods. One had a very significant wear spot that reduced the diameter and the others were slightly bent. Luckily, I had a box of old pushrods from other Stovebolts and found five perfect replacements. This engine has 11¼-inch pushrods.

Even after all that, the machine shop wasn't comfortable with some of the pitting, so new rods were obtained for this engine. This is why you should box up everything and take it to the machine shop for a proper inspection. My collection of pushrods is getting bigger!

Rocker Assembly

The rocker assembly is bolted on top of the head and consists of two shafts, the rockers, the springs, etc. This is the assembly for adjusting your valves. It goes together in only one correct way. Getting any shim or spring in the wrong place leads to excessive wear or premature failure. This assembly is notorious for being dirty, mostly or completely clogged, and the mounts can be stuck to the rocker shaft.

If everything looks in order after a cursory cleaning, it's time to get your hands dirty. You can never have enough pictures of this assembly because every shim, every washer, every spring, and every rocker needs to be assembled in the exact order it was taken apart.

If the parts are simply sitting in a box, reconstruct the assembly to make sure that you have all the parts and everything is serviceable. Once complete, take a picture, so you have a template on how to put it back together. You can also refer to the photo in the shop manual.

This engine is the newer-style 235 with a center-flow spout that has no second tube coming out and looping back to the bottom of the assembly. This newer style puts all the upper engine oil flow through the rocker assembly shaft system before dumping it back into the reservoir.

Cleaning

Here too, you need to clean things thoroughly before even thinking about a successful assembly. Too often, cleaning reveals something you need to address. In this case, I go out of my way to ensure that this assembly is perfectly clean. To do this, you really want to take it apart carefully and place components in the proper order. In this example, two rocker shafts meet in the middle. Once disassembled, these two shafts need to be inspected carefully for excessive wear. It's very common for these rocker shafts to be considerably worn where the rockers move on them. It's worse when there is no oil reaching the rockers. In this engine, both shafts have very little wear and look really good for their age.

Take about a 14-inch piece of 3/8-inch steel rod and push it all the way through the inside of the shaft. Do it very slowly and knock off all the crud with a small screwdriver (or similar) as you go past each hole. Use your parts washer's pump action to push kerosene through the shaft. Repeat this until the kerosene comes out clean.

This style of rocker assembly (the newer style) has no oil-return pipe. All of the oil going to the upper end goes through the rocker shaft assembly before being dumped back out into the reservoir.

On the outside, use double-O steel wool to make sure the entire surface is perfectly smooth. Don't expect to remove all the stains, but do clean it thoroughly. Don't use an aggressive grinding wire wheel for this. You need to keep as much of the finish as possible. Do not sandblast the shaft.

You need to clean all the rocker assembly parts. First run them through the kerosene wash, use a wire brush, dry them off, then remove the pushrod contact assembly from the

This super cleaning was accomplished by taping all machined surfaces with masking tape then bead blasting the outside of each rocker. Don't forget to chase all the passages and clean thoroughly after blasting.

rocker arms. You want to thoroughly inspect the ball that comes in contact with the pushrods to ensure that there is no damage or excessive wear. You also do not want to damage that part of the rocker. Once apart, clean the rockers including the valve contact area with kerosene and light oil.

You want to clean each rocker thoroughly. Chase the threads, use a piece of safety wire or a paper clip to clean the oil hole. Once blasted, run some 400-grit sandpaper through the shaft hole, on the flats of everything. When assembling, **remember that the shaft's oil holes face downward.** Once the entire assembly has been cleaned, put it back on the head to make sure each rocker contacts the valves exactly in the middle. Once you are happy with the cleaning job, spray some WD-40 all over the assembly to keep the rust at bay during the rest of the project. Set the assembly aside.

I like to leave about three threads showing on the rockers. This is a good neutral position for the valve adjustment procedure later. As this rebuild progresses, you will be glad you addressed these issues before going to the engine machine shop. Had any lifters or rods been damaged or you want a second opinion, you will have this information beforehand.

Head Machining Prep

You will save money and time at the machine shop if you remove the valves beforehand. One threaded plug needs to be removed and saved for later, and to make life easier for the machine shop, also take out the valves. You must do this at least once to appreciate how badly these valves can become abused.

To remove the valves, you need

The rocker assembly is now ready for the finished head. Spray the outside of any super clean assembly with WD-40 to keep things from rusting.

With everything cleaned and working like new, you can set the whole assembly aside awaiting the finished head. Notice how the WD-40 brings out the shininess and makes it look normal again.

a valve spring compressor similar to the one in the tools list. You may prefer a throat about an inch longer.

Be careful with the spring compressor. Lock the handle, then turn the crank handle, making sure you are solidly on the valve on one end and centered on the spring on the other. Once you turn the screw sufficiently, the keepers either fall out or can be retrieved with a small screwdriver. Break the plastic retainer and then let pressure off the spring the same way. The spring should safely come out, and the valve should slip out as well. If it doesn't, I use the handle end of my hammer to tap it a little.

CHAPTER 3

This is where you need to get to before you send the head to the machine shop. Everything must be removed. You will not be reusing the valves, and if the springs do not meet specs (as ascertained by the machine shop), they will be replaced too.

Place the valve spring compressor carefully in the center of the valve shaft. It is not as dangerous as with the suspension of a car, but always think safety first when removing springs under load.

Be sure to remove all plugs and fittings. Take it easy on the temperature sensor on top of the head. That fitting is very difficult to find. It is not a standard NPT size on pre-1955 vehicles.

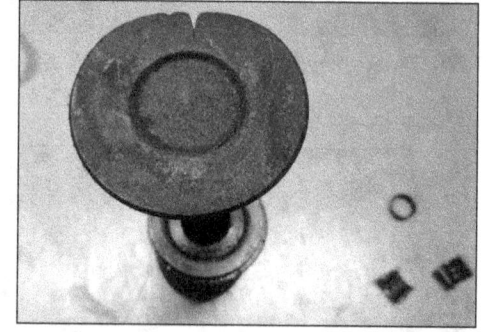

Damage from a poor-running engine looks like this. This engine is in need of a valve job. It never ceases to amaze me how these engines run anyway, despite the damage to a point.

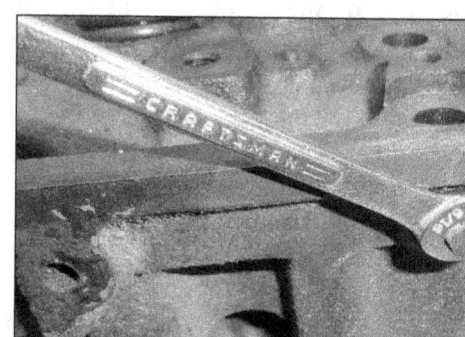

Be sure to remove any fittings on the head. When the engine shop cleans the head, the techs can do a better job with everything removed. If you cannot remove a fitting, let the shop know.

Once compressed, the keepers almost fall out. Carefully remove the keepers, then do it 11 more times.

All of this crud was attached to the valve. Something went terribly wrong. Discoloration of the metal proves that something was causing them to become abnormally hot.

Remove the temperature sensor carefully. This one is easy, but the ones used for vehicles prior to 1955 have a nonstandard thread size and need to be taken out with care. Any copper line to this sensor needs to be handled carefully because it contains a special gas and cannot be opened or crimped.

CHAPTER 4

ENGINE AND SHEET METAL PARTS PREPARATION

This engine arrived sitting on a pallet with the oil pan facing upward. I transferred it to one of my wheel dollies so I could move it around. This is a good beginning orientation. Once the head is removed, you have a nice, flat surface to set it down on.

The first order of business is to remove the oil pan. It should be bolted down with exactly 18 number-10 screws and four 1/4-inch hex-head bolts. Once you have that many screws in your hands, use a thick tool, such as a 1½-inch stout scraper, to pry it off the block. I don't like screwdrivers for this because of making unnecessary pry marks on the pan. Use the same scraper to scrape all the gasket material and crud from the block. Once the oil pan is removed, you can see the condition of the inside of the block.

I haven't found any better way to roll these engines around the shop. The low center of gravity makes it very stable.

Creating an Engine Cart

These engines are heavy and unwieldy. One good way to move them around is to use an engine cart. Also having an engine stand with hoist brackets allows you to lift and place the engine safely.

Materials

Start with at least 1/8-inch-thickness-wall 1-inch square tubing. Cut the pieces to:

Quantity	Length
4	26¾ inches each
8	6½ inches each
1	9½ inches each
4	18 inches each

You need 20½ total lineal feet of the tubing.

If you want to keep it right at 20 feet, remove 1/8 inch from the four 18 inchers. These are the wheelbases, so the difference isn't noticeable.

You need two 1/8-inch thick x 2 inch x 11½-inch steel plates to put on the ends.

To finish it off, you need four wheels that are 3 inches in circumference with a 275-pound capacity plus all the necessary hardware (Harbor Freight is a good source). This allows you to cart as much as 1,000 pounds.

Construction Procedure

Place the wheels over two of the 18-inch wheel supports. Make adjustments until you match the steel plate on the wheels with the edge of the tubing, then mark each hole with a Sharpie for drilling. (I used 5/16 x 1½-inch bolts with nuts, flats, and locks.)

The finished cart rolls smoothly, and because it's made out of 1/8-inch thick 1-inch tube, it is very stout. Do not be tempted to use thinner-walled stock. This engine with all of its accoutrements can weigh in excess of 800 pounds.

Prior to making any decisions on what to use for a project, I like to consult these rings of the different sizes I have available.

Once drilled, assemble the two-wheel assembly rails and set them aside. Doing it this way results in a squarer frame.

Place two of the 26¾-inch side rails on a flat table or workbench for welding. Place four of the 6½-inch pieces inside and between the two rails in the following order:

- First one, flush with the edge of the long rail and inside of it.
- Second one, 6¾ inches from the first one (inside between them).
- Third one, 8 inches from the second one (inside between them).
- Fourth one, flush with the end rail and inside of it. (If you did it right, that gap also measures 8 inches.)

Be sure to drop the end plates to 4 inches, so they do not interfere with the oil pan. If this cart is for a 216 engine, drop the intermediate bar from 4 inches to 5 inches. Otherwise the oil pan does not clear.

Clamp these pieces to the table for welding so you don't end up with warped side rails. When everything is straight and true, the cart is amazingly stable.

ENGINE AND SHEET METAL PARTS PREPARATION

Clean the mill scale and prepare the surfaces for welding. Do a really good job of welding these parts together because engines are heavy and you do not want a safety hazard around your shop. It's best to clamp the entire frame to a table or workbench to avoid warping. In the end, you want all the wheels to be on the floor.

Once that one side is welded, make an exact duplicate for the other side. The 6¾-inch gap is for the front of the engine.

Orient the two frames so that the 6¾-inch gapped end is across from each other. Set these frames on their sides 9½ inches apart from each other.

At 4 inches down from the top of the side frames, place a 2 x 11½-inch steel plate across the frame. (In other words, you have 4 inches of air space before the plate starts.) Clamp this plate into place, then do the same on the back with another 2 x 11½-inch piece of plate.

Finally, the 9½-inch square tubing goes on the second support (closest to the front of the cart) and 4 inches down. This just barely misses the oil pan and gives the entire cart more structural support. Once you have everything boxed in, you should be able to set a level across the whole thing and verify that each side brace is 4 inches from the top. Weld the braces on and make sure everything stays square.

Turn the new box assembly upside down and lay the wheel assemblies across and to the edge of the frame rails. The wheels being outside of the frame rails offers a wider stance and much smoother range of movement. Weld those into place, and the difficult part is done.

To show quality workmanship, make sure to use a flap disk and clean off all the slag, grind away any welding imperfections, and clean the entire piece for painting.

To finish the job, spray with a rattle-can coat of etching primer followed by some durable engine enamel, then install 1-inch caps on the ends. These caps are available at Amazon, and they are measured by the inside dimension.

If you have your engine sitting on the oil pan, which is never a good idea because it's made from thin sheet metal, make a small stand for it. Now you can properly drain the oil prior to disassembly.

You also want to purchase a few engine hoist brackets, so you can lift the engine off the stand. I used standard hardware store hooks with 1/2-inch threads on all four corners. ■

The side rails are 9½ inches apart to accommodate the width of the engine. This is standard for all Stovebolts. Only the oil pan depth on older engines is different.

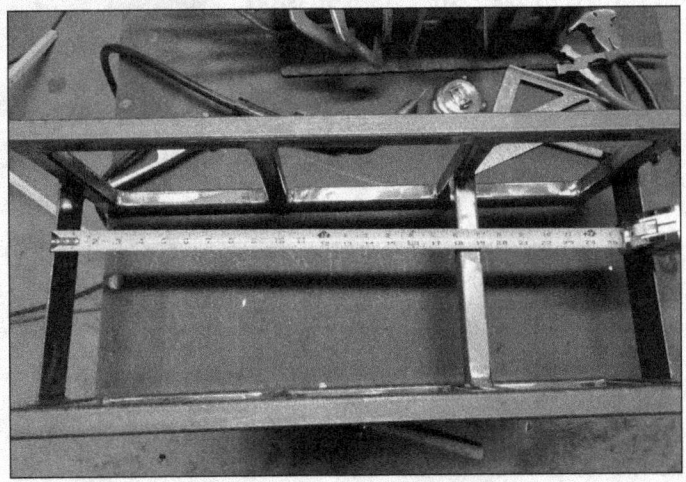

For the oil pan to fit nicely, you need the crossbar to be at 18½ inches.

The thin end pieces should be placed 4 inches down from the top. They are thin because they need to go between the oil pan and the bellhousing.

When you have several of these engines, and shop space is at a premium, this cart can be indispensable.

CHAPTER 4

Bellhousing Disassembly

The only way to separate the bellhousing from the engine is to remove the transmission, clutch assembly, and then the flywheel (if not already removed). You need to remove two bolts on the outside of the bellhousing, then four more on the inside, two of which you can't access until the flywheel is removed. You can get to all of this via the bellhousing access cover that has four screws directly under the bellhousing. Be sure to save the three tin lock-down plates that hold the flywheel bolts secure. They are necessary and difficult to find if you lose yours. Try not to bend off the tabs.

If needed, you can consult the shop manual for reference. It is easiest to remove the transmission, clutch assembly, and flywheel when the engine is still on the vehicle.

Avoid Catastrophic Failure

Being organized takes very little time and could help prevent a catastrophic failure. For example, use resealable bags to keep small items together. Mark one with "oil pan bolts." Mark the others similarly. You get the idea.

Also, take pictures of each assembly prior to the teardown. The images will help with reassembly. ■

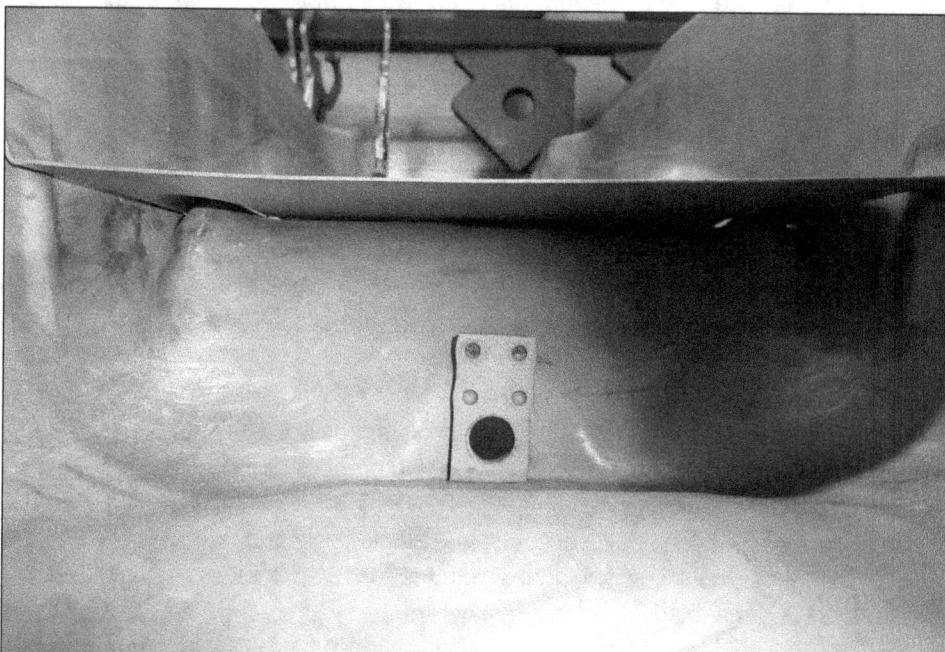

It is important to get every crevice completely clean inside the pan so you can assess its condition. This pan has suffered a lot of abuse.

Oil Pan

The oil pan is probably the most neglected piece of tin on the vehicle. Rocks dent it, stress warps it, and often you find an over-torqued drain plug. Water condensation causes major rust pits and even rust-through. I spent an entire day blasting this oil pan and inspecting it.

Once your pan is blasted, use 400-grit sandpaper to sand the entire pan inside and out. This makes it easy to see cracks, bumps, and abnormalities in the surface.

In this example, the previous owner didn't want to address the small hole made by a sharp rock and used Bondo to cover it. In all, there were three holes. One was from rock damage, another was rusted through, and another was an actual crack, about an inch long. These are not surprising because the pan is more than 60 years old.

It's down to the bare metal, so I can add some weld to seal these holes and cracks. First a little body work, smoothing and light hammer and dolly work to make things straight again. Once all the bumps and bruises are smooth, I weld the holes and cracks shut, redress the metal, and then it's time for another decision: How far I want to go with dressing up this oil pan. There are rust pits and various imperfections. My answer is always; no shortcuts!

If you perform metal working the same as if it were part of the vehicle,

This pan has lots of dents and damage due to the engine being set on the floor with the pan facing downward. It is difficult to seal these pans even without oil leaks, let alone trying to do it with a deformed pan.

ENGINE AND SHEET METAL PARTS PREPARATION

it becomes time consuming. I draw the line with putting Bondo on the oil pan because of rocks kicking up and making it look much worse than if you would have used an epoxy primer. Having the least amount of substrate the better.

When welding cracks, start about 1/4 inch before the crack on each end. This ensures the unseen start and finish of it is addressed too. Here, the rust-through was minor, and the welding went smoothly.

In this case, I had to address a stripped-out oil drain plug. Someone had already installed an oversize plug, and it stripped out. After redrilling out the oil pan's drain plug hole to 37/64 inch, I use a 5/8 x 18-inch tap.

As it turns out, this plug is available as a Dorman product (65313). It comes with the nylon gasket as well. This oil pan has a metal reinforcement at the drain plug that is plenty large enough to handle the size of the Dorman plug. Now the pan is like new.

This venerable old engine deserves the very best, and you don't want to get in the habit of cutting corners. I found many rust pits, dents, dings, deep scratches, cracked metal in the oil pan, side cover, and valve cover. They needed much hammer and dolly work to get them into shape.

Once they are sandblasted, you can use 400-grit sandpaper on a long board to check most of the surfaces of these parts. I recommend using a short Dura-Block to access other areas. You sand by hand if neither of those methods reach the spot.

You are checking for degree of flatness and smoothness. Once the metal is 95 percent there, apply a few thick coats of DPLF epoxy primer to the surface and then finish sand with 400-grit sandpaper. PPG's DPLF came highly recommended for engine tin because it is safe for up to 500°F. Once it's dry, you can apply rattle-can engine paint right over it.

Engine sheet metal often requires many hours of work but preserves the tin and makes additional rust virtually impossible. The oil pan, side cover, timing cover, and valve cover receive no paint on the inside. This

If needed, retap the pan plug, making sure there is an available plug to go with the size you choose. It's important to not over-torque the plug. Snug is fine because the plug's washer does most of the work. Replace the washer if it looks worn or out of shape.

avoids introducing possible contaminants into the engine internals, which is important. Once the outside is painted and dry, apply engine oil to the inside surfaces, letting the oil soak into the metal.

Valve Cover

The valve cover on the 1953–1955 engine has open slits on the top. General Motors wanted the engine to breathe but didn't take into account the severe damage that underhood dirt and grime getting into the valve cover could initiate. If your valve cover has open slits, a couple of ideas to remedy the situation come to mind. To preserve the look, close the slits from the inside using J-B Weld. It's even gray. If you clean the area thoroughly before application, it will stay there forever. Or, you can weld the slits closed. It is very important for a new engine rebuild to maintain a clean environment on the inside of the engine where sand and grit cannot ruin it.

If there are no slits, inspect for damage. The bottom of the cover should maintain its indentions that aid in sealing. The holes should be flat and not warped. It's a good idea to find some reinforcements for the cover screws so the pressure of the screw head is spread out.

Side Cover

Check the corners of the side cover and inspect for any leakage. Improperly installed side covers often cause leaks all over the garage floor! Flatten the screw hole areas, but maintain the natural indentions. A little tin work goes a long way.

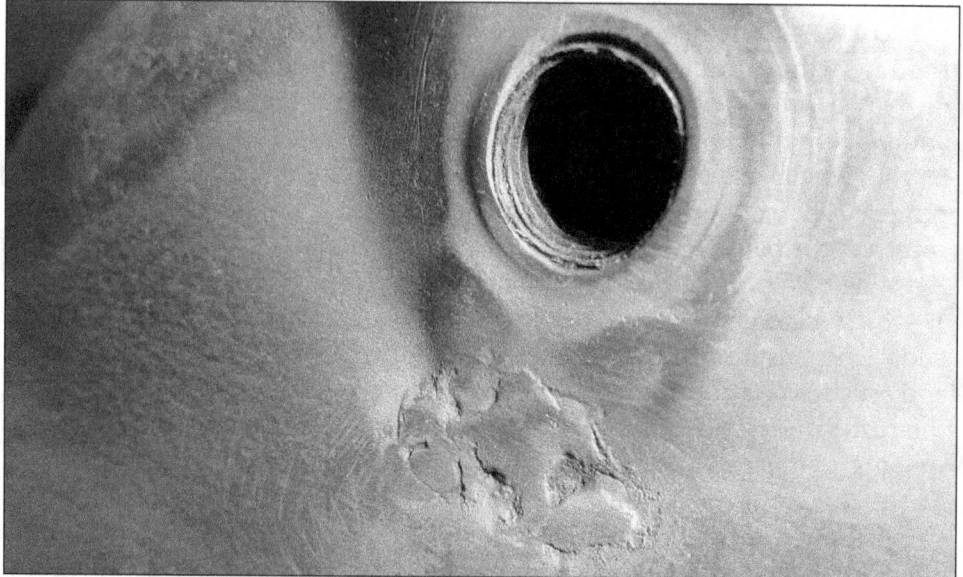

Thread damage, holes in the pan; everything takes time but time well spent if it prevents an oil leak.

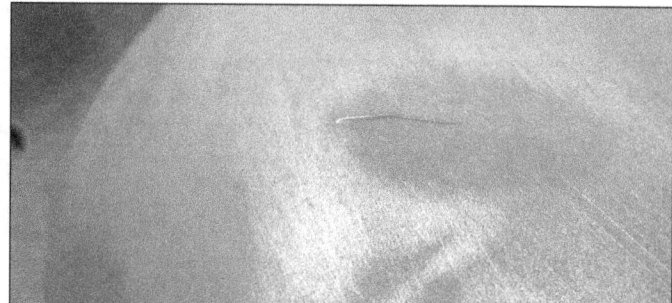

After blasting and sanding, a crack is revealed that goes all the way through. I could have replaced this pan, but I didn't want to take another vintage oil pan out of circulation.

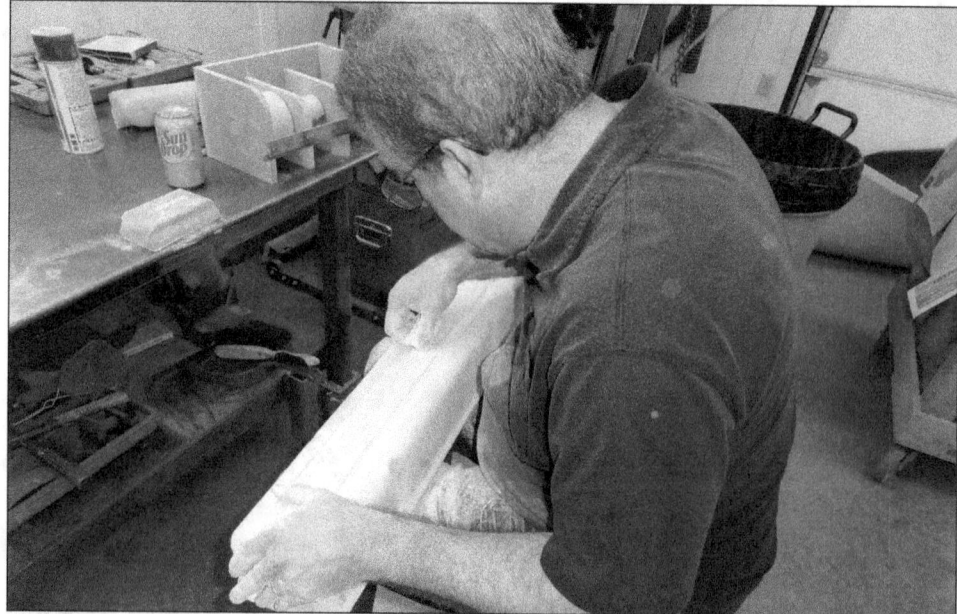

Final sanding after metal work, epoxy primer, and high-build primer. This cover is going to look good.

CHAPTER 5

ENGINE TEARDOWN

In this chapter, I will explain how to tear down the engine without doing any inadvertent damage. Certain things need to happen in order for you to be successful. For example, the timing cover does not come off when you remove all of the outside screws. That would have been too easy! There are two more screws inside the engine only accessible if you drop the oil pan. These little nuances can have you scratching your head without guidance. The shop manual is helpful, but there is nothing like learning from the experiences of others.

Harmonic Balancer and Oil Pump Removal

The next order of business is to remove the harmonic balancer. If you know the secret, this is easily done. Some of these balancers have been on the engine a long time and you might over-stress your puller if you don't lightly tap on the edge of the balancer as you are tightening your puller. If you lightly tap the edge, it smoothly walks right off the crankshaft. If you lodge a piece of wood into the crankshaft's rotation, it makes the crank stop so you can remove the balancer.

The balancer has two 3/8-inch threaded holes for using the proper style of puller (pictured earlier) in accordance with the shop manual. If you use a two-prong puller, make sure you center it. The balancer will come off easier.

The shop manual is a great guide for doing this but understand that it

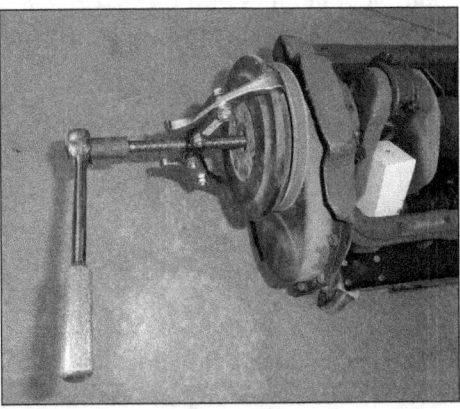

These balancers usually come right off, which is a concern when you think about it. The best idea is to have the machine shop drill a 7/16 x 20 x 1½-inch hole in the crank for a bolt to hold the balancer in place. You don't want the balancer falling off at speed; believe me.

The wooden block keeps the crankshaft from moving during the harmonic balancer removal process. This is the wrong puller for this job, but I broke my good one and hadn't replaced it yet. Be careful when substituting tools. You want to use a three-jaw puller (see page 17).

was written 58 years ago and there are very few tools that are described in that manual that are even available today. When they are, they are typically found in engine machine shops, not in yours or mine. You read the shop manual and then use the tools you have that are as close as possible to the originals.

In the case of the harmonic balancer puller, I had one and broke it taking off a stubborn balancer. Moral of the story? Use the proper puller.

Remove the oil pump next. Follow this sequence because items are protruding above the block's surface that you want to protect.

Start by removing the 1/2-inch pipe with fittings. It may be difficult to remove. Loosen the brass nuts completely. The oil pump is held in by a bolt with a locking nut. If the crankshaft is in the way, put your balancer back on as far as you can by hand and turn the crank until you have access.

By the way, the oil pump has four slotted screws on top and the pickup screen sticking out. Put your wrench on the bolt and loosen it. You should be able to spin off both the bolt and the nut by hand after that. Remove the bolt and nut then wiggle the oil pump until your 1/2-inch tube can drop right off, then pull out the oil pump.

Dipstick Tube

I have not found a successful way to get the dipstick tube out of the engine block without doing damage to the tube. However, a length

Take care not to bend anything relating to the oil pump and oil pickup screen. Because these parts are always exposed to oil, they are usually in good shape.

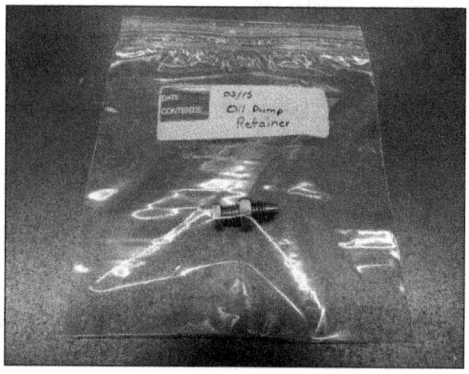

This is the special locknut and screw for the oil pump shaft after cleaning and bagging. Take care of the hardware on these vintage engines. Some of them are difficult to find.

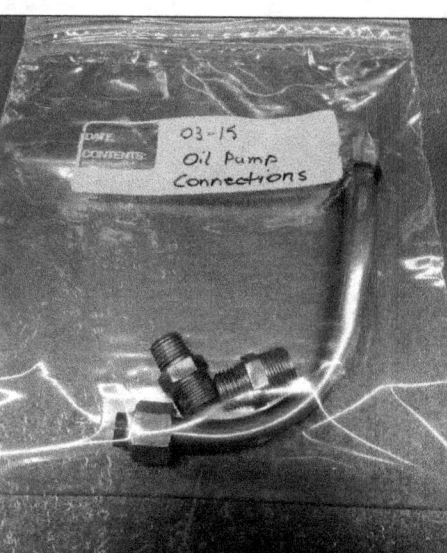

Once thoroughly cleaned, bag the oil pump connectors and parts. Check for cracks or anything that seems out of place.

Loosening the special locknut and screw (center, near the cam gear) allows the oil pump to pull out directly.

Oil Pump and Balancer Cleaning

The oil pump has an indention; this is where the bolt locks it in place during reassembly. Take all nuts and bolts, the oil pump, and the pickup screen (which you can unthread from the pump) to your parts washer and give everything a good cleaning. Use steel wool on the 1/2-inch tube including the brass nuts. Brush off the fittings with a fine wire wheel on the bench grinder, and do the same for the pickup assembly. Bead blast the harmonic balancer. When bead blasting the balancer, tape up the inside where the shaft goes as well as the outside where the timing cover seal rides. There is lots of dirt inside and this is the best way to get it out. Clean and clean some more!

Go easy on the rubber dampener between the two parts of the balancer that you will not remove. Finally, remember to use bags to sort and store the small components. ■

of 3/8-inch metal tube goes right in. Take the old one out as carefully as possible. Run a 5/16-inch bolt down the tube, then put a vise-grip over the area where the bolt is backing up the tube, and tap it out with a hammer.

The idea is to preserve the length measurement and the measurement of how far down in the block it went. Some engines have a 5/8-inch-deep stop at the bottom of the block; others have a 7/8-inch-deep stop.

Making a Custom Dipstick Tube

The dipstick tube on a 1953–1962 235 or 261 engine was 8.1094 inches long. The engine block has a stop that keeps the tube from continuing too far into the block; it is at 5/8 inch on most blocks, but a few have been known to have a 7/8-inch-deep stop. The tube is 3/8-inch steel, so any 3/8-inch fuel hard line made of steel works well. I prefer to make dipstick tubes out of stainless steel because they will outlast everything else on the engine, and they look really nice!

The trick is to get a straight length of 3/8-inch stainless steel fuel line. Because I purchased the stainless for this project in 20-foot rolls, I have a straightener for this purpose.

All 216/235/261 engines from 1949 through 1962 had roughly the same length and diameter tube. The official length is 8.1094 (8 7/64) inches. Your tube may be shorter, which is a good problem to have because all you need to do is cut off the excess.

I have a couple of tips that will make you feel more comfortable making a custom dipstick. First, the engine block has a stop inside of it so that when you drive in the new dipstick, it stops where it's supposed to. The other thing is that because it is pressed in tightly, it is highly unlikely that you will leave your old one in usable condition.

You may think that this is just a dipstick tube, but this one will outlast the engine, and give the engine some bling. The dipstick tube is a 3/8-inch piece of stainless steel tube. Originally it was made of regular steel.

Removal Steps

Before you replace a dipstick tube, fill the oil in your engine to the full line. To be sure of the oil level measurement, put the correct number of quarts in your engine, run it up, and then check the oil level. If there is any discrepancy between these dipstick measurements, you can fix it now if you choose.

The tubing must be straight to look right. Straightening stainless steel rolls like this without the appropriate tool is much harder than it may seem.

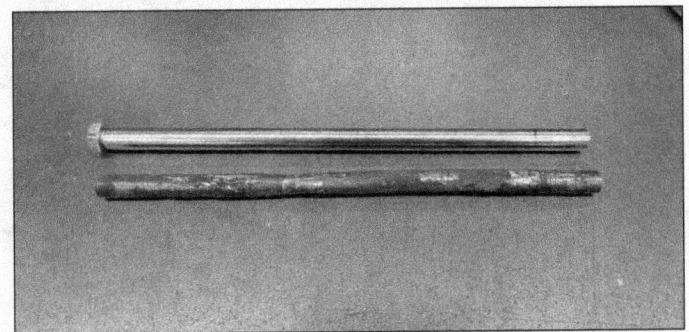

There is no good way to remove the old tube. To keep it from collapsing, inserting a 5/16-inch bolt helps, but don't plan on keeping the old one in good condition.

Making a Custom Dipstick Tube (continued)

If the oil is below the full mark, you will want to shorten the new tube; if it's above the mark, you cut the new tube longer by the amount of difference between the measurements. Remember, measure twice, cut once!

Because the dipstick itself is almost exactly as wide as the tube, it is important to know that squashing the tube in any way makes it unusable. If you use a tubing cutter, do it less aggressively than usual. It's best to use a metal-cutting band saw. Also, important to note is that the new tube is nonmagnetic. Be sure to keep any cutting or adjusting away from the engine and blow out all the metal fragments prior to installation.

Clean thoroughly around the dipstick tube so that you don't introduce a bunch of crud inside the oil pan. Remember, there is no good way to get to dirt and crud out once it's inside the pan, including metal shavings, etc.

Use a clean 5/16-inch bolt and drop it down the tube so the head sticks up out of the tube. Estimate where the end of the bolt is, go above it a bit, and grab the tube tightly with a vise-grip. This procedure almost ensures that you will ruin your old tube. But this is insignificant because it's just a piece of regular steel fuel line that you can get at your local auto parts store. Work the tube left to right to free it up. It's press fit so it will come out eventually.

Because you used a bolt to reinforce the old tube, you can use it to measure the length of the new one. If you use the exact measurement above, chances are you won't need to do anything, but it's wise to compare the two. Any difference will show on the dipstick when checking your oil.

Once you are satisfied that the new tube is the same length as the old tube, or you have decided to change it, check the oil level one more time.

The time to polish your new stainless tube is before installation. If you try hard enough, you can polish it to a mirror finish. Use the same methods you are accustomed to using for any polishing step: super-high-grit wet paper, buffing wheel with compound, etc. Be sure to tape the "press fit" area before polishing.

Installation Steps

Insert your dipstick into the new tube before installing. Make sure that it slides in and out easily. If it doesn't, there is a problem on one end or the other (probably some less-obvious damage). The correct drill bit to use to clean out any imperfections caused by the tubing cutter squashing the ends is a 5/16-inch bit. Blow out and clean the new tube thoroughly so you don't inadvertently put metal shavings in your oil pan. This is a straight piece, so no bending is necessary nor desired because the bend can bind the dipstick. This vintage of dipstick is not designed to flex.

Some engine blocks of this era had 5/8-inch-deep stops; others measured 7/8 inch. This may have to do with the depth of the oil pan because some years' versions were different. You should be able to tell the depth of the stop by looking at your old tube.

Measure down 5/8 inch (or whatever number you measured) and use a Sharpie to mark the tube all the way around (you can also use a piece of painters' masking tape). This is to give you an idea of when to stop driving it in. You should be able to feel when the tube stops moving, but it's good to mark it so you know what is happening.

With a clean 5/16-inch bolt on the top and your marking on the bottom, you are ready to drive in the tube. You want to retain the angle closely so there is no squashing at the bottom. Once it's started, you can tap it all the way in place. It's a good idea to use a smaller hammer so you can get the feel of the operation. Since you used your old tube to measure, the only difference is that your new tube is prettier, stronger, and rustproof and probably will outlast even you! ■

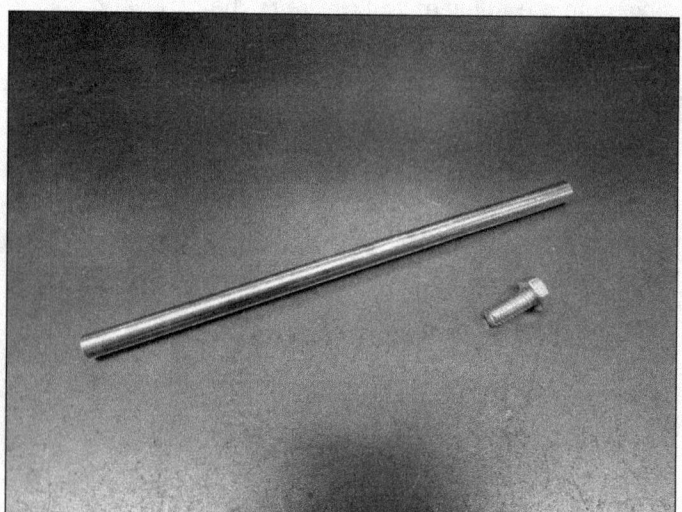

A 5/16-inch bolt is essential in tapping the tube into the block. Remember, this is a nonmagnetic tube so any metal shavings cannot be removed with a magnet.

Timing Gear Cover

The timing gear cover is held on by eight short screws and two longer screws that you can access from the outside. Two more hex-head bolts are found on the inside. The timing cover is not removeable from the outside only. You want to preserve the bolt-head retainer tin, so you lightly tap on the tab with a screwdriver and small hammer. If you tap in steps, it doesn't break as easily. Once you have both tabs bent slightly outward, use a wrench to remove the bolts.

You may have to turn the crank to get the bolts out. Also remove the locking tin, clean everything thoroughly, and put the hardware in a labeled bag.

The cover needs a little prep work before you move on. First remove the crankshaft seal that is embedded into the cover. Do not try to muscle this seal out of the hole with a big screwdriver, hoping not to damage the cover. Set your bench vise to about 4 inches open and place the hole in the cover over the open jaws. Then with a punch, lightly tap all the way around until it comes out. You want to preserve the tightness of this cover-to-seal connection.

Once the seal is out, tape the inside area of the hole where the seal will be pushed back in, and blast the cover. This removes all the gasket residue, old dirt, and grime but preserves the tightness.

With the timing cover removed, you can see the oil spout tube and the gear set. This poor old engine was ridden hard and put away wet. Wet is a bad thing and you can see the pitting that has occurred where the timing cover seal rides on it. These grooves are deep, and I will probably put a stainless steel sleeve over

These two bolts are the culprits responsible for you not being able to remove the timing cover from the outside. Bend the retainer slowly so the tabs do not break off. That retainer is there to keep the bolts from backing out in a pretty inaccessible location.

Be careful not to damage the little tube that is sticking out of the block. It has a small hole in it pointed at the gear junction for oiling the gearset. The tube is pinched on the end and is located between the two gears.

My favorite tool for bending the tabs is a screwdriver. Bend slowly and carefully. Use the back of the wrench for a hammer to very gently move the tabs.

That damage is due to the rubber seal rubbing on the metal. The accepted fix for this is a stainless steel sleeve called a Speedi-Sleeve. It's very thin, but it does add diameter which is good for a better seal anyway.

the shaft to be sure I have no front seal leakage. This is the engine's front main seal.

The tin often turns out to be time consuming, with lots of dents, holes, and unacceptable anomalies. If you want something perfect, you must put in the time. It pays to do this in steps, and do not move on to the next step until the other one is finished. Too many steps being juggled can lead to missing something important.

Camshaft

The camshaft will be replaced along with the cam's gear and all the cam bearings. When you pull it out, you will notice all the journals it has to go through to get it in and out. Remember this because when installing a new one, it will be imperative that you take your time and be careful not to ruin the new bearings.

To remove the cam, rotate the crank until you see two Phillips-head screws through the gear. These are for the camshaft's thrust plate. Remove the screws, and then carefully pull the cam (with the gear still on it) straight out. Clean the screws and put them in a separate labeled bag.

Even though you may not be using the old cam or gear, you need to retrieve the thrust plate. That's the plate that you removed with the two screws to release the cam for removal. To get to this important plate, you need to press out the gear. I found it useful to have a 20-ton shop press in the shop for removal of U-joints and other things that are press fit.

You want to also retrieve the crescent-shaped key that helps keep it in straight. You can pry it out with a screwdriver. Don't forget to save it for when you are ready to press on the new gear.

A shop press and a hardened impact socket make short work of pressing out a cam gear. This is necessary to access the thrust plate because it will be reused.

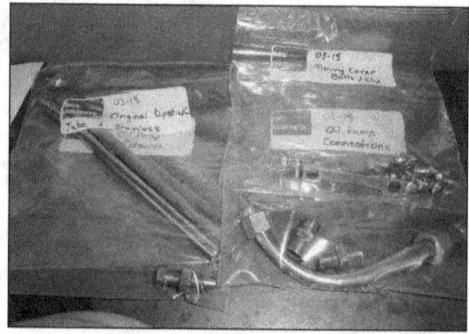
Our zippered bag inventory is starting to look impressive. This will make the assembly much easier than guessing where things go and the misery of getting it wrong.

To turn the engine so these two holes line up, you can reinstall the harmonic balancer temporarily by hand.

Timing Plate Modification

This sidebar applies only if your vehicle has a front (of the engine) engine-mounting system. If your vehicle does not require mounting the engine under the timing cover, you can skip it.

Adding Mount Holes to the Timing Plate

During the later years of the series (1958–1962), the engines present a problem concerning motor mounts and the fact that newer engines were mounted differently. The good news is, Chevrolet kept the design of the engine the same as in earlier years, so you can still use it with a minor modification. You need to address this difference, while the engine is apart. The difference is where the front motor mounts were positioned in 1947–1955. The bolts were 7/16-inch fine-thread carriage bolts. The missing holes are the problem.

The plan is to drill the 29/64-inch holes using a standard drill bit, then with it marked carefully, use a Dremel tool and a carbide rasp to finish the holes to accommodate the square part of the carriage bolt. Of course, you could use a different-style bolt, but where would be the fun in that? The idea is that when you are done, you won't be able to tell whether Chevrolet did it or you did it. Use a hand triangle file to really get those corners sharp.

The placement of these holes is important. They align the engine left to right on the frame, so it must be centered to the center of the engine's crankshaft. To do this, you put the plate back on the engine temporarily and measure from the crankshaft's cap bolts to find the center of the plate. You remove the front crankshaft cap bolts and replace them with longer ones that you can screw in and have the head of the bolt high enough to grab the edge of the T-square. This allows you to place the T-square straight and even.

Transfer the center of the bolt's head to the plate with a thin Sharpie. Turn over the T-square and mark the same on the other side. Measure precisely between the two lines; that is the center of the engine. Mark the center with the Sharpie.

From the edge of the plate, using the T-square as the guide to compensate for its curve, measure using the upper part of a caliper to .955 inch. Put a mark where it intersects with the engine cap line. Do this on both sides. Now draw a line all the way across the plate to each mark that you just made.

From the engine centerline, place a mark at exactly 1.535 inches to the left of the centerline and again to the right of the centerline. This is the 3.070 inches you need between the center of the holes. As it happens, I have a good friend in Washington State who lives and breathes these engines, and he sent me a series of pictures to properly align these holes. He uses a Chevy original plate that already had the holes drilled in the right place.

Do not use the edge of the plate as a reference for anything because they can differ enough to make them unreliable. Always measure from the face using a T-square.

It's a good idea to dimple the centerline for future reference. Dimple the cross-line intersecting between your 3.070-inch mark and your .955-inch mark for drilling. Use a 29/64-inch drill bit. I recommend using about a 3/8-inch bit to start with and move up so as not to have problems with the bit wandering.

Once you have the holes drilled, you need to make them square. This is difficult to do for a home garage mechanic like myself, but a Dremel tool with a carbide rasp gets the job done. The slower you go, the nicer the holes turn out. Use the proper 7/16-inch carriage bolt to check your work.

While you are going to all of this trouble to be correct, it probably makes a lot more sense to keep the hole round, weld a 7/16-inch fine-thread weld nut to the inside of the plate, and then bolt the engine to the frame from underneath. The reason this is a popular idea is because if you forget to put that carriage bolt into that hole before you put the timing cover back on, you are in sort of a pickle.

To avoid the dilemma, drill a small hole for a cotter pin in the bolts so they stay in, no matter what. I would use safety wire and route the wire through both holes at once. Also be careful not to use bolts that are long enough to puncture the timing cover. ■

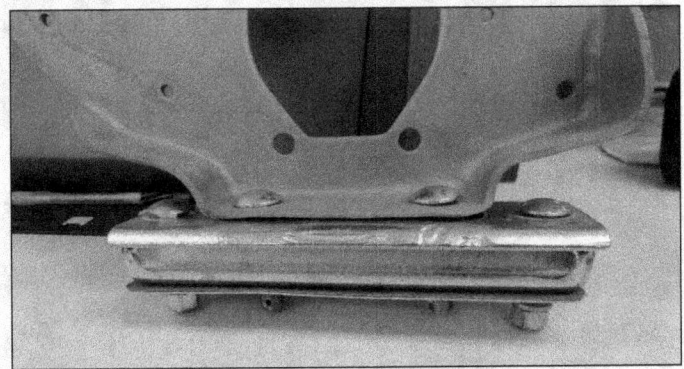

1 The two holes in the timing plate for the front motor mounts are important for vehicles with front motor mounts. Be sure to install the bolts before you put on the timing cover.

Timing Plate Modification (continued)

2 One challenge is finding the center of the engine's crankshaft and then transferring the mount holes to the other plane.

3 Finding the crankshaft's center is imperative. You do not want the engine to sit at an angle in the vehicle. That would cause many problems with drivetrain parts.

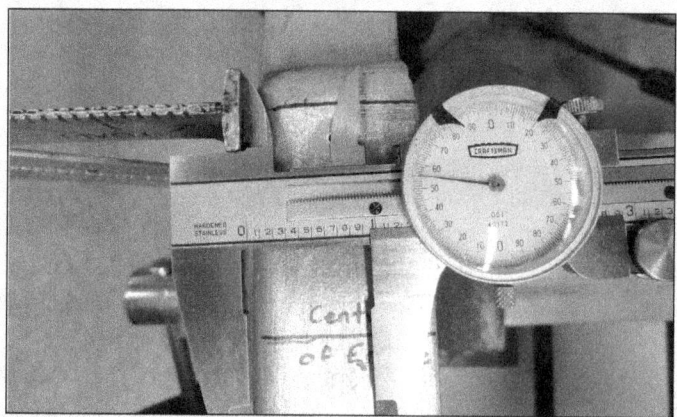

4 Vernier calipers are a good way to get accurate measurements.

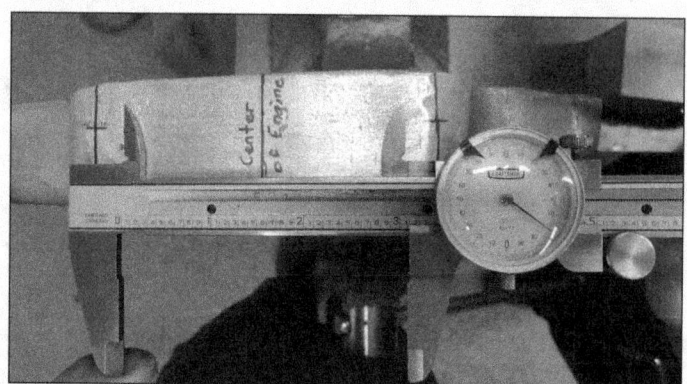

5 Once you know the center, you need 1.535 inches on each side of it for a total of 3.070 inches.

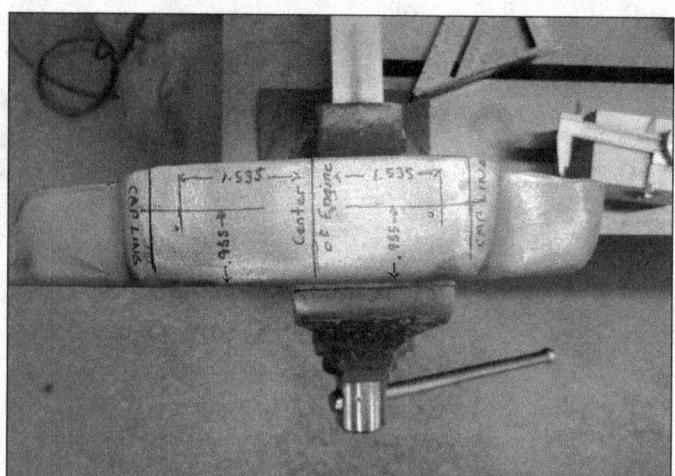

6 X marks the spot. Be sure to begin with a small bit to prevent drill bit wandering.

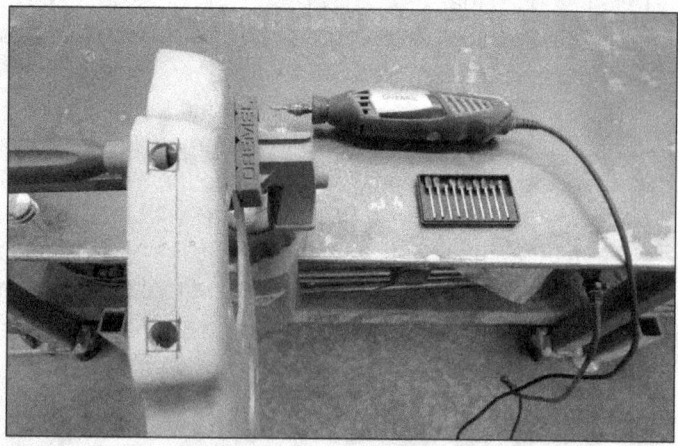

7 A Dremel really comes in handy here. Making round holes into square holes is difficult without it.

ENGINE TEARDOWN

8 General Motors retained the same front timing plate until the end of the Stovebolt era, so you don't have to locate an older timing plate, making this project an easy conversion. The exception is late 1962.

Crankshaft and Pistons

Your engine is starting to look a little bare. Everything is now out of the block except a small tin shield, the pistons, rods, and the crankshaft. So, removing the crankshaft and pistons is an important stage to do correctly. This is a step that needs careful attention to detail. Each piston rod belongs in its original cylinder. It is not a good idea to put them anywhere else. Each piston rod and cap that attaches to the crankshaft must be oriented in the same direction as it was originally.

Your first order of business is to clean around the sides of the piston rod and cap area so that you can see the original markings. You want to mark the rod and cap connection so that you know exactly how they go back together later. You can't use a Sharpie for this because when the engine shop cleans them for inspection, they disappear. A number punching kit for stamping steel is relatively cheap and handy to have around the shop.

Sometimes engines are stamped already, but not always. Upon close inspection I saw that this engine was marked completely. This is a critical step and can't be omitted if you expect to have a top-notch build.

This means that on the side connection between each rod and cap on the same side, it should be marked

This 1/8-inch letter/number punch set can be used when the markings are ambiguous.

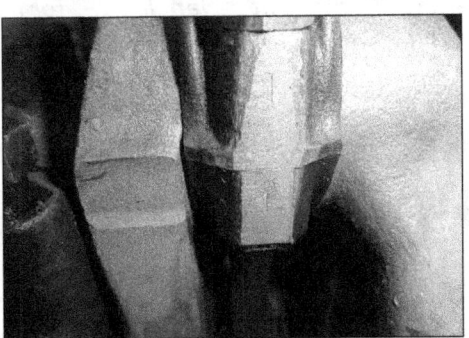

It's important that the piston rods and caps are oriented in the same way they were when removed and that they are used in the same cylinder. Marking both halves on only one side helps you with reinstallation. The "1"s stamped here denote the number-1 cylinder's piston rod and cap.

This piston rod cap is marked with a "1." Also notice the orientation of the number. It is read standing over the engine, so the engine front is in front of you and the back of the engine is behind you. All the caps should be oriented in the same direction. If not, be sure to make a note of that so you don't install them incorrectly later.

twice: once on the cap and once on the rod itself. In this case, the cap has a number in the middle on top as well.

Each crankshaft bearing cap needs to be marked. Since you can't confuse the front and the back, no indication stampings are needed, but the two center caps must be marked with an "F" for front and "R" for rear.

To remove the crankshaft, use a 1/2-inch-drive breaker bar with 3/4-inch socket because these bolts are torqued down well. Remove the bolts on each cap, bag them in a labeled bag, and keep them with the cap they came out of.

Before you move on to the next cap, check to see if any shims are between the block and the cap. If there are, count them, write down the exact location they were in, and keep them with the cap in their location. Give this information to your engine shop when you drop off the engine. This vintage 235 came with no shims. None is good. If you find shims for 1954–1962, someone other than Chevrolet put them there. It's time to take them out!

Once the caps are off, place them aside (in their original order) to prepare for cleaning.

Now you have a crankshaft with the pistons still attached. Remove the piston rod caps. Use a 1/2-inch-drive 9/16-inch socket on a ratchet to remove each cap, one rod at a time. Leave the nuts on the rod, but unscrewed all the way to the end.

Tap the two nuts/rods with a short piece of 2x4 wood. Never use metal on metal. Once the cap is loose, you can pull it off. Chance are the bearings will fall out. Othe than inspecting them to see thei wear pattern, they are trash. Loo carefully at the cap orientation. You will see that there is only one way to put them back on correctly.

After each cap is removed from the crankshaft, remove the nuts and let the piston drop away. When all o them are done this way, your crank shaft is free. This is a heavy crank shaft, and it's important that you don't drop it. Remove the crankshaft and stand it up in a corner where nobody will touch it. It's not good to lay a crankshaft flat any longer than you must.

With the crankshaft out, you now have six pistons and rods to

The crankshaft bearing caps are also marked "F" for front and "R" for rear. They too must be oriented the same way as before.

Though difficult to see, this crankshaft bearing cap is labeled "F" for front. This means that it is the first intermediate bearing cap from the front. Because there are only four bearing caps, it's second from the front.

This overhead shot shows the correct bearing cap orientation. It's not a good place to make mistakes.

ENGINE TEARDOWN

Piston Removal Process

1 Ridges about 3/16-inch wide of accumulated crud keep the piston from coming out of the top of the cylinder. Time to get out your handy ridge reamer.

2 The ridge reamer uses a cutting blade, and the three stabilizers are moved simultaneously toward the edge of the cylinder by turning the center screw. The lock bolt keeps it in place during the process.

3 As you turn the ridge reamer, the included scraper precisely scrapes the tops of the cylinders without doing damage. This removes the carbon buildup so you can remove the piston.

4 Pushing the piston with a wooden hammer handle is a good way to slide it out. Be sure to support the rod so it does not scratch the cylinder walls when removing. You can do that using both hands reaching around from both sides.

5 Once past the rings, you can grab the piston with one hand, guide the piston rod with the other, and remove the piston and rods together. Nothing wrong with having a helper either.

CHEVROLET INLINE-6 ENGINE 1929–1962: HOW TO REBUILD

work on. To perform the next step, you need to be able to get to the top and bottom of the engine block.

As nice as it would be to simply push the pistons out the top of the block, you must use a reamer first. If you run your fingers inside the cylinder, chances are good that there will be a ridge at the top of the cylinder. This is because over time, the pistons push crud as far up as the top rings can push. This leaves a ridge about 3/16-inch wide or so. It can be so packed you simply can't get the pistons out. You do not want to ruin the cylinder walls by forcing the piston.

The reamer adjusts to the size of the cylinder, then a single blade with a pad on one end cuts the ridge out of the cylinder. It only goes in the cylinder one way. Set it in place and turn the center bolt until the reamer is semi-tight in the cylinder. Using oil liberally, switch to the larger socket and turn the reamer in the cylinder. Give it a few complete rotations, then tighten just a little, and do it again.

After a few more rotating and tightening sequences, the ridge should be removed. Do not force it, use smooth and easy movement. The job is finished when there is no ridge left. Then the piston slides right out.

In the case of this engine, it had no ridge at all. This is the first time I have seen this. Cylinders almost always need the ridge removed.

With the cylinder oiled, you can tap the pistons/rods out with a wood hammer handle (or similar), being sure to guide the rod out without it scratching the cylinder walls.

You are almost done preparing the block for the machine shop. Now you need to clean the rods, caps, and all the pieces that you just removed. Remember: no harsh treatment of anything that could affect measurements. Clean everything in your small parts washer, put all the hardware in labeled bags, and prepare to take them with you to your engine machine shop.

Separating the Rods and Pistons

The pistons and rods come apart easily. There is a 9/16-inch hex-head bolt inside the piston/piston rod connection. To loosen this bolt and nut, do not put the rod in a vise. You can potentially bend the rod and cause real problems. Rather, put a long punch in the vise, sticking out so you can put the piston via the piston pin hole over it giving you the leverage to remove the bolt. The bolts are tight, but a 3/8-inch ratchet is adequate for the job. Loosen the bolt but do not remove it. By loosening, the pin should push right out.

The pistons and rings won't be reused, but you should remove the rings and clean up the pistons anyway. (I do not like dirty stuff sitting anywhere in my shop.) At this point, it's a matter of cleaning everything to your satisfaction. After this round of cleaning, you can begin preparing the engine block.

Piston ring pliers makes removing and installing piston rings easy. They are inexpensive and worth having in your tool arsenal. They are available nearly anywhere engine tools are sold.

So, other than addressing a few remaining engine block and head issues, you are just about ready to make the trip to the engine machine shop. No matter what the machine shop says as far as whether your block and head are healthy and worthy of the effort, most of the work you have done so far is still time well spent.

Rod and Piston Separation Process

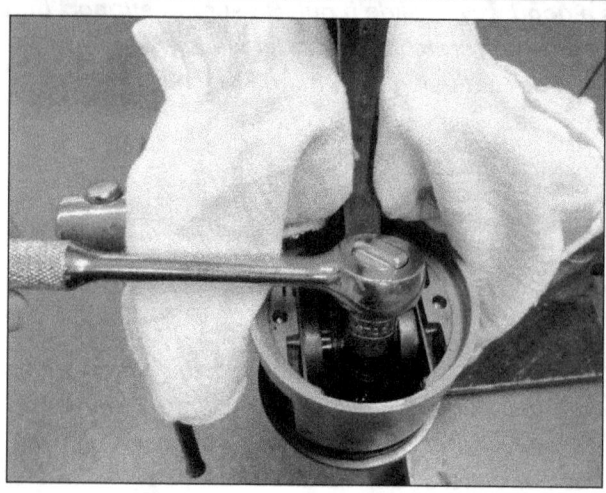

1 These rod bolts are pretty tight. Be sure not to bend the rod when separating them. Don't clamp them in a vise; rather, clamp a long punch in the vise and slide the piston into it via the rod connection hole. The piston is easily removed from the rod once the bolt is loose. The piston pin slides right out.

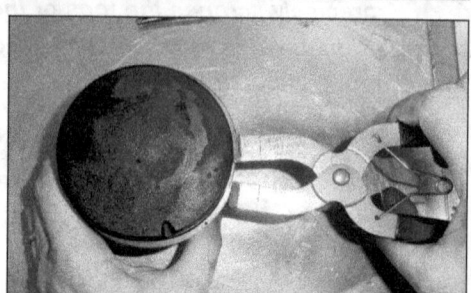

2 Removing the piston rings is easy with these piston ring pliers. The rings will not be reused but there is a slight possibility the pistons might be.

ENGINE TEARDOWN

3 Piston ring pliers hold the piston rings. They provide for an even spread, and that also spreads the stress on the ring. Only spread the ring as much as you have to.

4 With everything you see here cleaned and ready for reassembly, you can move on to the next phase. You have a lot more to do.

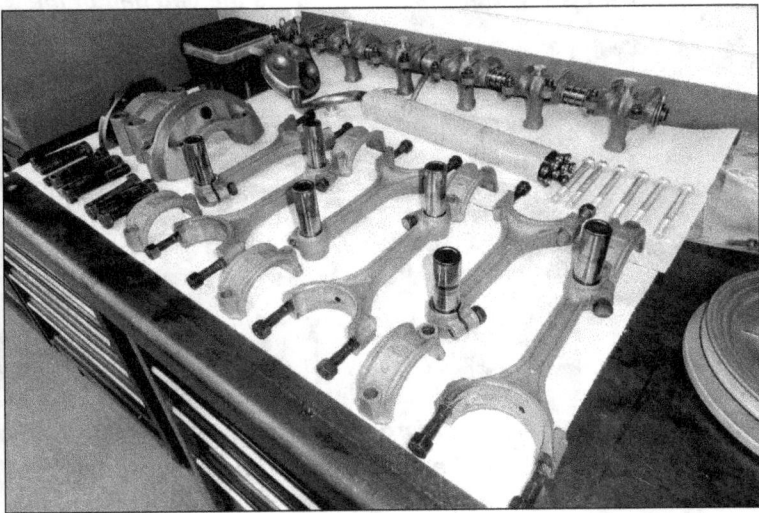

5 These parts were bead blasted where appropriate, which means that no machined surfaces were blasted. Everything was carefully taped off that has to do with machined surfaces beforehand.

Final Block Preparation

Make sure all freeze plugs are removed, all threaded ports open, anything that can aid in getting the internals of the engine as clean as possible.

The accelerator linkage pin can be removed. You need to remove four freeze plugs and four oil gallery plugs. To remove the freeze plugs (two in the side and two in the front) do the same thing that the shop manual suggests for removing the four oil gallery plugs, which is to drill a 3/8-inch hole in the center of the plug, then pry it out with a long punch.

When drilling, remember that you are only interested in drilling a shallow hole. This is important, so you don't drill into a water jacket or something. There is about 5/8 inch between the shallowest freeze plug and the water jacket. The bottom right freeze plug is the cover for the camshaft on that end.

You can use a magnet to catch the metal shavings, so they don't get spread all over. When prying these plugs out, do not rest the punch on the edges of the plugs. That can cause ugly gouges in the block that could make fitment a problem. You want to use another thin piece of metal or another freeze plug. Anything to protect the surfaces.

If the rear main seal is still inside its groove, push it out with a small screwdriver. Then, remove all of the threaded plugs. Also remove the little metal shield that is just below the road draft tube and is attached by two slotted screws.

Inspect the block to make sure you didn't miss anything. There should be nothing removable left. Place all the small parts, plugs, etc., in a labeled bag. I use brand-new threaded plugs during assembly, but it's good to have the old ones in a bag so you can account for them.

Remember to remove the pilot bushing. This is easier than most people think if you simply screw a 5/8-inch tap into the bushing. When the tap bottoms out, it pulls out the bushing. Modern pilot bearings are available that can replace the bushing for a nicer mechanical connection.

CHAPTER 5

Preparing the Block

1 Remove the freeze plug by drilling a 3/8-inch hole in the center of the plug and then use a long punch to pry them out. Don't drill any deeper than you have to.

2 This engine has a rubber rear main seal that easily slides out using a screwdriver. Not shown is the cap half of the seal, but it comes out the same way.

3 Remove all miscellaneous plugs, caps, etc. and the oil baffle that prevents oil from slobbering into your road draft tube.

4 Don't forget to remove the accelerator pin and any screws or fittings. The engine will be cleaner when it comes back from the engine shop if they boil it out with everything removed.

Water Jacket

When you have worked with these engines long enough, you begin to see the anomalies that Chevrolet didn't address. One of them is water jacket access. The drain plug near the back of the engine is used for draining the coolant out of the engine block. The problem is, sediment seems to congregate right in the back of the engine because the engine was installed with a 3-degree back slant toward the firewall. This means that when you need to drain the block, you can't because it has rock-hard sediment plugging that hole.

With freeze plugs installed, there is no way to get to this area of the water jacket from anywhere other than through that drain hole. I have spent hours with a coat hanger routing out the crud. So, before you take the engine to the machine shop, remove the freeze plugs, remove the drain plug, clear the drain, and spray it with a garden hose to make sure it is free flowing.

Before you assume that the engine shop will do this for you, let me tell you that every engine I have taken to many different engine machine shops and specifically told them about this problem and asked them to address it, came back still plugged up. They do not have any better way to get to that area of the engine than you do.

Remember that the water jacket is thin, so don't be tempted to jamb a drill bit in there. A coat-hanger-size wire through the freeze plug holes

This is the style of 1/4-inch NPT drain plug you need for the drain port on the engine block. While you are in the vicinity, you can also add an expandable freeze plug to the bellhousing just to cover the hole.

and the drain plug hole eventually clears it. The engine shop's boiling process is good but not that good!

CHAPTER 6

CHOOSING A MACHINE SHOP

The engine machine shop you use matters. Be sure to ask all candidates in your local area if they are familiar with these vintage engines. You want them to treat your engine as if it is going into a concours car. You will probably not be asking for the bare minimum service they provide so they must be competent.

Preparing for Machine Shop Work

Carefully box up and label everything you have taken off the engine. Have the shop inspect all the parts to determine what can be saved and what will have to be purchased. For example, if the cylinders simply require honing, the shop may able to keep the pistons, but they need to be checked individually to ensure that they are still serviceable. You may have questions about some parts, such as the hydraulic lifters. Write down all your questions and make a list of things you want the shop to do. The following are things to put on your list.

- Can you save the hydraulic lifters by resurfacing them? The cost is typically the same for a new set of lifters as it is for resurfacing the old ones.
- What assembly lube do you use? Lubriplate No. 105 is a white, waterproof, NLGI No. 0 grease lubricant that possesses exceptional anti-seize properties and is recommended extensively for coating all moving parts for engine assembly and rebuilding. You need both assembly grease and assembly lube. A good combo is Lubriplate Grease and Royal Purple Max Tough Assembly Lube or an equivalent.
- Is there anything you can tell me off the top of your head that I should know about assembly? There is always something you should know that they know. They might share information with you such as how to ensure that the rear main seal doesn't leak or common problems they see all the time. Never pass up an opportunity to learn about your engine.

Then if you want the shop to do special work, you must tell them exactly what that may be. For this engine, here is my wish list.

- Please install the freeze plugs and oil gallery plugs. Use threaded oil gallery plugs (for a small extra cost).

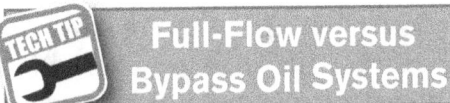

Full-Flow versus Bypass Oil Systems

There is a lot of confusion between full-flow and bypass oil systems. Both are full-pressure oiling systems, so it has nothing to do with pressure. It has everything to do with how much oil is getting filtered. The first full-flow oil system for a Chevy 6-cylinder was introduced in 1958 with a new 261 design. This was the first time all of the oil was sent through the filter. In contrast, the bypass system is the only one available for the 216/235 engines and sends about 12 percent of the oil through the filter.

Any filter at all was a dealer-installed option in those days. Because this is unacceptable to me for a new rebuild, I am having the machine shop do the mod. Performed by a competent machinist the mod allows for 100-percent oil filtration. This helps ensure longer engine life.

CHAPTER 6

- Please install cam bearings because they are pressed in.
- I would like a 1½-inch-deep, 7/16-20 fine-thread hole drilled in the crankshaft for bolting down the harmonic balancer. The shop should be able to do this for you. I was quoted $50. It's a small price to pay for being able to turn your engine with a ratchet (only with the spark plugs out) and the added safety of the balancer not falling off at highway speed because it's usually pressed on.
- According to the how-to steps outlined at devestechnet.com/Home/FullFlowOil (you can even print this out for them), can you mod this engine for full-flow oil filtration? The answer should be yes (I was quoted $100). I feel much better knowing all my oil is being filtered, not just 12 percent as is the case with the stock bypass system. This modification is the same thing that comes stock on the newer 261 engine and is how all modern engines work.
- If you have a 216 or 235 engine with a bypass system but want the benefit of a spin-on oil filter (still bypass but easier to change the filter), you have two options. A good choice is to get the WIX Model 27455 spin-on adapter that mounts to the intake manifold just as the bypass filter did. The WIX 51050 filter is used with that system. This 51050 filter has a built-in .0625-inch-reduced orifice to keep the proper oil pressure. It's a good kit. The only disadvantage is that it uses a nonstandard thread and does not work with other brands or types of filters. The other choice is to purchase a Trans-Dapt 1028 spin-on adapter, which uses an everyday PH8A, FL-1, NAPA1515 spin-on filter and then somewhere in the line you add a .0625-inch restrictor. It's not difficult at all; you just tap the inside of one of the fittings for another fitting with a 1/16-inch hole in it. Per the instructions in chapter 10.
- At this point, consider purchasing the overhaul kit from the machine shop. It comes with everything needed for the complete rebuild in the over or under size the engine was machined to. Pistons, rings, bearings, push rods, gasket set, cam gear, and the works. When it comes to purchasing a cam for this engine, a common mistake people make is ordering a performance cam. The best performing cam through all RPM ranges is the stock cam. I always order a new cam from the same shop that did the machine work.

Every part labeled and at the machine shop for its inspection and processing. More careful disassembly may translate to fewer problems later.

These are things I am either uncomfortable doing myself or feel the job would be done more competently by the machine shop. The extra cost of them putting in the freeze plugs, for example, is minimal and since this is a possible source of leaks, why not let the pro do it? Cam bearings are pressed in and if you don't have a good way of doing this, ask them to do it. Drilling the crank for a bolt serves two purposes: It ensures that the balancer doesn't slip off, and it also gives me the ability to turn the engine with a breaker bar during timing and setup. Between that and the fact that there are horror stories out there about people's pressed-on harmonic balancers coming off at highway speed, it seemed prudent.

So now, the engine, head, crank, cam, lifters, and two full boxes of engine parts are all at the machine shop. They have instructions to

Displacement Numbers

The formula for calculating overbore is:

$$(\text{bore} \div 2)^2 \times \text{stroke} \times \pi \times 6$$

Where pi equals 3.14159.

Here are the displacement numbers for various overbore sizes.

Overbore Size	Jobmaster 261	Thriftmaster 235
.000 Stock	260.930 ci	235.490 ci
.010 Over	262.323 ci	236.813 ci
.020 Over	263.721 ci	238.141 ci
.030 Over	265.121 ci	239.472 ci
.040 Over	266.526 ci	240.807 ci
.050 Over	267.934 ci	242.146 ci
.060 Over	269.346 ci	243.488 ci
.070 Over	270.762 ci	244.834 ci
.080 Over	272.182 ci	246.184 ci

1954–1962 Stovebolt Specs

	Jobmaster	Thriftmaster
Displacement	261 ci	235½ ci
Bore	3¾ inch	3 9/16 inch
Stroke	3 15/16 inch	3 15/16 inch
Firing Order	1-5-3-6-2-4	1-5-3-6-2-4
Compression Ratio	7.8:1	8:1
Horsepower	33.7 (AMA) 148	30.4 (AMA) 140
Number of Main Bearings	4	4
Wrist Pin Diameter	0.927 inch	0.866 inch
Rod Shaft Thickness, front to back	.595 inch	.595 inch
Rod Shaft Thickness, side to side	.975 inch	.760 inch
Crankshaft Journal Diameter	2.435 inches	2.435 inches
Engine Color in Trucks	Green and some later yellow	Gray

inspect everything that would have an impact on tolerances and machine work. Now that your precious engine is out of your hands, you can expect at least a month of time at the machine shop, but don't forget to ask for a specific timeframe.

Standard Shop Procedures

The following is a list of things that the shop can do for you.

Magnafluxing: The engine is cleaned then coated in a magnetic powder that attracts to the engine and shows clearly any cracks in the block.

Cylinder Honing: This is where they rough up and pattern the cylinder walls but do not take off any thickness. This allows the piston rings to seat better, and with new rings, possibly eliminate blow-by. Generally, this is not possible by the time you are ready for a rebuild and cylinder boring is necessary.

Cylinder Boring: The cylinders become worn over time and not evenly due to the geometry of the engine's motion. (This is usually the reason for the engine requiring a machine shop in the first place.) Re-bore sizes are limited and this is generally performed in steps of 10 thousandths of an inch. (When someone says their engine is bored "10 over," that is what they are referring to.) The machine shop determines how much needs to be taken off the cylinder side walls to give you a perfectly round cylinder.

In addition, the shop does the same on all cylinders so the pistons and rings you purchase are the same for each cylinder. This means that the worst cylinder on the block determines the end bore size.

Crankshaft Grinding and Surfacing

With time, your crankshaft will go out of true and require rebalancing. It is long, and there is always some inherent wobble. This helps eliminate that problem. Once this process is complete, the machine shop tells you which undersize bearing set is needed for both crankshaft main bearings and piston rod bearings.

Line Honing the Camshaft Gallery

This is done to true up any changes in the cam gallery over time and tells the shop the proper cam bearings to order.

Decking

The block is resurfaced by removing just enough from the mating surface for the deck to be perfectly flat.

Head Work

The head is also resurfaced, and then the valve guides are bored and replacement seats and valves are installed. It is also Magnafluxed and pressure tested to ensure that there are no invisible cracks that could cause problems.

Machine shop costs are going up like everything else. This is why you must be diligent in taking good care of your engine. The other problem is that there are only so many rebuilds available for each engine block because there is only so much metal on the cylinder wall. Once you get to .060 over, it's time to start thinking about a new engine block.

And because "new" is relative, it may take some research to find one that has more life than the one you have. It is possible to go .080 over, but that is the limit.

This is the second page of the machine shop invoice. I would rather not install the Speedi-Sleeve that renews the surface of the harmonic balancer/front main seal surface myself because they are pretty finicky to press on correctly. So, I felt $10 was a reasonable price to not have to go through sleeves.

This is page one of the actual invoice for this trip to the machine shop. The first two entries are for the modifications I requested. The full-flow oil option and drilling the crankshaft for the bolt for holding on the balancer. Notice how this engine is bored to .080 over. This is the end of the road for this engine.

CHAPTER 7

WHILE THE ENGINE IS AT THE SHOP

You have much more to do to prepare for the engine to return from the shop.

You need to address all the engine sheet metal; each individual system needs to be completely refurbished.

The old rusty bolts are replaced with a stainless steel engine bolt kit. You may feel this is overboard, but for $50, it's well worth it. Think about this bolt issue for a second. You can't sandblast the old ones or even deep clean them because the CAD plating has been compromised years ago. If you use the old bolts after cleaning them, they rust quickly. The exceptions are the head bolts and the flywheel bolts because hardened steel is preferable to stainless.

You can purchase new head bolts or clean up the old ones. I purchased new zinc-plated flywheel bolts. Finally, you can sandblast all your old bolts and take them to a plating company. If you decide to acquire the bolts piecemeal, perhaps from a hardware store, look carefully at the bolt heads to be sure they are of the proper strength. For engine parts, some must be Grade 5 and some must be Grade 8. The top of the bolt heads are marked appropriately.

The intake and exhaust manifolds on these old engines can be problematic. They should be thoroughly addressed before reinstallation.

We will tear down the distributor and carburetor and rebuild them from the ground up.

We will install a new one-wire alternator, a new starter, fuel pump, and water pump. The engine will receive the water pump adapter plate with the short-shaft water pump to relocate it to the center of the radiator.

Cooling system components need to be gathered, cleaned, painted, and ready for reassembly.

While the engine is at the machine shop you have the opportunity to make all the parts look like factory new. You want to use a good epoxy primer then a sandable primer over it. Epoxy primer adheres to bare metal and gives the sandable primer a good surface to hold on to.

CHAPTER 7

Much time and effort later, you can see clean-looking engine tin. Well worth the effort. Arguably, I am not certain they looked that good from the factory.

A PCV valve will be added as well. PCV removes combustion gases and decreases sludge in the oil pan, and it's an inexpensive way to ensure long engine life.

A spin-on oil filter adapter kit will be added to go with the new full-flow oil system (you can pay a little extra for the machine shop to machine it). This spin-on adapter will be placed at the side motor-mount location. You must make a special adapter for this as well.

By the time you are done, the engine will look as good as it runs and, because you are meticulous, you can expect to get longer life and better performance out of it with the upgrades. You will also have a unique upgrade to high-energy ignition (HEI) using the stock distributor.

Next, you need to address all the miscellaneous parts that go on the engine, such as the thermostat housing, alternator bracket, etc. I opted to go with a 12-volt, one-wire alternator. I do not like that it doesn't look stock, but trouble-free operation and lack of a regulator make it a stronger choice. This choice is necessary because the other improvement will be high-energy ignition using the stock distributor. To do this right, you need a decent alternator bracket and a 12-volt .7-ohm HEI coil. Here, I use the stock-looking type.

We will also need a few ignition parts, including a reluctor, reluctor pickup, mounting plate, HEI module, and heat sink. If your engine did not come with a generator or a starter, you get to choose the most efficient options. This allows you to customize the engine the way you want.

New Parts List

Following is the list of parts that needed to be purchased to complete this engine. The cost per item is what I paid in 2015; things have surely increased by now! You should do your own research into cost and item numbers for your engine. You may also want to use another supplier; these are the ones I used.

- Exhaust manifold spring: Classic Parts of America No. 89-425, $26.95. This is the circular spring that opens and closes the large valve on the exhaust manifold. They are most often broken and need to be replaced.
- Exhaust manifold stud kit: Dorman No. 03147 (use the long ones), $6.00. Now is a good time to ensure your exhaust manifold studs are in good shape.
- Intake manifold carburetor riser: Classic Parts of America No. 81-212, $8.95. This is the plastic riser that sits on top of the intake manifold before the carburetor.
- 180-degree thermostat with jiggle valve: AC Delco 12TP1D. This is a great thermostat. A jiggle valve allows a small amount of water to pass through it while there is flow, allowing for fewer air bubbles and cooling problems.
- 12-volt one-wire alternator: Tuff Stuff Automotive No. TFF-7127NE, $104.97. Something to be aware of when purchasing an alternator is whether your vintage vehicle has an amp gauge; if so, it is probably rated at no more than 50-amp capacity. Be aware that under certain conditions, going over 50 amps could cause a fire or damage to your vehicle. Larger is not better. A 42-amp alternator runs an air conditioner and most common accessories just fine. In that case, get a REMY 20040.
- Alternator bracket: Fargo Automotive No. 9450712, $49.95. This bracket is made to bolt any 10- or 12S-type alternator directly to the 235/261 engine block.
- Spark Plugs: E3.52, $24.95. E3 plugs performed better in my detailed tests. No gapping necessary. They are all gapped at .040 inch.
- Plug wires: Accel Superstock Series Points/HEI No. 4021K, $40.99. This plug set allows you to use the HEI system with full benefit. It also works great with a stock ignition system.
- HEI system kit: DTN, $176.50. This kit comes with everything you need to convert to HEI using the stock

WHILE THE ENGINE IS AT THE SHOP

New Parts List

distributor, including cap, rotor, reluctor, reluctor pickup, ignition module, heat sink, brackets, and all wiring.
- 12-volt .7-ohm HEI coil: MSD No. 8202, $47.95. This is a full 12-volt coil, so you want to remove the ballast resistor on the firewall. It provides for a 45,000-volt spark.
- Vacuum advance unit: Classic Parts of America No. 83-274, $29.95. It uses the current bracket, so don't throw the old one away.
- Spin-on oil filter adapter kit: DTN, $174.50. This kit contains your choice of mounting options for a spin-on WIX 51515 oil filter, stainless braided hoses, and stainless steel hardware.
- Water pump adapter plate: Dave Folsom, eBay search for water pump adapter 235, $50. The plate is used to put the fan in the center of the radiator for better cooling. If you have a tall radiator, this plate is necessary for proper cooling. The 1947–1955 pickups need it for sure.
- Water pump 3/8-inch belt, 53/54 style: Airtex No. AW108N, $66.79. This is the water pump that enables this engine to fit into older vehicles without modification. It is a short-shaft pump that uses the old 216 cooling fan. It is imperative that you purchase this one if using the water pump adapter. They are available from Rockauto.com.
- 1/2-inch fan belt: NAPA Premium XL No. 25-7440, $12.95.
- Fuel pump: Spectra Premium No. SP1080MP, $39.95. DTN also sells an electric fuel pump kit that uses an auto-priming circuit for faster starts after the vehicle has been sitting awhile as an alternative to the basic mechanical one.
- Exhaust donut: Felpro No. 8194, $3.95.
- Harmonic balancer repair sleeve: Felpro No. 16202, $7.95. If your balancer has a groove worn around it where the seal rides, this is a good idea.
- Upper radiator hose (formed): Jim Carters No. ME199, $11.00. This is a 1947–1955 pickup part. Use your preferred vendor for your vehicle if this one isn't right.
- Lower radiator hose (formed): Jim Carters No. ME239, $22.00. This is a 1947–1955 pickup part. Use your preferred vendor for your vehicle if this one isn't right.
- PCV conversion kit (deluxe): DTN, $112.50. The road draft tube is removed, and this kit is installed to remove crankcase gasses. These were the last engines in Chevrolet's history to not have native PCV. It comes with a stainless steel, preformed line, valve, and all necessary stainless hardware.
- Air filter for dry stock 1950 air cleaner: NAPA Gold No. 2373, $11.77.
- Stainless steel engine bolt kit: Totally Stainless 1955–1962 235/261 Original Style, $50.
- Accelerator return spring: Classic Parts of America No. 89-521, $5.95.
- Thicker valve cover gasket (7/32 inch): Felpro VS50190C, $7.95.
- Valve cover retainer set: No. 92612799, $19.99.

If you don't care about HEI, here are the part numbers for the stock ignition parts:

- Tall distributor cap: Standard Motor Products No. DR428, $15.95.
- Newer-style rotor for tall cap: Standard Motor Products No. DR308, $6.95.
- Points: Standard Motor Products No. DR2227PT, $8.95.
- Condenser: Standard Motor Products No. DR60T, $9.95.
- Spark Plugs: AC Delco No. R45, $14.94.

To purchase DTN products, go to devestechnet.com/Services/index. If a vendor is not listed in this book, I generally use rockauto.com and summitracing.com for generic parts.

CHAPTER 8

DISTRIBUTOR

In this section, I am going to rebuild a Delco tall-cap distributor from the ground up. This means taking apart everything, thoroughly cleaning and replacing any broken or unusable parts. This also applies to short-cap distributors. The only differences are the cap itself, spring hold-downs for the cap, and the length of the upper shaft assembly.

I decided to rebuild a batch of them because I had them lying around the shop and will need them eventually anyway. This gave me a good understanding of how things go back together.

Distributor Rebuild

The first order of business after removing the distributor cap is to remove the points and condenser. Go easy on the phenolic (black plastic) pieces because they are becoming difficult to find. If the condenser wire pulls right out, great, but if it's stuck, first remove the nut on the outside and the conductor plate. This reveals a round nut with slots on both sides of the screw. With something small, rotate it out a little, and the condenser and points should come right out.

Next, you need to remove the plastic pieces. First remove the nut and conductor plate, then the round nut and the lock washer behind it. Once you have all that removed, take out the screw (carefully), and the two plastic pieces should pull apart from each other and come out as well. The plastic pieces are probably the most difficult pieces to find, along with that round nut and special screw, so don't lose anything!

Now remove the top plate assembly by removing the three screws on the outside. Two of these are opposite each other and hold the distributor cap clips. These screws are the same and each has a lock washer.

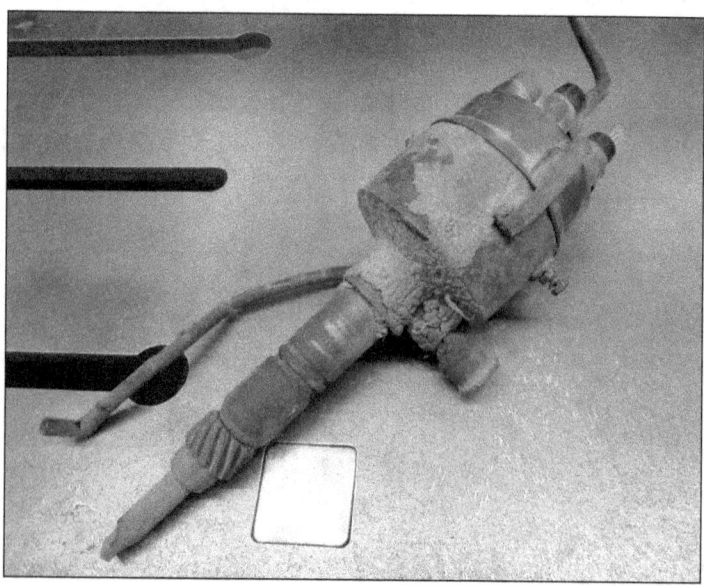

Wait until you see what they look like when they are in pristine condition. In this condition, you do not yet know if the internals are good; however, unless they are frozen, these Delco distributors are easy to rebuild.

This tool was designed to remove the circular nut inside the black plastic housing. They are very rare. Most people just use a small screwdriver.

DISTRIBUTOR

This is the typical condition of the distributor under the top deck. The problem is, the weights work using centrifugal force and cannot stick if you want the engine to run correctly. A good cleaning goes a long way.

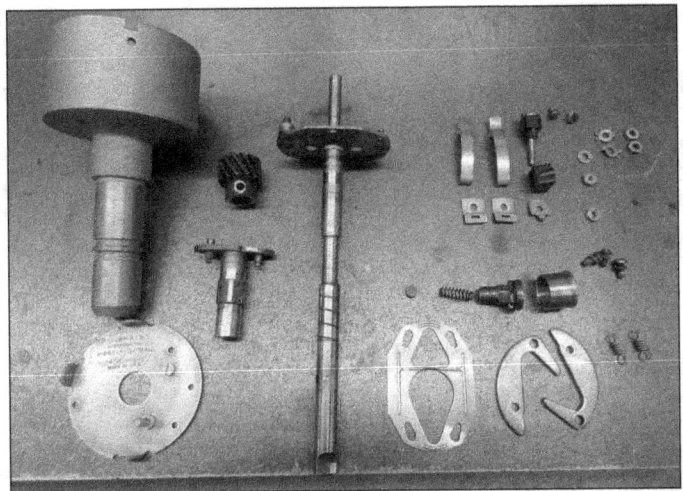

This photo shows all the parts removed from the distributor. Be sure to remove that small circular biscuit (to the left of the grease spring) from the cavity so you don't have to find a replacement. Nobody sells them anymore.

The mechanical advance cover, lock tabs, and springs. Be sure to take care in removing the lock tabs. They need to be intact later.

A 7/16-inch wrench makes quick work of removing the grease cup assembly. Once removed, there is a spring and a hard-to-find pad next to the distributor shaft inside.

Once the top plate is off, take a close look at what you have. Notice how the plate is oriented. You want to put it back the same way when you rebuild it.

Two nuts hold the assembly together. The nuts have lock tabs, which is important because once it's together, they are difficult to access. Carefully bend the two tabs out far enough to remove the nuts.

Once you have the two lock tabs out, pull the plate straight up and out. Notice how the indentions face downward. You want to put it back together the same way.

Remove the springs, and don't lose them. I was able to reach in there and pull them out by hand. You don't find much tension on them at all.

Finally, remove the mini shaft with the lobes, then the two counterweights. That should be everything on the inside.

On the outside, remove the grease cap, then with a 7/16-inch wrench, remove the threaded grease assembly. You need to remove two parts inside it: a spring and a plastic bushing that pushes against the shaft.

To make the bushing retrieval easier, remove the drive gear. Be gentle grinding off just the head of the pin that's holding it in. Use the appropriate-size punch to knock out the pin after grinding. Be sure your punch is small enough for the hole, and it should come out with moderate effort. It is critical that you do not bend the shaft.

Once the pin is out, work it around a little, and the gear should slide off.

Now you can remove the inner shaft assembly. You should be able to use the punch to push the little plastic bushing out into the center of the shaft housing, then push it out with the shaft. The plastic bushing is important, and if it's worn out, you can usually use one from your local hardware store. You do not want that spring to push against the shaft without a bushing.

CHEVROLET INLINE-6 ENGINE 1929–1962: HOW TO REBUILD

CHAPTER 8

This is the proper orientation of the mechanical weights. The two pieces are identical and interchangeable, so it does not matter which one goes on which post.

Tape up the shaft so you don't get paint or primer on the machined parts.

At this point, you should have everything apart.

Cleaning and Painting

You can clean all of these parts with a 3-gallon parts washer with kerosene. Use wire brushes and really take your time. Tape and sandblast the nonmachined surface of the housing to remove all traces of crud. Shine the top plate with 400-grit sandpaper. Once everything is clean, use compressed air to dry the parts, then paint the housing the color of your choice.

Flat black was used originally. Paint with the tape still on the machined shaft. Use etching primer to start. After the paint cures, overnight preferably, spray WD-40 on all the parts and inside the housing.

Place the shaft in the housing and move it up and down to ensure that you don't have any remaining crud in the housing. With the WD-40 on it, it should spin freely. You can use WD-40 as a rinse to remove any contamination as the last cleaning step.

Putting Things Back Together

To start reassembly, put the inner shaft assembly in a vise with plastic jaws, or protect it in another way, and reinstall the bottom part of the inside. You can do this because the gear goes on last. You can use white lithium grease as sort of an assembly lube. Slather it over every part. The distributor doesn't get any oil and little grease, so you want those weights to be slick and free from rust in the future. Place the counterweights on first.

Once the counterweights move freely, place the upper shaft assembly so that it occupies the same plane as the weights. Then install the plate with the locking tabs and nuts. Tighten securely and carefully bend the tabs to lock the nuts in place.

To reinstall the gear, be sure you

The mechanical advance cover is oriented with the indentions facing downward. Makes sense, really.

You can set the top shaft assembly on the bottom shaft and hand-twist the top shaft to see the movement of the mechanical weights. This is a good check to ensure that nothing is binding or put together wrong.

have the proper length and size of roll pin. (I use high-strength, stainless steel ones from McMaster-Carr.) The 3/16-inch pin is tight in the shaft, but don't rely on that single roll pin. Put another M2.5 (x30) pin inside the first one, making sure the openings are opposite each other. This almost guarantees that the gear isn't going anywhere.

Test it to make sure there is no slop introduced by the pin combination and then cut off the pins flush; the same as the original one. If by some chance there is any slop in the gear-to-shaft connection, drill out both the gear and the shaft to the next size of roll pin combination, which is 7/32 and 1/8 inch. You can use a 3/4-horse bench grinder with wire wheel to brush off many of these parts after cleaning with kerosene.

Reinstall all the remaining parts as they were originally. Attach the top plate by the three screws and lock washers and install a clip retainer in the two across from each other. The slot in the retainer goes down, and the retainer follows the curve of the distributor housing.

Next, install the black plastic pieces. Put the screw in the inside piece first, feed it through the hole, then on the outside, add a lock washer, then the round nut, then the conductor plate, then the regular nut.

You can install the points and condenser anytime. Leave them out if the plan is to add a round plate inside to accommodate HEI.

That completes the distributor rebuild. You should test this when you get the engine back from the machine shop.

Vacuum Advance

The vacuum advance bracket for cars is different from the one for trucks. The truck's bracket comes out at 90 degrees; the car version comes out at 45 degrees. The bracket

The fancy pins used by General Motors are not available, so you need to use roll pins for fastening the gear to the shaft. Use a roll pin within another roll pin for added strength. Just put the openings 180 degrees from each other.

After you have the two pins driven in and carefully cut off close to the gear (I used a Makita grinder with thin wheel), there should be no play whatsoever in the gear/shaft connection. If there is, plan B is in order, which is to drill the gear/shaft for the next larger-size pins.

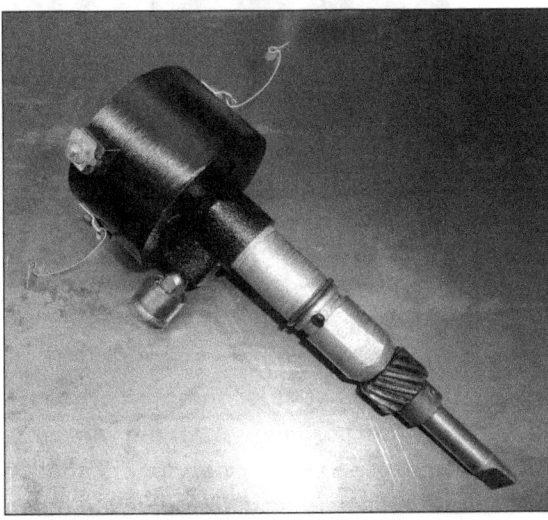

Here is what the finished distributor looks like. If yours has an O-ring on the shaft as this one did, remove it. O-rings do not belong on the distributor shaft even though one of the main rebuild companies sends them to you that way.

I think I am getting the hang of this!

determines which angle the vacuum advance line to the carburetor points. Whichever one you currently have is the one you should use. The reason I mention this is because vendors do not provide the bracket when you order a new vacuum advance. The vacuum advance has a rubber membrane inside of it that decays over time, causing the engine to run poorly at higher RPM.

Ignition System

High-energy ignition was introduced by General Motors in the mid-1970s and revolutionized this critical system. Prior to the mid-1970s, the stock points system was relegated to 6-volt operation. The large ballast resistor on the firewall reduces the voltage so that 1940s coils and points systems work just fine on a 1970s vintage engine.

Removing this resistance-based ignition system did several things that really moved us forward. They are more consistent firing, no points to adjust, and fewer moving parts. Because the spark is much hotter, wider plug gaps and thicker spark means a more complete burn of leaner fuel mixtures. This improves engine performance and reliability.

As Jim Linder, an ignition systems instructor, put it: "The HEI as built by General Motors could very well be the best overall ignition system out there ever. It has a varying dwell based on engine RPM and a ramp and fire circuit using 3.6 ms and 5.5 amps output with current control. Arguably, this will improve engine performance and reliability."

To explain further, before this advancement, the ignition coil only had time to produce a 12,000-volt spark. By going to a 3.6 ms ramp and fire circuit, we can shorten that time and allow for a full 45,000-volt spark. What's more, the dwell is now based on RPM, so timing is more precise at all engine speeds.

From Points/Condensor System to HEI

You can take a stock distributor from a 1959 235 engine and convert it from a points/condenser system to an HEI system without modifying any of the vintage parts. If you do not like this mod after you have tried it or (for any reason) want to go back to a points/condenser system, you can. That's because of the following:

- You will use the stock distributor you already own.
- You will not modify the distributor or any of the vintage parts.
- The distributor will look the same from the outside when this is completed.
- The engine will run better and more efficiently than before the modifications.

This is a 90-degree version of the vacuum advance bracket. It is the common bracket used for Chevy trucks from 1940 to 1962. The car version is at 45 degrees. This means that the hard lines from the vacuum advance to the carburetor are shaped differently to accommodate the output of the vacuum advance.

Here is how the vacuum advance bracket was originally put together. Also, be sure to remove any O-rings that are on the shaft. That space is designed so that oil cannot creep upward and not for an O-ring. O-rings cause problems when installed here in ease of movement and determining if the distributor shaft is completely down into the oil pump slot.

With HEI, no moving parts touch each other. The voltage is created by a magnet in the reluctor pickup that precisely fires when the lobes come close to the pickup. A very ingenious system.

DISTRIBUTOR

Parts List

After doing a little research on parts, these parts seem to be the most available and the easiest to fit into this tight space. To be more specific, the reluctor and reluctor pickup units are out of the 1972–1985 slant-6 Mopar. The brains (HEI module) for of all this is a GM design. The parts list is as follows:

- Ignition reluctor pickup: Standard Motor Products LX-103
- Ignition reluctor: Standard Motor Products LX-105
- HEI replacement module: Standard Motor Products LX301T or Speedway Motors 91012338 Stock
- HEI module heat sink: AC/Delco 10474610

Tools List

The brand names in the following list are my preferences; other brands may work as well for you.

- Dewalt Portaband with Swag Offroad table
- Dremel model 220 drill press attachment
- Dremel model 4000 rotary tool
- 1/8-inch straight rasp for the Dremel
- Small metal ruler (straight edge)
- Makita 4-inch grinder with both grinding wheels and flap discs
- Allen wrenches (fractional)
- Screwdrivers
- Hammer and center punch for locating hole placement
- Multimeter
- Tap and die set for 6-32 and 8-32
- Drill bit set (both fractional and numbered)
- Small jewelery file set

Mark the reluctor for the hexagon shape you are going to make. Fortunately, it's simply a six-point star pattern.

Generally, when you think of HEI for this vintage, you think of a large, foreign-looking (nonstock) distributor, or Pertronix adapters. Both are fine, and I encourage you to do your research, but in this case, I want to use the stock distributor without ruining the points mounting tower, the points cam lobes, or the points cam screw that is affixed to the internal distributor plate. In fact, you will do no modifications to the distributor itself.

The cost for everything is about $90 and available at RockAuto, eBay, Summit Racing, or your favorite supplier, except for the HEI module, which is available at Speedway Motors. The only reason I use the Speedway unit and not the GM OEM is due to pricing. They are otherwise the same.

Reluctor

Drill the reluctor for two 8-32 (1/4-inch-long) set screws. Use a number-29 drill bit. These set screws require a 5/64-inch Allen wrench. Back them out or remove them entirely for the next operation, which is the lobe grinding process. Remember, make no modifications to the distributor itself.

Drill for these set screws on the thick part of the reluctor. Drill both at the same time to position them across from each other perfectly. If you set the reluctor flat in the vise, the holes come out really nice. Use a standard clean and sharp 8-32 tap to finish the part.

The actual lobes on the distributor happen to be 5/8-inch hexagon. You can turn your distributor all day with a 5/8-inch 1/2-inch-drive long socket.

Using the Dremel model 220 drill press attachment, with a fine, straight-shanked rasp with 1/8-inch diameter, makes pretty easy work out of cutting the hexagon shape out of the center. Remember not to take off much material. The reluctor is already 5/8-inch round diameter inside, and you are making it 5/8-inch hexagon. This takes about 45 minutes to do because there is a lot of fitting and refitting involved. It must be tight when you are done.

Start by marking across the reluctor. Then, keeping the reluctor so that the lobe you are attaching is

As you can see, there is just enough left on these reluctors to make a 5/8-inch round hole into a 5/8-inch hexagon.

CHAPTER 8

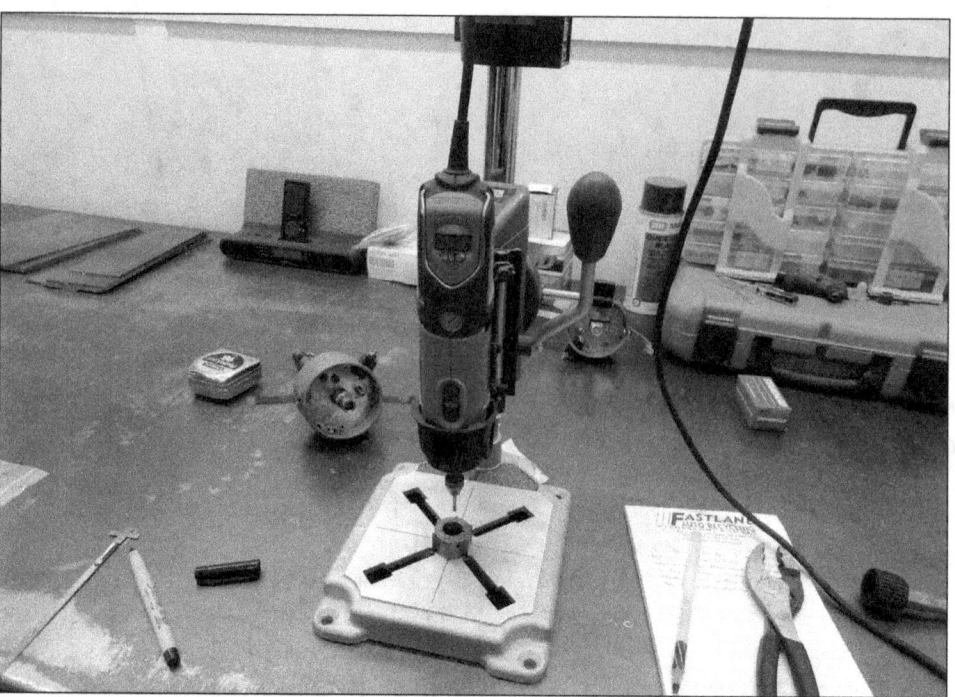

The Dremel drill press and a narrow-diameter spiral rasp roughs out the hex shape. The reluctor becomes hot, so wear gloves. Take it slow and be precise.

directly across from the line in front of you, push it gently into the rasp, and move the Dremel's lever up and down to make a groove top to bottom.

If you don't have a Dremel model 220 drill press attachment, use your drill press with the same bit. Be sure to use the highest RPM you can.

Be sure to notice the placement of the reluctor on the tool. You want to make six equal such grooves. I can't say enough the importance of taking this slow. Remember it's a 5/8-inch hole already. There isn't much to take off and still have it fit tightly. And, it needs to fit 100-percent tight, otherwise you will have trouble with the .007 clearance on all six lobes between the reluctor and pickup. Do all six lobes with equal pressure and depth then dry fit on the distributor, over and over.

When all lobes have a distinctive six-sided shape, carefully move the reluctor on the tool from side to side to square the sides with the grooves. Do this very slowly. When you are done, it should fit tight without the set screws. You shouldn't have to hammer it in, but a snug push in and pull out by hand.

With a tight and consistent fit, you next tighten the set screws and test for wobbling or hitting any-

Use the drill press table's guide marks to help keep the reluctor in line with the drill. This requires checking many times and being careful not to go too far.

thing. Mine came out nice the first time. (Truth be told, if I can do it, anyone can).

No sense in letting the reluctor scrape the bottom plate. Pull it up a little so it turns smoothly and doesn't bottom out. If you did it right, your rotor sits on top as always and your reluctor isn't hitting anything (even if just barely).

I learned something very important after doing this procedure on various distributors: There are two distinct types of distributor lobes depending on the engine and the year. The old-style 216/235 engines prior to 1954 have sharp lobes on their distributors. The 1954 and later ones have rounded lobes. This is not due to wear. This is important because the lobes are also different sizes.

The older ones can vary between .615 and .618 inch and the newer ones are consistent at .620 inch. The .625 is 5/8 inch, and you do not want the reluctor to be sloppy once it's in place. This means you may have some filing to do to get the reluctor to fit once you have roughed it out.

After the hole is roughed out, the final process is hand filing for sharp corners. You want this to fit nice and snug.

DISTRIBUTOR

General Motors made a few different sizes of shaft lobes. The tall-cap distributor is the only one that works with this HEI system (post 1953), so you will probably only encounter the .620. The picture shows a 216-distributor on the left and a new-style 235 distributor on the right.

The Allen set screw is accessible even when everything is placed in the distributor.

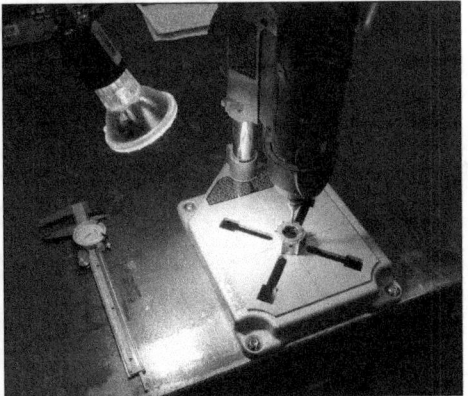

Be sure you have enough light on the project; it requires precision.

This is what the Dremel bit looks like and how careful you need to be to get this as exact as possible.

This reluctor is made for this distributor now, allowing for the rotor to go to its stop perfectly.

Pickup Adapter Plate

The reluctor pickup assembly for this engine is made to drop into a 1972–1985 Mopar Slant Six so you can't use the plate that it came with. I found nothing redeeming about this plate, so I removed it and started designing a plate for the Delco distributor. Do not randomly remove the plate. Follow the procedures below. Set the assembly aside for now.

All you must do now is redesign the pickup plate so that the pickup sensor is directly across from any of the lobes. Because this thing fits directionally so that each lobe also corresponds to each reluctor bump, I

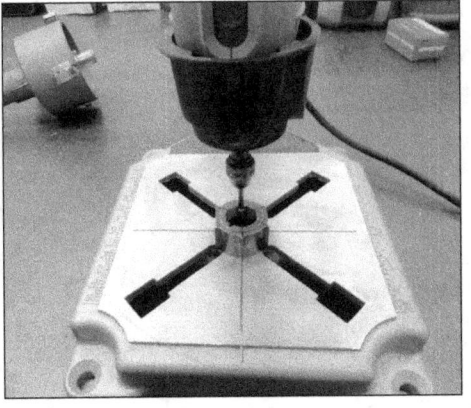

Using an up-and-down action on the drill press is what makes this possible. Be sure to use the star pattern of the reluctor as your guide. The material is hard, so expect it to take some time.

CHAPTER 8

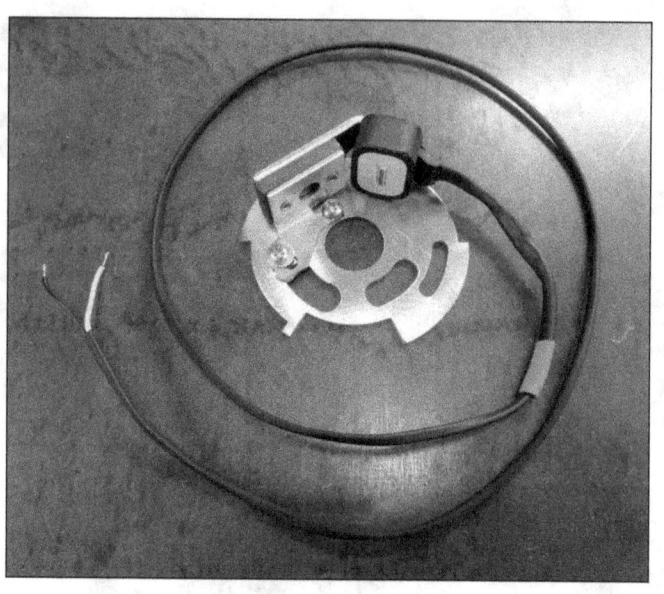

You make the plate out of 11-gauge stainless steel. Tapping for number-6 and number-8 screws with that harder stainless steel makes for a better plate. This is the completed reluctor pickup assembly.

the vintage parts, you must figure out how to use the condenser hold-down screw and the points hold down screw for the plate hold-down because those are the only two tapped holes on the surface of the vintage distributor.

Use the template so your plate comes out better than my early ones because I had to figure out all the geometry, which required adding weld, taking it away, etc. A roll of

This is the resulting plate cut out of stainless steel using the waterjet process for really fine results.

will refer to them as lobes from now on.

You need about an 11-gauge metal plate that cleanly accomplishes the following four things.

- Ability to rotate within the distributor 5 degrees left to right for proper phase adjustment.
- Allow the pickup assembly to move in or out to adjust for the .007-inch gap that is recommended.
- Not interfere with items not needed such as the points pin and cam screw.
- Make the adjustments stable so that one adjustment doesn't interfere with another.

Of course, in keeping with the philosophy of no modifications to

HEI Adapter Template for Delco-Remy Chevy Distributor 1937-1962

Full size Template, Be sure you are printing at 100%! That is not the default of most printers, so be careful! The largest diameter of the radius should be 2-15/16".

Large Oblongs are 5/16" x 5/8"

Small Oblong is 3/16" x 9/16"

DRILL No. 29 TAP to 8-32

DRILL 3/4"

DRILL No. 36 TAP to 6-32

Here is the template for the distributor's internal adapter plate. Trace around it and transfer it to a piece of 11-gauge steel then cut to size.

blue 3M masking tape has the same inside diameter as the distributor (3 inches). When you are through, the 11-gauge metal plate should fit perfectly inside the distributor with no play whatsoever.

Putting It All Together

Next, you mount the pickup assembly on the new plate. To remove the pickup assembly from its original plate, drill out the rivet using a number-36 drill bit. Do not make this hole larger than number-36. You will be tapping this hole and the new plate corresponding to this hole for a 6-32 screw. This takes the place of the rivet quite nicely. You can Loctite it in place later.

Remove the hold-down screw on the old plate and you should have just the pickup assembly free. Reuse the hold-down screw because it is short enough to be flush with the bottom of the plate when it's mounted. The 6-32 rivet screw needs to be shortened to be flush with the bottom of the plate as well.

There is zero room for error in making this adapter plate because of

Grind off just the bumps from the plastic above where the reluctor pickup is close to the edge. Use a Dremel with a thin cutoff disc.

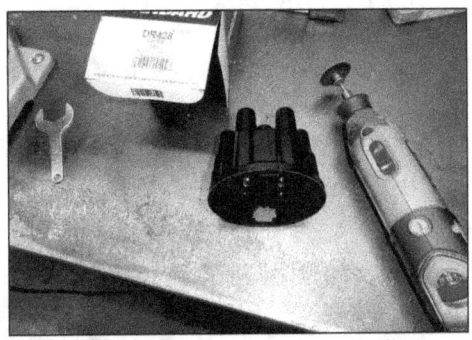
Use lots of care not to take off too much. Distributor caps are still being made, so you don't need to feel too bad about this necessary minor modification.

the space. Using this new plate, you may still have to grind off a small ridge from the distributor cap to get enough room. It's probably about .020 inch deep, almost nothing, but it has to be done. It will have no adverse effect. You probably need to grind off both of those bumps about the first 3/8 inch of the inside of the cap where the reluctor pickup bends out.

When you have the adapter plate in place with the pickup assembly, install it and make sure the magnetic pickup is lined up with the marks you made on the top rim of the distributor. If you rotate the plate, you have 2½ degrees on one side of the mark and 2½ on the other side. Install the reluctor and set the gap to .007.

This is the correct feeler gauge (.007) for the reluctor-to-reluctor pickup gap. It is not terribly critical; anything from just not touching to the thickness of a few strips of bond paper will do.

Rotate the reluctor through all six lobes to make sure it maintains .007 or so through all of them. If you need a little adjustment, very little, you can loosen the set screws on the reluctor and wiggle it a bit for ultra-fine tuning.

Rotate the distributor. If you hear a noise, the reluctor may be bottomed out, scraping on the new plate. No problem, loosen the set screws and pull it up a bit. Move the reluctor up a bit higher than the pickup's sensor. You have plenty of room so that it does not interfere with the rotor.

Wiring and Details

So, you have established that the distributor cap and rotor fit nicely and the distributor turns quietly. The gap is set to .007 and the lobes are indexed to the pickup assembly. It should work right? You don't know yet because there are still a few loose ends.

Here, the adapter plate, reluctor, and reluctor pickup are installed with just enough room.

What do you do with the two wires that go out of the distributor? Use the stock parts. After the reluctor pickup is properly installed, simply seal the plastic parts to the hole, let them dry for 24 hours, then thread the wires through.

One of the conundrums in dealing with this project is trying to keep it looking stock. Here's what you can do with the two wires coming out of the distributor.

You can Permatex the black plastic pieces back in the hole and to each other. The distributor works as advertised for points if you keep the screw assembly part in your toolbox, and you can get two wires out to the outside this way. If the Permatex ever came loose, you can't lose your parts because there are wires through them. This enables you to get to the bottom end of your distributor without problems.

If you were to use a long piece of black shrink tubing around the two wires, you would have a hard time noticing at all. I was able to obtain a few schematics of the system (see images on page 66). This really makes it clearer and should help in understanding the whole system.

High-Energy Ignition System

Another modification that I felt was necessary has to do with where to put the HEI module and heat sink. You want it close to the coil and distributor, so everything is in the same place if possible. After spending hours thinking about it, I devised a bracket that places the unit exactly where it should go.

This spot is unused real estate, has airflow across the module as well as behind it, and it's the right size if you choose to cover the module and heat sink with a stripped-out Delco-Remy regulator box. You could even chop the box a bit to make it look flatter, just like it belongs there.

The plate is made of 11-gauge steel and the dimensions start at 7 x 8 inches. The width at the widest point of the coil bolt pattern is 3½ inches. The first bend is at 3¾ inches down from the top, while the second bend is at exactly 4 inches. That is a difficult bend to make with rudimentary shop tools. You cut that part off at 4 inches, then measure 1/4 inch up, then use a vise to make one bend angled at about 45 degrees.

You then weld it back up and do the whole grinding and dressing thing. The coil mounting holes are 2.375 inches between them center to center. You make 3/4-inch relief cuts to make it easy to remove the spark plugs, and then round the corners with a band saw. The top profile is the same profile as the coil bracket.

Cut the first fin off the HEI heat sink to mount it. Grind it completely flat. Place the heat sink in the center of the plate and mark the four holes

This solution is barely visible under the hood and is the best compromise for a quick place for the HEI module plate. You can also get creative and use an old voltage regulator cover and place it anywhere you want.

This bracket bolts to the coil mounting holes and allows air to pass over and under the module.

DISTRIBUTOR

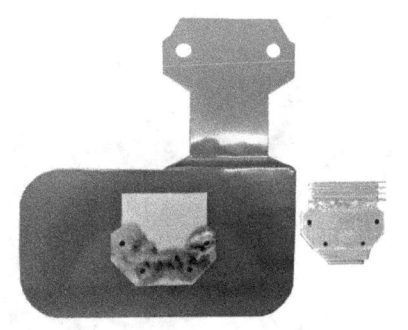

I prefer to have bare metal where the heat sink meets this plate. Although I do not think it is necessary, it adds more heat transfer.

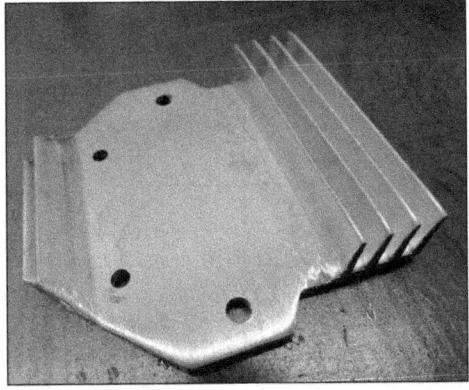

Here, the fin has been cut off and the holes properly drilled for installation.

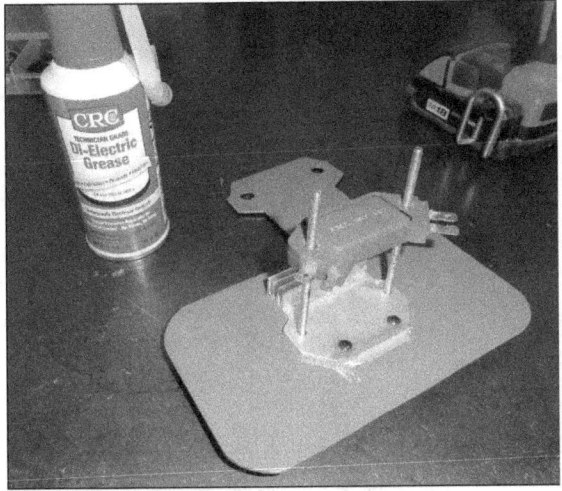

The liberal use of dielectric grease keeps the bare metal from rusting and the module properly conductive.

Cut off the first fin so the HEI module can sit flat on the heat sink. Also cut off the two plastic nubs on the bottom of the HEI module so everything sits flat.

on the plate. Drill the top two with a number-29 drill bit, the bottom two with a number-36.

Tap the bottom two holes on the plate with a 6-32 tap and the top holes with an 8-32. Place the 6-32 screws from the front of the unit and the 8-32 screws from the back. This is not only a secure way to mount this unit, it also ensures a solid ground.

Tape the area and around where the heat sink will go before painting. You want that heat sink to sit on bare metal. Bolt the heat sink to the adapter plate and, using a sharp X-Acto knife, cut closely around the heat sink. Remove the excess tape, then primer and paint the plate your choice of color. Warning: When removing the tape, first run the X-Acto knife around the tape so you don't peel away your precious paint.

The 8-32 screws enter from the back. You need 1¼-inch-long screws because you want to ensure that they are long enough. They do not end up being the same length. One holds down the module with a washer and nut; the other side needs washer, nut, washer, nut. This is to give the length you need to add a ground wire.

I chose the screw on the right to be the longest, but it doesn't matter. Checking continuity with a multimeter when you are done ensures that you have solid ground from anywhere on the engine or frame of the truck to that ground screw is a really good idea.

You can consult Schematic One, which is a generic four-pin HEI module setup.

Schematic Two is the actual GM HEI module that confirms what Schematic One shows you. I always feel better when I have two independent sources, especially when wiring is concerned.

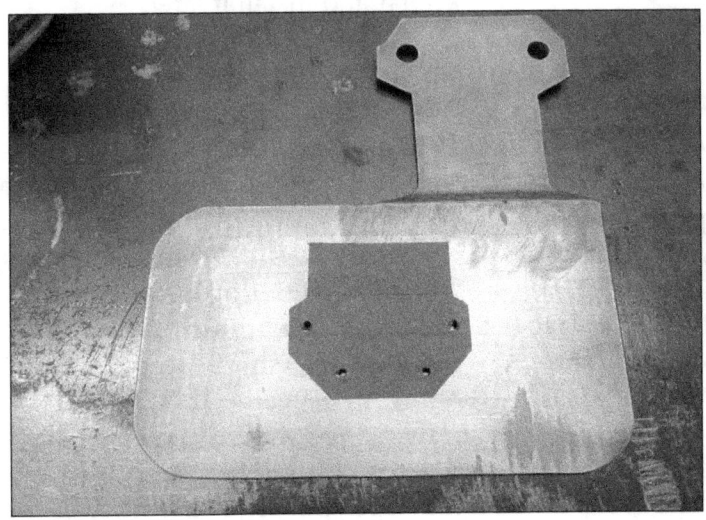

Before painting the plate, trace around the heat sink, then place tape over the area so the heat sink can sit on bare metal.

CHAPTER 8

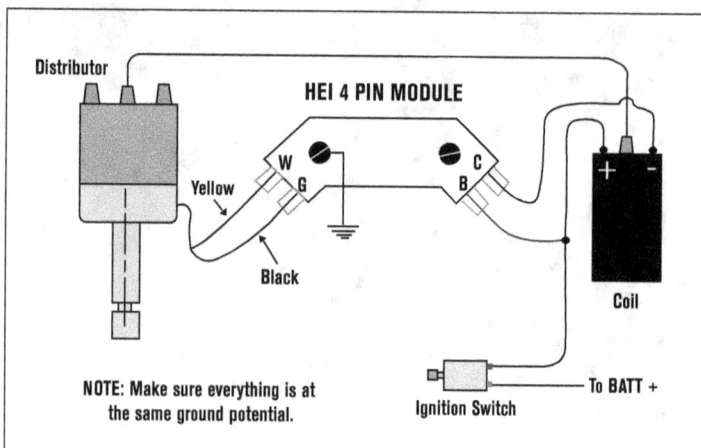

Use Schematic One to confirm that you have the wiring correct.

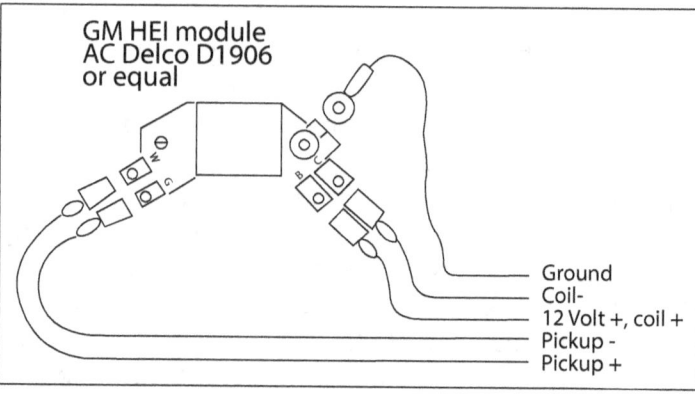

Schematic Two confirms what you know from Schematic One.

The MSD 8202 is a good choice for a hot 45,000-volt .7-ohm coil. When repainted, it looks stock and fits in the stock coil holder.

This reluctor pickup system uses a yellow wire and a black wire. That means pickup (+) is yellow and pickup (-) is black. It matters which is which because doing it backward can change the phase as much as 30 degrees.

Troubleshooting Wiring

If your engine refuses to run perfect when you start it up, but it does run, chances are you have the two wires (from the distributor to the HEI module) backward. This could be your fault, or the manufacturer of the reluctor pickup. I have run into this often! Make sure your timing is close before swapping these wires. ■

The Speedway Motors HEI module comes with a big connector with a capacitor. This is for engine noise suppression, and I am opting not to use this connector at all. I suppose if you have a radio in your vehicle that is affected by the RF noise, you can keep it and install it later.

HEI Coil

The stock GM coil from 1955 to 1959 was a 6-volt coil. If you measure across the two terminals of the coil, it is approximately 1.5 ohms. If you measure from the other side of the ignition resistor on the firewall to the minus terminal on the coil, you should get about 3.5 ohms. In other words, GM ignition resistors are 2 ohms. If you have a resistor coil and no ignition resistor on your firewall, measuring across the two terminals will get you about 4 ohms.

The breakdown for the stock system is as follows: With the charging system running about 13.8 volts, the current in the circuit is at about 3.94 amps. When the charge hits the ignition resistor on the firewall, the voltage is reduced to 7 volts. After it has gone through the coil, you have 5.94 volts at the points. If you have a resistor coil, it's less. It is a balanced system, but not what you are looking for with an HEI system.

This is important because the ignition resistor and 1.5-ohm coil keep the current limited to make the stock parts last longer. But now you have a more modern system with its own current-limiting circuit. The HEI system limits the current to between 5.5 and 5.8 amps. Also, the HEI system functions best when running at as close to 12 volts as possible. These two facts make the old coil obsolete.

It also means that the idea of bypassing the ignition resistor during cranking, and all that was sacred for the points system, is now a detriment. Your new HEI system does not require the firewall ignition (ballast) resistor. This can be bypassed with a new piece of 14-gauge wire jumpered across the resistor at installation.

The new HEI technology craves 12 full volts during regular operation. The HEI module has its own current limiting (5.5 to 5.8 amps), so you aren't concerned with excessive current. You want full voltage, so the coil you want is the one with the least primary ohm value. The problem with using an ohm value too low, however, is that your HEI module is dissipating more current, thus becoming hotter.

You have two choices usually associated with a stock points system:

- 13.8v (max) input with 1.5-ohm stock coil with 2-ohm ballast resistor for 3.94 amps
- 13.8v (max) input with 4-ohm replacement resistor coil for 3.45 amps

You are interested in maximum voltage input because you are determining wire sizes and want to err on the side of caution. These are the lower ohm values that work best for an HEI system (based on 13.8v max input):

- .7-ohm (R) coil = 19.71 amps
- .6-ohm (R) coil = 23 amps
- .35-ohm (R) coil = 39.42 amps

As you can see, there is a point where it gets pretty scary. Because the HEI module you are using for this limits the current to between 5.5 and 5.8 amps, you are not concerned about amperage, to a point. The .35-ohm coil would obviously be the closest to the goal, so you might think that's a good choice.

The reason it is not has to do with the HEI module's heat-sink dis-

Selecting a HEI Coil

When you purchase a stock coil for your 1955–1959 (or AD with 12v system), parts stores have them listed as 12-volt coils. A prominent "12V" is even stamped on the side of the coil. This was done because there were so many purchasers who insisted on a 12-volt coil, the company relabeled them as 12V to eliminate argument.

Vintage coils are not voltage rated. A 6-volt coil from the 1940s or early 1950s can make your 12-volt stock system run just fine. This can be proven mathematically. The 6-volt system didn't have a 2-ohm ignition (ballast) resistor, so the numbers come out exactly the same.

After HEI was invented, the industry did start rating coils by voltage as well as ohms. So, when you purchase a new 12-volt coil, don't end up with the same coil you already have.

The MSD 8202 is a stock-looking 45,000-volt high-performance HEI coil that is perfect for your purposes. You can buy them at Summit Racing. ■

sipation rate. It would become too hot and fail prematurely. In the end, the sweet spot from a mathematical perspective appears to be a 12-volt coil between .6 and .7 ohms.

One of the main reasons you are doing this upgrade is to achieve a much hotter, wider spark that allows you to run .045-point gaps so that you can ignite leaner mixtures and greatly improve engine performance. The new coil and balanced wiring system make a big difference.

HEI Wiring

The gauge of wiring in your vehicle was fine for the 6 volts and 4 amps or so that it was designed for. But now, you want to run 6 amps through those wires. This is why General Motors beefed up the ignition wires on HEI systems. You want to prepare for more current than your system is used to. New wiring is probably okay, but old wiring could cause a fire, so please look hard at your wiring. My recommendation is to go with 14-gauge wire clear through the ignition system to be safe.

If your plan is to keep a points distributor as a backup, you should retain the ignition resistor on your firewall and the stock coil then remove the jumper from the ballast resistor.

Hooking it up is straightforward. Take the wiring slow and check and double-check it to make sure everything is wired correctly.

HEI System Testing

The reluctor and reluctor pickup that you have replaced your points with is merely a trigger to let the GM HEI module know when it needs to fire the coil. It needs a minimum of 9 volts peak AC to trigger the module. If you have the reluctor setup gapped properly (.007 or so) you easily achieve 14 volts peak AC or more. Each time a reluctor lobe aligns with the reluctor pickup it causes this voltage spike, which is the trigger for the GM module.

You see, this is a simple system and most of the work has been done for you as far as getting its operation down to a science. The reluctor lobes are spaced exactly as they need to be, the reluctor pickup is monitoring the reluctor and spiking at the right moment. This is really an ingenious

CHAPTER 8

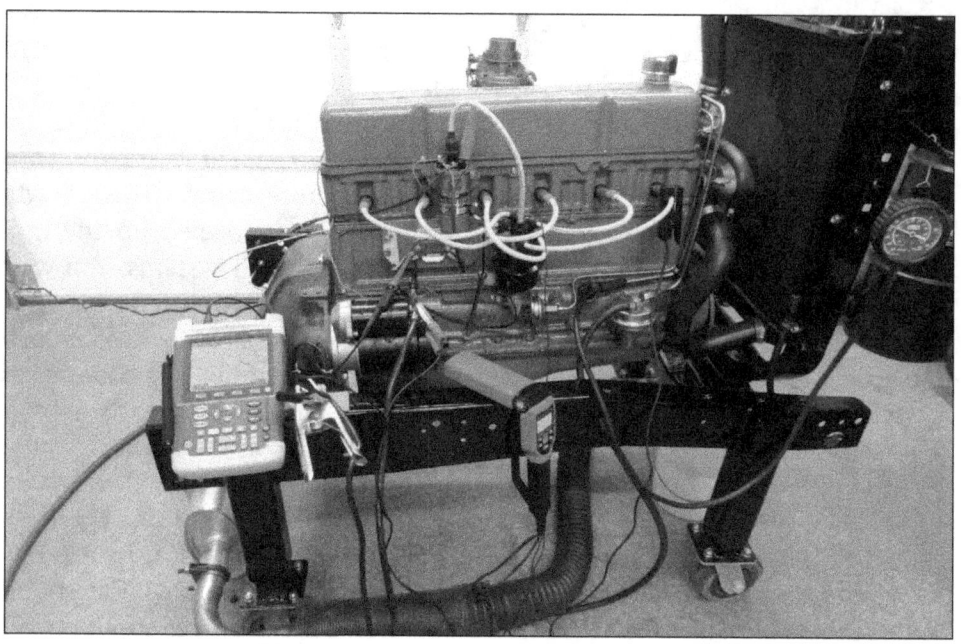

Using an oscilloscope, you see a uniform waveform to verify that the engine is firing properly. This engine is quiet due to the hydraulic lifters and because the engine is firing correctly every time.

The reason for the ballast resistor is that this is a test engine. The first thing you can remove forever when going to HEI is that paint-melting ballast resistor on your vehicle's firewall.

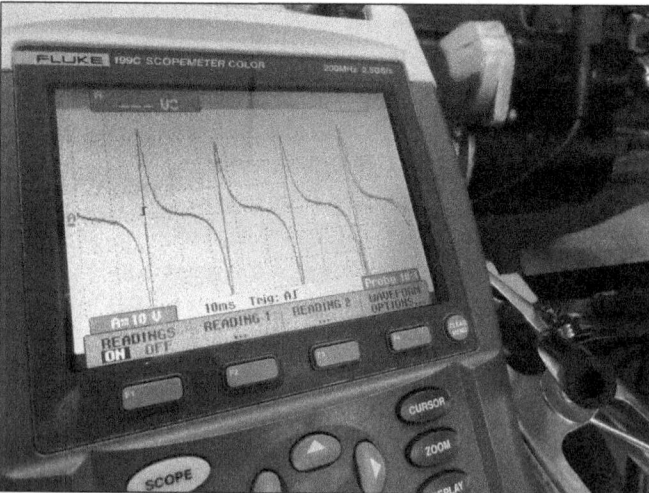

Each spike represents the reluctor lobes coming around and moving past the reluctor pickup in a precise manner.

way of eliminating points. No parts coming into contact with each other, and the power for the trigger is provided by a magnet.

The two wires coming out of the distributor should not draw attention to the fact that the internals in the distributor have been modified. So, aesthetically, it looks pretty much like one black wire coming out of the distributor. If that HEI module's bracket and looks is something that you just can't stand, you can hide

The two wires coming out of the distributor are concealed under a single piece of 1/8-inch heat shrink to make it look like a single wire. This distributor looks 100-percent stock but has never run this well in its life!

Adding a screen allows for more airflow past the HEI module. I did not use a heat sink for nothing.

DISTRIBUTOR

it anywhere you want, even under the dash. But keep in mind that its location under the hood will not be obvious.

The shorter the wires, the better. Because this is a test engine, it also has a ballast resistor. If it wasn't there, you could put the cover of an external regulator over it and it would look pretty cool I think. While you are at it, get a regulator cover with the Delco-Remy script on it. Also install a coil shutoff switch.

You can read the whole article for this process at devestechnet.com/Home/HEIgnition. It includes extensive controlled fuel mileage testing and much more. Then, if you decide this is too ambitious of a project to take on yourself, kits are available at devestechnet.com/Home/HEIInstall, which also serves as the installation page.

If your interest is in keeping the stock ignition system, more information is available at devestechnet.com/Home/TuneUpGuide.

This is what the system looks like when you cover the HEI module with an old Delco regulator cover. It is not that big of a deal under the dark hood, but it adds detail.

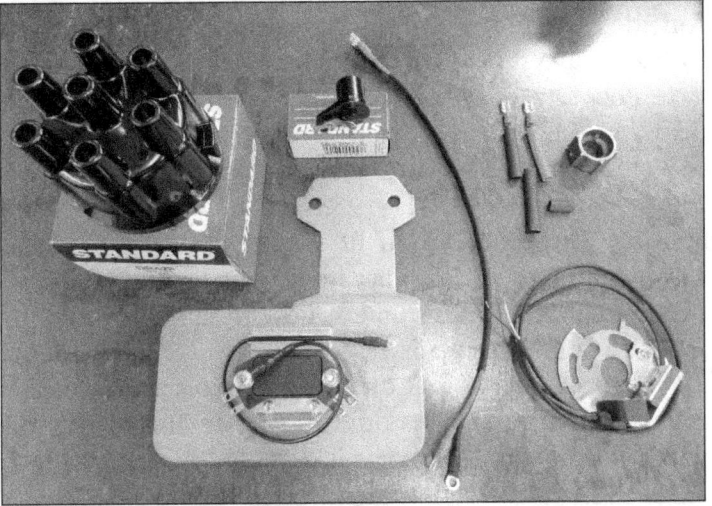

Here are the contents of a kit. Notice that a ground wire from the distributor to the HEI mount plate has been added.

These kits are popular, and I can say after three years of selling them, we have had only a few failures that we can't explain. That is also a testament to the owners who purchase them because this isn't just a plug-and-play kit.

CHEVROLET INLINE-6 ENGINE 1929–1962: HOW TO REBUILD

CHAPTER 9

CARBURETOR

Because I work on these engines from 1953 through 1962, I have several of the newer-style Rochester Bs lying around. The older-style Rochester B carburetors had a smooth neck; you can place the older era air filter assemblies by tightening a clamp around the throat. The newer-style Rochester Bs have a center bar across the throat with a threaded nut. The older air filter units are not compatible with this new style, so you have a choice. You can go with a newer-style air-filter assembly, or you can adapt the carburetor to allow the use of the old-style filter assembly.

Your choice depends on the vehicle. If you are putting it in a 1947–1955 truck, you want to use an air filter unit that was made for those years. The first thing I will do is document how to make the adapter. The newer-style throat is 2 5/8 inches; the older one is only 2 3/8 inches. This does not mean the newer-style throat sucks in more air because of

On the same Rochester B you see the carb adapter to allow older air filter assemblies to be clamped to the top.

the bridge across the throat for the attachment of the air filter unit; they function about the same.

New-Style Carb to Old-Style Filter

To modify a carburetor for an older-style filter, purchase two sizes of steel exhaust tubing at your local muffler shop. You need some tubing with an outside diameter (OD) of 2 3/4 inches and an inside diameter (ID) of 2 5/8 inches. You also need some 2 1/2-inch OD (2 3/8-inch ID). The overall height of this unit will be 1 1/4

The 1959 Rochester B prior to the rebuild. First and most importantly, save the tin tag that is fastened to one of the four top screws. This number is the only way to ensure that you have the correct carb kit.

This completed refurb with the carb adapter mounted on it was simply polished and then clear coated so it doesn't rust. Good luck finding a carburetor with its original plating.

CARBURETOR

A metal-cutting chop saw makes it easy to cut metal tubing of almost any kind. They produce almost no sparks or smoke, which is good.

Both of the 2½- and 2¾-inch OD sizes needed for this project are cut to 5/8 inch.

Trace around the larger of the tubes to make the OD for the flat washer.

inches, so you don't need much tubing (I bought 12 inches of each size, so I could make a few extra ones).

Cut a piece of the 2¾ inch to be 5/8-inch long. Cut a piece of the 2½ inch to also be 5/8-inch long. Slice the 2½-inch one in half down the seam. Using your air filter assembly, resize the smaller one to fit snugly inside with the adjustment bolt turned about halfway out. This should be close to 2⅜ inches. Make a mark on this sleeve, and after cutting to size, weld it closed again.

With two proper-size rings, make a washer that fills in the 1/4-inch gap completely. You want this washer to fit exactly inside the larger ring (2⅝-inch OD) and exactly on top of the smaller one (2¼-inch ID). This strategy gives both rings the proper height.

With some strategic welding you can do this so that it functions perfectly. Start with the large ring and place the washer inside level with the lip, then weld it on the outside only. Be sure to get good penetration so that after you are done grinding all the weld back off to level, it is still secure.

Once you are finished grinding the weld smooth again, turn the washer upside down, placing the smaller ring on the table or work bench, but in the center of the larger ring. This makes it easier to position the Metal Inert Gas (MIG) wand in the correct position for welding inside the hole. Again, good penetration is essential because you will grind all that weld smooth too. Weld it slowly and use proper welding technique to avoid warping.

Test fit the unit to make sure it fits properly. If the larger ring just barely fits over the carburetor, you can grind out the seam for a perfect fit. Once you have a good test fit, you need to make sure it doesn't come off the engine. To do that, weld a 1/4-inch nut near the bottom and exactly where the thicker part of the carb flange is located on both sides.

Mark in the center of the meatiest part of the throat and 3/16-inch up on both sides to about where the old mounting bridge is located. Place the nut where you want to weld it, and then fill the 1/4-inch hole as if using it for a spot weld. You fill it

CHEVROLET INLINE-6 ENGINE 1929–1962: HOW TO REBUILD

CHAPTER 9

If finding the perfect washer of the correct size eludes you, you can do this the hard way. Using a hole saw on the drill press takes care of the inside, now on to the Porta-Band saw for the outside.

Here's how the older-style filter assemblies are mounted. It's also true for the oil-bath type. Both simply clamp around the outside of the new adapter.

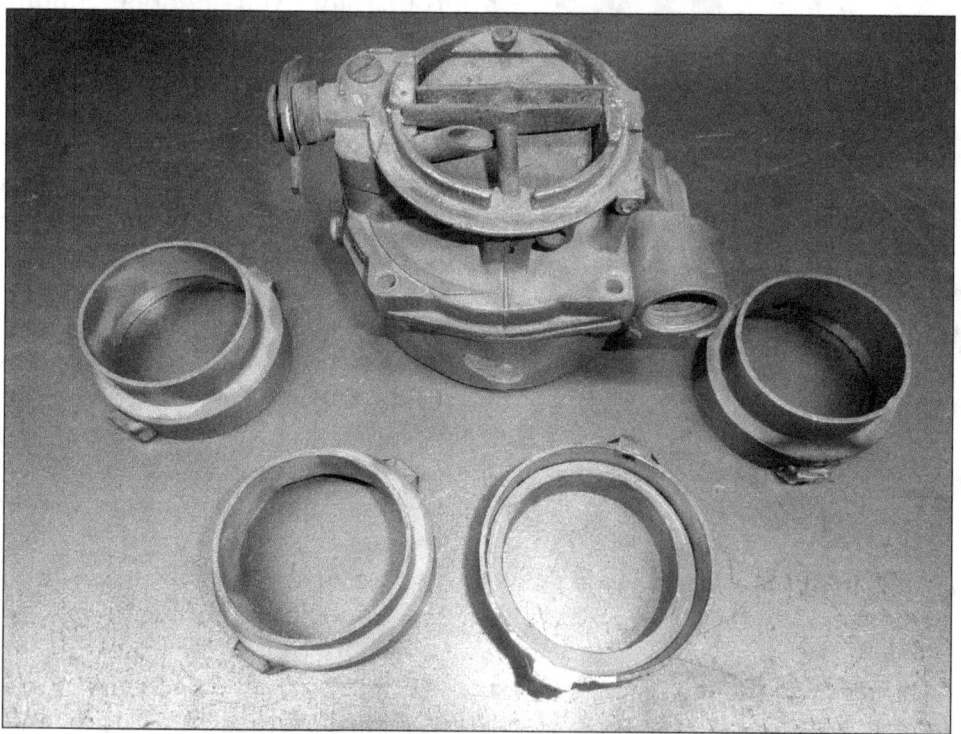

Once weld nuts and all parts are welded together, drill for a number-10 Allen set screw. This solution works nicely, and now you can use the vintage air filters on the newer carbs.

The Allen set screws are not necessarily exactly across from each other. What governs this is the fattest part of the carb's throat in that area.

with weld so you can redrill for a number-10 Allen-style set screw.

When the weld is cool, mark the center of it for drilling and center punch it. Mark 3/16 inch from the bottom in the center of the nut. This should place the hole exactly where you want it. Drill using a number-21 bit used for a number-10-32 tap. Tap and place the unit on top of the carb in the correct location. Make a mark through the hole on the carb.

Using a 1/8-inch drill bit, put a shallow dimple (less than 1/16 inch) to allow the set screw to protrude a little inside the carburetor. Install the set screw using Loctite.

Now you can use these newer-style carbs with an older vintage filter assembly or a newer one. The choice is now yours.

This modification is solid and, with Loctite on the Allen set screws, it will provide you with years of service. This mod may be difficult for you if you lack sophisticated machinery.

You may only have a 2-inch hole saw. In that case, cut the holes, trace around the inside of the larger ring,

CARBURETOR

then use a Porta-Band saw to cut a round circle. Next, use a 3-inch air rasp to whittle away the 1/4 inch that your hole saw didn't get. I am all for having the right tool for the job, but you may have to do it the hard way. Either way, it's satisfying to know the end product will be useful for our niche years of 1947–1955.

Rochester B Carb Disassembly

General Motors used several companies as a source for its carburetors, but Rochester was the main provider during those years. An argument can be made that Carter made a better carb, but Rochester won out with sheer quantity. My apologies to you Carter fans.

The Rochester B was very popular back in the day, and many versions are available. Your Rochester B may look a little different, but for the most part, it's the same. You may find exceptions such as a third check ball, or another small anomaly, but if you use common sense you can do this. A good idea is to take pictures as you go for future reference.

First you need to do a really good cleaning job. The best is to use carb cleaner or engine degreaser (I use my 3-gallon parts washer with kerosene.) Further cleaning will be necessary after the carb is completely apart.

Start by removing the bottom of the carb. To do this, using a needle-nose pliers, pull the clips from the small linkage, and remove the linkage, keeping careful track of all parts and their positions. Take off the bottom by removing the two large screws.

Next, remove the top. The top contains the float assembly, so be very careful when separating them.

Four screws hold the top on; be sure to notice where the throttle and choke bracket are located on one of the corners. Carefully lay the top cover upside down on your work table or bench. Several items protrude up from the top, but one of them will remain even when everything is apart. This includes a brass tube that needs to remain straight and true. Since it is a vintage (and unavailable and unreplaceable) part, be very careful with the assembly. You need to protect it from damage while you clean and restore the inside of the carb.

With the three main bodies separated, you can begin removing components.

Save Money

Carb Plating Options

These carbs are so old that it is very unlikely you will find one with the gold anodized plating intact. Of the five in my inventory, none have any plating left on them. This means you will have to do one of the following:

- Have them re-anodized at a plating company. This is expensive.
- Purchase an anodizing kit. This is cheaper but leaves you with some nasty chemicals and possibly not-so-perfect results.
- Purchase a can of carb paint from a vendor such as Eastwood. They are chemical resistant.
- Purchase a can of high-temperature clear coat and retain the natural color. This keeps it from rusting.

I chose to go with leaving it the natural color of cast steel. I am not making this one for a show truck, so leaving it natural gives me the options later if I choose to go another route. ■

Removing the carb base starts with removing the wire clip that keeps the linkage in place. Take plenty of pictures so you are reminded later how all these small parts go together.

Two large screws hold the base to the carb. Once the single linkage is removed, this can be separated from the bowl.

CHAPTER 9

Four screws hold the top. Be sure to save the metal tag that is supposed to be attached to one of those screws. That is the only way to be sure you are getting the correct carb kit. Take good care of this tag and make sure you put it back on later.

Removing the float assembly is simply a matter of pulling out the connecting pin from either side. The pin slides right out with no need for tools.

Careful disassembly is important so you don't bend parts or lose them. Give yourself plenty of workspace and elbowroom.

Remove the float valve carefully using a screwdriver large enough to bridge the gap.

Begin by removing everything from the top cover. Start with the float assembly. The pin holding the float assembly should be loose and easily pull out of its holes. If you can't do it by hand, you should be able to pull it out with needle-nose pliers without marring the surface. Wiggle it carefully until it comes out. Keep track of the orientation of the float.

Float Inspection

Inspect the floats for any visible damage. These floats are still available as of this writing so if yours has sprung a leak, or just to be precautionary, replace it. Remove the float valve and seat, which is the brass carrier with slots on both sides for a wide screwdriver.

Tower Check Ball and Power Piston Removal

Carefully remove the tower check ball cover, the spring, and the smallest check ball, then the jet. The jet should be marked with a number. Remove the power piston tower. Be careful not to lose anything as you place the pieces so you know how they will go back together.

CARBURETOR

The ball bearing under the tower cap can pop out, so be careful. Simply unscrew the top cap, being careful to catch the spring under it, then tip it over to collect the bearing.

This is the actual jet. They come in different sizes and are made to meter the amount of fuel allowed to pass through the carb. The number on the jet is probably the one you need; however, others have been known to drill out that hole. Bad idea. You can verify that the size is correct by checking the Rochester factory specification for your vehicle or using a wire gauge.

This rare power piston and spring is difficult to find. This can be hard to remove but a critical part. The power piston simply moves up and down with fuel pressure, but many of them are rusted in place. Soak it in a product such as PB B'laster to get it free, for days if necessary.

Some models have a screen inside one of the holes in the tower. Clean it well and leave it in place. Next remove the power piston. This is usually stuck and difficult to remove. Be very careful because they are not available. Take your time and try every trick in the book to keep that power piston intact and serviceable.

To do its job, this power piston should move up and down freely. The spring under the power piston is not available either, so be very careful when removing them. The top of that power piston is important because the check ball sits on top of it and meters the gas intake.

If the butterfly assemblies are working freely and have no end-play or wobbling, I leave it up to you whether you want to go to this trouble.

Once the power piston tower, the piston and spring, jet assembly, etc., is removed, you can move on to removing the butterfly assemblies.

Cleaning Kit Option

A good thing to have for the internal cleaning process is something you may have but haven't thought of for carburetors. It's the large-size cleaning kit for HVLP paint guns. If you don't have one, take this opportunity to get one.

In it, you find things that are important to properly rebuild a carb. For example, the kit has a tube of different-size orifice cleaners (basically 2-inch pieces of strong wire of different diameters) as well as bottle brushes and other important cleaning aids. It turns out that the holes in these carbs are small, and this kit works perfectly!

Removing the T-clip is as easy as simply pulling it straight out. Under it is a spring and another ball bearing, so be careful.

Remove the plunger assembly and set it aside. Don't throw anything away yet, in case you have the wrong carb kit with the wrong plunger assembly.

The butterfly on the air horn, or top of the carb, is held in by two screws that may strip out and cause you great pain and misery if you do not grind off the ends a little. Try it gently to see if they break loose. If they don't, use your Dremel and grind the excess threads off the end of the screws. You want to use Loctite Red to reassemble them once the screws are ground. Once ground, they should come out easily.

The same is true for the lower butterfly valve. Check first, but if you think you might strip them, grind the ends off. It will save the screws and prevent you from having to drill out and retap an intricate assembly.

Carburetor Body Removal

Now that you have removed all parts out of the air horn (top), move on to the body. Remove the little T-clip (called the main discharge tube) that holds another check ball. Many times the check ball gets stuck and doesn't come out easily, but it must be removed. It is the other steel larger check ball in your carb kit. Remove the large plunger mechanism with tower bracket and spring, and place them aside.

Base Assembly

The base assembly is the only part that is different between a 250 engine and a 235. It has to do with the spacing between the two mounting flange bolts. Never toss a Rochester B carb that has the wrong mounting bolt pattern. Get the correct one and the rest of the carb is good.

Remove the brass idler screw with spring and the vacuum advance fitting. If you remove the bottom butterfly assembly, you should have a completely stripped base unit. The only reason for removing the butterfly assemblies is having slop, either from side to side or in and out. Sometimes a brass drift punch moves enough material to stop the slop where the steel and brass converge. If you remove them, be sure that you fully understand the workings of a shaft and its supporting mechanisms and how to proceed. Ideally, you want no slop on any plane. You also want to assess if it's tight because of rust or dirt buildup, or if it's clean, and tight. I usually opt to remove both butterfly assemblies.

Rochester B Carb Reassembly

The hardest part of this was remembering how the springs go back on. You don't want to install the butterflies for example and have something backward. Especially since you put Loctite Red on the threads. These are the only four screws I recommend Loctite Red on. This is because you ground them down to get them out, ruining their self-locking nature. Remember, to remove Loctite Red you must heat the screws up to 500 degrees. Please don't get this far and make a mistake.

Base Reassembly

Start with the carb's base. Install the idler screw (the one with the pointy tip and spring). Screw it all the way in, then back it out one and a half turns. This is a good place to

CARBURETOR

Carburetor Kit Anomalies

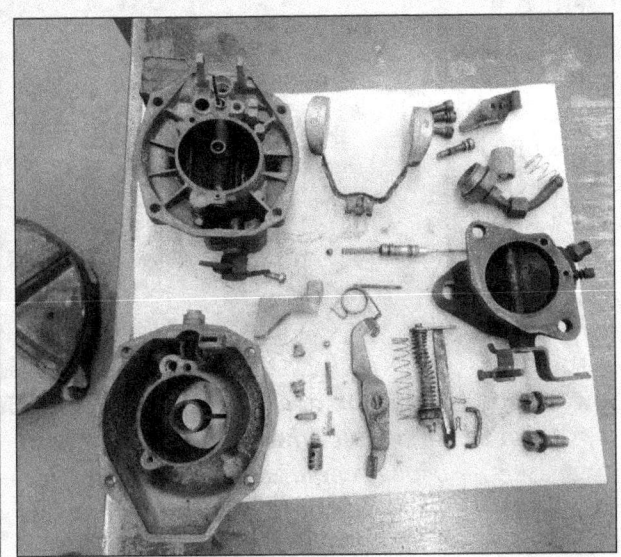

Here is an important shot of everything disassembled. I do not recommend bagging and tagging right away; rather, do it after you finish the process. Having the parts spread out on the table or workbench enables you to locate the correct part quickly.

Here you see the disassembled butterfly valve assemblies and all items after cleaning.

If you are one of the lucky 30 percent who have a metal tag affixed to the top of the carb on one of the bolts, be thankful! All you must do now is tell the parts person at your auto parts store the number, and he or she can look it up and give you the correct kit. If you're not so lucky, you must do some investigation. Sometimes, that same number is stamped on the underside of the body assembly.

That's about another 20 percent of you. The unlucky of us must source a carb kit from the same year model of the original engine. This is an inexact science, but thanks to someone thinking a tin foil tag was a good idea, we are stuck with it.

Purchasing a carb kit for a 1959 235 (in this case) will probably get you home. I pay about $30 for carb kits these days for this vintage. They come with pretty much everything you need, but if you need other parts, check out Mike's Carbs. He stocks a lot of hard-to-find parts and could save the day. The carb rebuild kit I purchased for this one is NAPA PN 2-5194A (V15049). The fuel filter is NAPA PN 3050.

Thorough cleaning ensures that your carb will work correctly. The carb in this case had lots of green corrosion. This is what happens when gold anodized parts lose their anodization and meet steel. It's a mess, but Chevrolet didn't anticipate you would be rebuilding a 60-year-old carburetor.

Clean all surfaces, no matter how difficult they are to access. Use light blasting, a Dremel with fine wire brushes, bench grinder wire brush, sandpaper, and some very fine files; whatever it takes to achieve a shiny and new look. ■

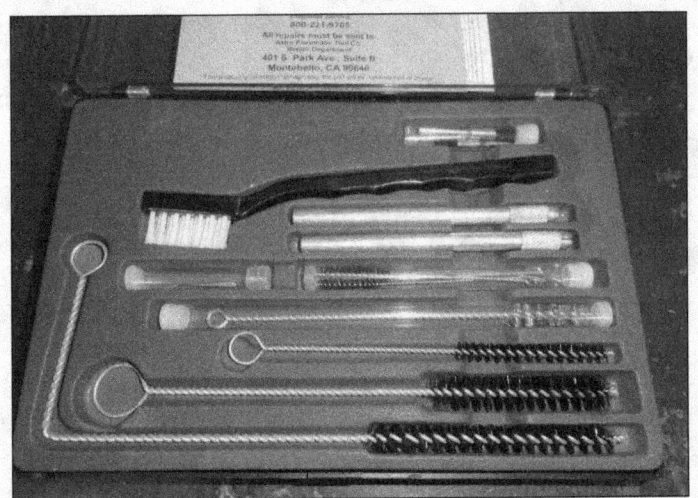

I find that a good paint gun kit has many of the tools you need for cleaning hard-to-reach places including passages and ports.

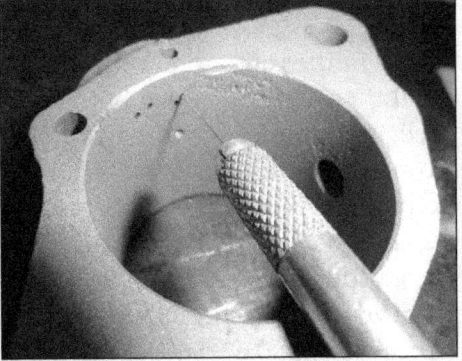

The wires that come in the paint gun kit work perfectly for ensuring all the internal passages are free of crud. Use air to blow them out to be sure.

CHAPTER 9

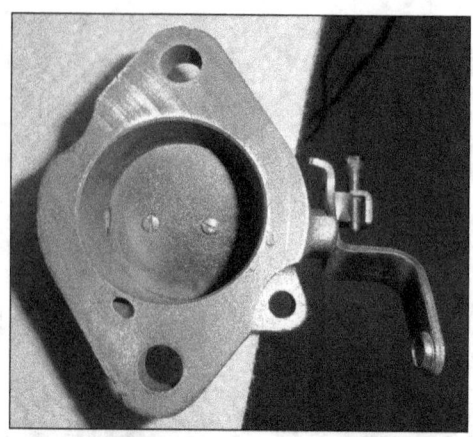

This is the reassembled carb base. The valve should seat perfectly, and the movement should be smooth. Use WD-40 to bathe the parts so everything is extra clean and free.

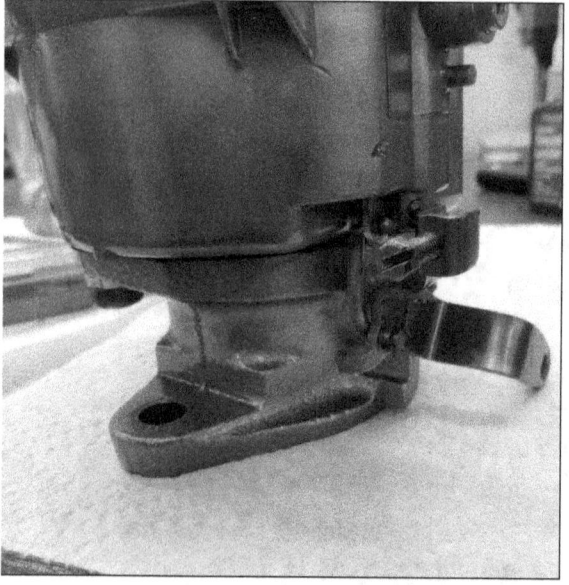

This is the carb base mated with the carb body so you can see the orientation of the linkage between the two.

correct spot. Turn it around and check again.

You will find that it is settled in only one way. The screws faces are viewable from the underside of the carb if that helps. Once you are sure you have the assembly right, use Red Loctite to hold them in place. Remember, before they had expanding nubs on the ends of the screws to keep them from getting sucked down into your precious engine. Now, choose the gasket that mates up to the float bowl. Use the correct one. You will see where the old one used to be, so don't plug any holes with the wrong gasket. Once it's in place, go ahead and put the two screws back in that hold it on the float bowl. Tighten securely. I personally do not put anything on these gaskets. They work fine without adding sealers or something that could contaminate your fuel system.

Float Bowl and Air Horn Reassembly

Before you begin reassembly, take look at some of the disassembly photos to make sure you are on the right track.

Look at the float bowl, or body, of the carb. You may want to put the accelerator pump back where it belongs. But there is one in the kit, so you should use the new parts. Install the spring that goes under the pump. Then the heavy spring goes around the pump itself. Push it all down in the hole and put the pump bracket in its slot in the body. Push them both down until you can place one of the U-shaped keepers in its slot to lock it all down.

This is much easier to do on the carb rather than wrestling with it on the table or workbench. Don't forget that the lighter spring goes in first. Squeeze the U-shaped locker to keep it from coming off.

start and is recommended in the carb kit's instructions. Install the vacuum advance fitting as well. Get it nice and tight. If you removed the butterfly, now is the time to put it back on. Choose orientation carefully. If you aren't sure which way it goes, set it in, then look to see if everything is tight with it sitting there and make sure the screw locations are in the

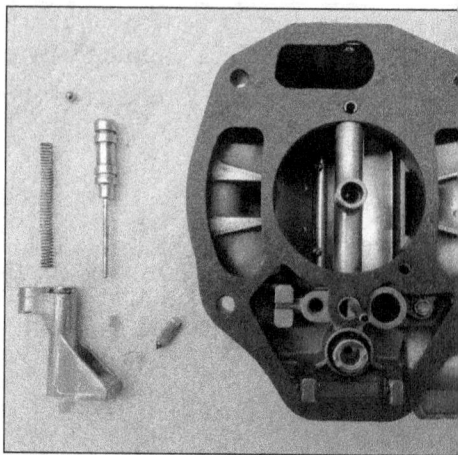

Install the gasket before the tower. Be sure to use the correct gasket; kits usually come with two of them. This is why I said not to throw anything away. Your old gasket tells you which new one to use.

Now that the assembly is put together, from the outside, reattach the little linkage from the bottom of the accelerator pump assembly to the butterfly assembly on the base. The linkage points should be in with the dogleg facing out. Use the smallest clips in the new kit to secure it. You should now have an accelerator linkage that springs back by itself smoothly.

Setting the float bowl with the base in front of you, install the first check ball. Place it into the larger hole near the accelerator pump where the T-shaped keeper goes. Next, place the large (not the aluminum one) check ball, then the new small spring (looks like the spring from an ink pen), then the T, which goes down into the spring and then pushes flush with the hole. That's all there is to the float bowl.

Turn the air horn (top) upside down on the table or workbench. You see one tube sticking up that was not removed during cleaning. In front of that is where you want to install the

CARBURETOR

This keeper goes on the end of the protruding shaft on the end of the butterfly assembly. Be sure to notice which way the spring goes along with all other associated parts.

Imagine how well this is going to work when it is clean. This upper butterfly shaft is being removed for cleaning. Remember, there is no need to remove that shaft unless it is worn and feels sloppy.

float valve seat, which has two slots for a large screwdriver. The carb kit has a new valve seat with a gasket. Be sure to install the new gasket, then position the new seat into place.

Tighten securely. You do not want any leaks. Be careful not to bend anything. Put the new float valve aside for now.

Place the correct gasket from the new kit. Make sure it doesn't plug any holes or sit in the way of anything. To install the power piston, put the spring inside, set it in, and check for movement. You want it to move smoothly and freely. Also, the thin end of the piston needs to be straight. If it isn't, it may not push the check ball out of the way properly. Set the spring and then the power piston in place (in the small hole at the end), then install the tower.

Once you are certain that the piston moves freely in the hole by turning it and watching the movement, set the smallest steel check ball in that hole. Then from the carb kit, place the little spring that has tapered ends in the brass cap.

After the power piston, check ball, and spring/cap are lined up, tighten the cap securely. Install the jet (the brass piece that has a number on the top rim). Tighten securely. Install the float assembly by first dropping the float valve in its place, then properly orienting the float assembly and sliding the keeper bar to center it. The little tab in the center protrudes downward.

When the float is sitting flat with the top upside down, so you can see where it is resting, there should be $1^{9}/_{32}$ inches from the top of the float pontoon to the gasket. Use the measuring square that comes with the carb kit. To change that measurement, delicately bend the center tab in or out so that when it sits on the needle valve, you have the proper measurement.

Next, turn the assembly upside down and let the floats dangle. Measure from the gasket to the top of the float pontoon; it should be $1^{3}/_{4}$ inches. If it is different, another tab can be bent for that in the center of the assembly. Once you have both sides perfect, you are done.

If there is a difference between the two floats, you need to make a delicate bend on one side. In any

This photo will help you understand how the spring is wrapped around the shaft and how the parts go together again.

case, you want to be sure the floats are not interfering with the gasket or anything else.

You can probably take fewer pictures of the final assembly because you can look at the disassembly pictures to figure it out.

When you have everything adjusted, carefully mate the air horn with the float bowl, taking care not to bend or bind anything. Place two of the four screws to secure the top adjacent to each other for now.

The upper butterfly assembly is next. This takes some concentration

This is the orientation of the butterfly to the butterfly shaft. The two brass screws are hard to find, and you will strip them unless you grind off the deformation that keeps them in place. Use Loctite Red to hold them in once fully assembled.

Drilling out these pins allows you to remove the bridge, so the engine breathes nicely with the smaller adapter. Only do this if you are planning on using the carb adapter discussed at the beginning of this chapter.

because you don't want to install the spring backward, forget the keeper on the end of the shaft, or place the wafer backward. To do this correctly, lay out all the parts as they are in order of assembly. First the spring, then the wafer. Hold them up to the hole and then lock them down with the round keeper that you removed earlier. You need to wind the spring one revolution so that everything springs together properly. Of course, wind in the direction the spring is wound in, and don't bend it.

The proper butterfly shaft has visible indentions where the screws go. Slide the butterfly between the shaft slots and put the screws back in. Hold off adding Loctite until you are certain the screws are in correctly.

With the butterfly assembly in place and rotating smoothly, install the lever assembly to the side of the carb. It also has a spring that needs to be installed correctly. This is the bridge between the lower butterfly and the upper one.

If you want to use this carb with an older-style air filter assembly, you want to remove the nut bridge assembly by drilling out the pins that are holding it. It restricts airflow for your purposes, so no need to have it in there. You can always replace it later should you need this awesome carb for an engine that requires it.

I have to say, this is a neat mechanical device when you think about it. It's beautiful in its simplicity. Yet it is critical that all parts are assembled correctly.

In Summary

This finished carb is quite fitting for this project. In this process, I chose not to change out the float assembly. Even though it's only about $15 for a new one, I will try this one first, then if it's bad, I can change it easily since I didn't slather a bunch of gasket sealer all over it. You can get an entire Rochester B carb rebuilt for about $180 with the core, but what would be the fun in that?

Things are changing out there folks, 60-year-old parts are becoming harder to find. It's imperative to have the proper respect for vintage parts and understand that they are not an unlimited commodity.

Fuel Delivery System

The mechanical fuel pump has been a good mainstay and works well; however, it does have its problems. They can go bad and, depending on how they go bad, create severe problems. Because the mechanical pump relies on a diaphragm that can leak fuel into the bottom of an engine, it has been known to cause premature engine failure. This is another incentive to always check your oil. This rarely happens, but it's possible.

On the other hand, going to an electric pump does not change the reliability statistics much. It can go bad too, but it is an alternative to the common mechanical pump. Spectra Pre-

CARBURETOR

mium makes an OEM electric pump that works nicely with these engines, and the actual pump statistics are the same in gallons per hour, etc.

Also consider this common problem: Have you ever let your vehicle sit for a long time and notice that it takes a lot longer to start? This is because the carburetor's fuel bowl is empty or depleted from evaporation, and it is no longer primed to start immediately. The electric pump and a circuit called AutoPrime solves this problem by pumping the carb bowl full prior to engine start.

Kits are available, but they have drawbacks. One is that an electric pump takes more room to mount where the old mechanical pump used to be, thus requiring removal of the road tube (or the fuel pump can be moved to the frame rail). Removing the road tube is a good idea anyway because that is how you can install a PCV system in these engines.

Also, as these vehicles age, the fuel tank can begin to shed rusty crud into the fuel line. To protect your engine, install a glass fuel filter, such as the Spectre Performance Products 2369, between the fuel tank and the fuel pump. It allows you to monitor for dirt.

Beyond the Stock Stovebolt Fuel System

The stock 1947–1955 GM fuel system consists of a fuel storage tank, a 6-inch rubber hose (1/8-inch NPT female to 5/16-inch flare), 5/16-inch fuel hard line, a mechanical fuel pump, more 5/16-inch hard line, a glass bowl fuel filter, and a carburetor. The electricals include a gauge and a sending unit. This system worked quite nicely for its time. With the advent of modern technology, however, you have ways to make it much better, and it is nice to have something solid to work with.

The reason for the rubber hose coming off the in-cab fuel tank is that the cab floats on cab mounts that allow for movement separate from the frame. At the tank, there is a fuel shutoff valve. This valve, when turned all the way in, keeps fuel from flowing to the fuel pump. One of the improvements you can make is to put a short soft line from the frame to the pump. Because the engine moves independently from the frame, it causes excessive pressure on the hard line.

The pros are that it is a simple and mostly reliable system. Hats off to the engineers at General Motors. The cons are that starting is difficult after the carburetor's fuel bowl contents deplete because of evaporation, a lack of a filter between the tank and the fuel pump, and short pump longevity due to today's more caustic gas formulas.

What do I mean by more caustic gas? Every lawn mower and small engine manufacturer in the world includes a warning that says if you use ethanol, be sure to drain your gas tank after 30 days because the gas becomes unusable after that. Ethanol is known to corrode some rubber and neoprene products at a substantially higher rate.

My suggestion is to avoid ethanol for your vintage vehicles at all costs. Nothing good can come from a 30-day restriction on fuel usage. If you do not have a no-alcohol gas pump available, use a product called Sta-Bil with every fill-up.

The stock fuel system was well designed and has withstood the test of time. But there is more you can do.

Fuel Pump Basics

The way to eliminate the real and annoying problem of harder starting after a vehicle has been sitting awhile begins with a discussion of the use of electric fuel pumps. First, you need to understand fuel pump flow behavior, fuel pump pressure, and fuel pump safety precautions.

The stock mechanical fuel pump works off the engine's camshaft. Due to the cam action, the pump's lever being in contact with the cam allows for fuel flow in the direction of the carburetor. The stock mechanical fuel pump is rated to deliver a maximum of 25 gallons per hour (gph) and provide between 3.5 and 4.5 pounds per square inch (psi) of pressure against the carburetor's float valve. This means that no more than 25 gph is consumed by an engine with that fuel delivery system. It also means that the pump is not responsible for pushing more fuel into the carburetor than can be consumed due to the carb's float valve only allowing enough

CHAPTER 9

Beyond the Stock Stovebolt Fuel System (continued)

This is one way to mount an electric fuel pump using the stock location and adding a glass inline fuel filter before the pump.

Two of the most common styles of mechanical fuel pump: post-1953 on the left, pre-1953 on the right. They both fit these engines, but the older ones have ports straight across from each other.

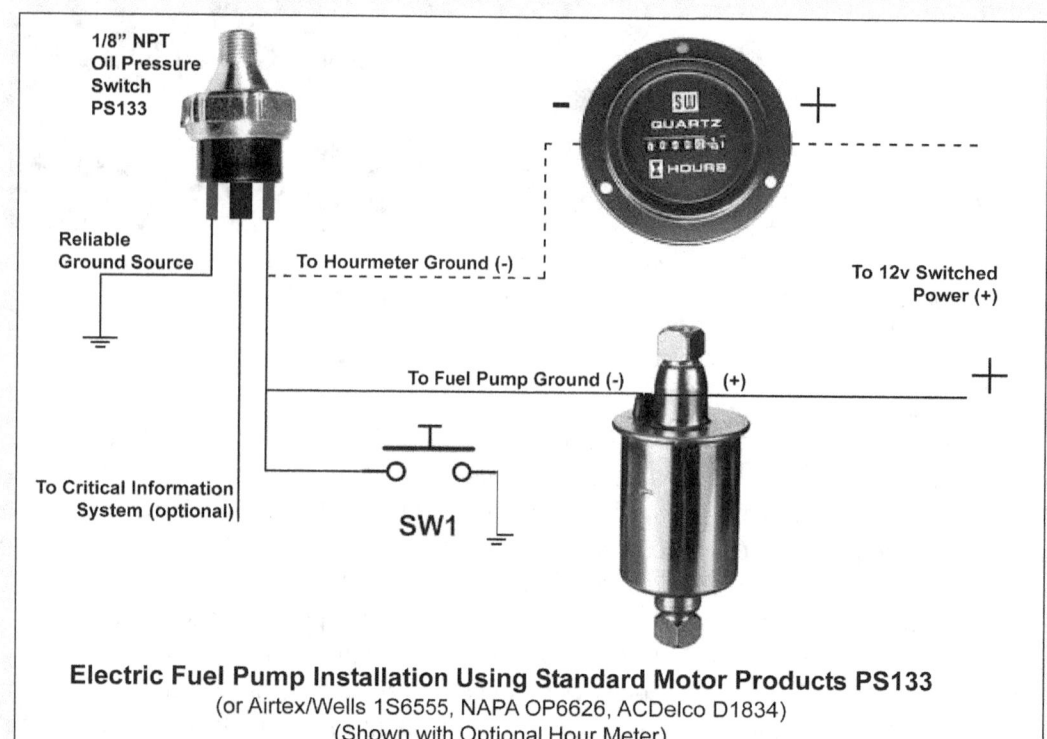

Electric Fuel Pump Installation Using Standard Motor Products PS133
(or Airtex/Wells 1S6555, NAPA OP6626, ACDelco D1834)
(Shown with Optional Hour Meter)

This is one way to update your fuel system so that it is safe. A switch that relies on oil pressure to control the fuel pump means that the fuel pump does not spew explosive gasoline all over the place in a rollover accident without engine oil pressure.

When I say, "fuel flows in the direction of the carburetor," I mean only in the direction of the carb. Fuel is restricted from flowing backward by the mechanical fuel pump's check valve. There is no check valve in the other direction, which is significant because it means fuel can freely flow past the mechanical pump if another pump is used to augment the existing one. This enables you to do some pretty cool stuff to make this system better.

The mechanical fuel pump has gone the way of the dinosaur, as they say, and mechanical fuel pumps have not fuel in to keep the carburetor's fuel bowl full.

What happens to the fuel pump's pressure when the float valve closes? The same thing that happens when you pinch off a garden hose. Liquid stops flowing with no penalty to the workings of the pump.

CARBURETOR

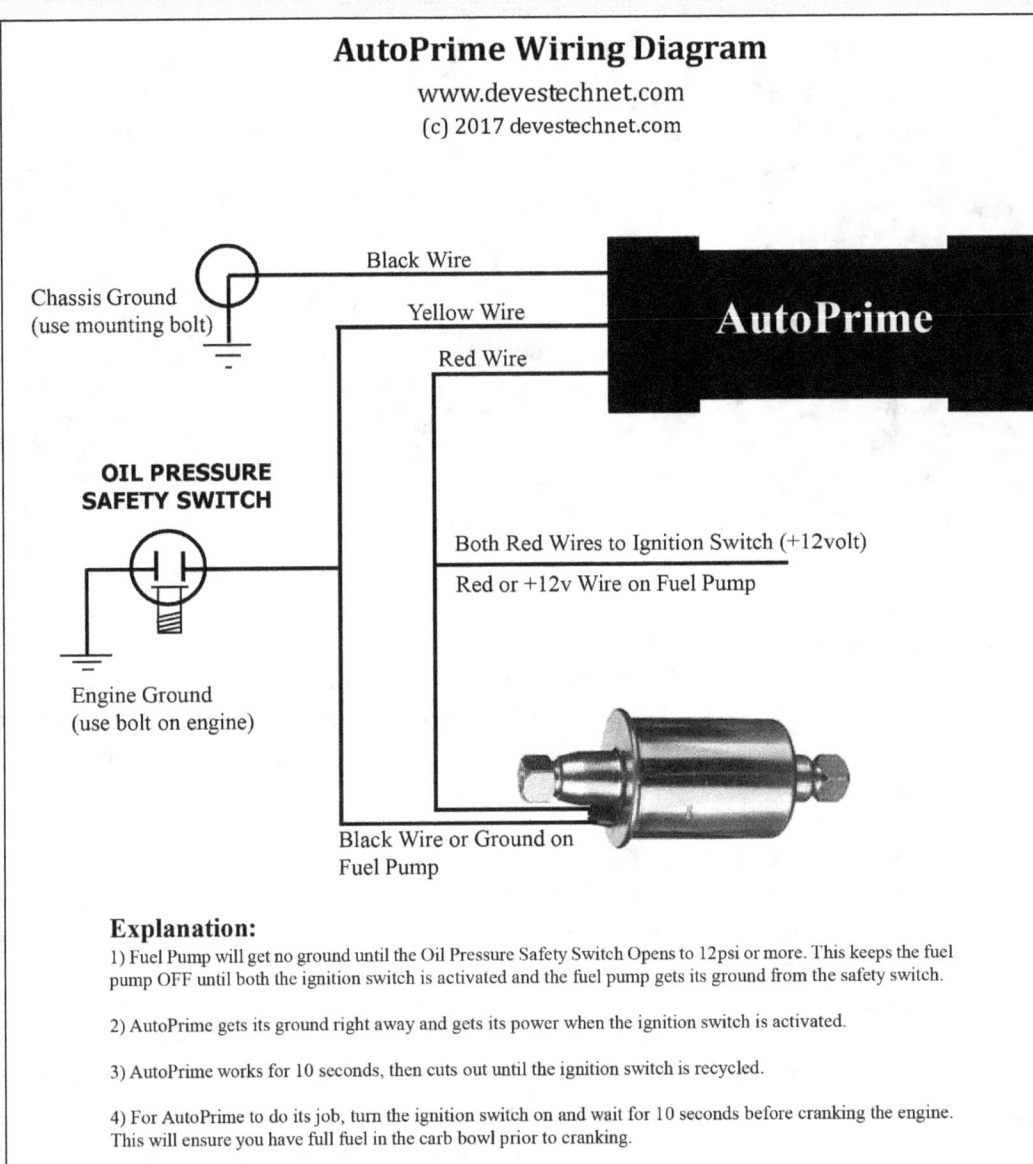

This is the accepted way to wire an entire electric fuel system using OEM parts from the late 1970s through the mid-1990s.

oil pressure switch used for this purpose. The two terminals across from each other are connected internally only after 12 psi or more of oil pressure is present. Properly wiring this switch into the system prevents the electric fuel pump from coming on until the oil pressure is at or above 12 psi. This puts the mechanical and electrical pumps on par with each other, allowing them to behave the same in the fuel system.

Electric fuel pumps work similarly to their mechanical counterparts in that they pulse fuel through the system. The diaphragm that pushes the fuel is smaller and the pump is OEM, so it has been engineered for modern fuels. Electric pumps work the same as mechanical ones in the vehicle's fuel system; when sufficient fuel is pumped into the carburetor to bring the carb's float to maximum, the fuel pump stops pumping. This is because the carb's float valve holds back about 10 psi of pressure, and the pump is only rated to put out 3 to 5 psi. Really, the only difference between mechanical and electrical pumps is the method by which they are powered.

been used for OEM purposes since the mid-1980s. They do, however, have one advantage: They stop fuel flow when the engine stops. For you to consider an electric fuel pump, you need a way to stop fuel flow when the engine stops. It is not safe or desirable to hook an electric pump to 12 volts and let it run all the time. In the case of an accident, you do not want fuel pumping out of the tank, so you must devise a way to ensure that the fuel pump stops upon engine shutdown.

The way the General Motors got around this in the 1980s and 1990s on OEM installations was to use a fuel safety switch that was based on the presence of engine oil pressure. The Standard Motor Products PS133 is a good example of an

Electric Fuel Pump Installation

Installation of an electric fuel pump can be accomplished by it mounting to the frame rail or, if you are replacing your existing mechanical pump, you can make a bracket that

Beyond the Stock Stovebolt Fuel System (continued)

This is one method for mounting an electric fuel pump to the frame. Use a soft line to the hard line that goes to the carb so there is some flexibility to compensate for engine movement.

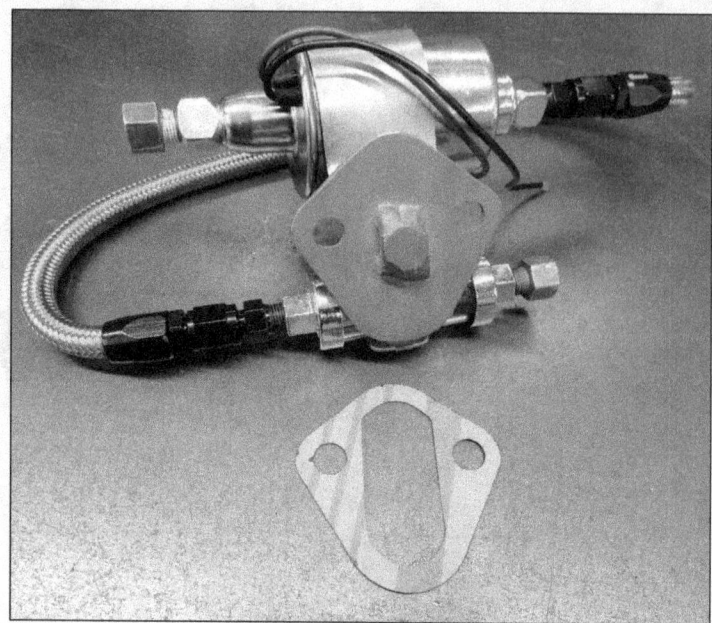

Welding a bolt into the plate means no leakage and a solid platform for the new electric pump. A –4AN stainless braided rubber hose is a good choice for connection.

This bracket installs in the mechanical pump location for the new electric model. It features a welded stud to ensure nothing ends up inside the engine.

places the new pump exactly where the old one was located at the side of the engine. The advantage to mounting it in the same place is, with a little tweaking, you can use the same hard lines to connect it. This bracket can easily be made from 5/16-inch steel.

Trace around a fuel pump gasket for the pattern, drill the two holes for mounting, then drill a third hole in the center for a 3/8-inch bolt, weld the bolt into place from the inside, and you are good to go. Welding is the safest way to do this because you do not want the situation where the bolt could drop into the engine.

Using the same mounting surface and bolt holes for the electric pump as where the mechanical pump used to be works great. There may be some minor tweaking of the hard line to get it to fit but may save you from having to recreate hard lines. This is truer with the 1940–1953 pumps (mechanical) that have the inlet and outlet directly across from each other. If you have a pump that has offset ins and outs, you may need (at least) new hard lines to the carb.

One important caveat is that the electric pump works great in the same location as the mechanical pump if you went to a PCV system. The road draft tube gets in the way and cannot be used if mounting the electric pump there. If you are not running PCV, you should be. (See the chapter 10 sidebar "Installing a PCV System.")

The front side of the mounting bracket. The gasket is optional. A good sealer does the job without a gasket.

CARBURETOR

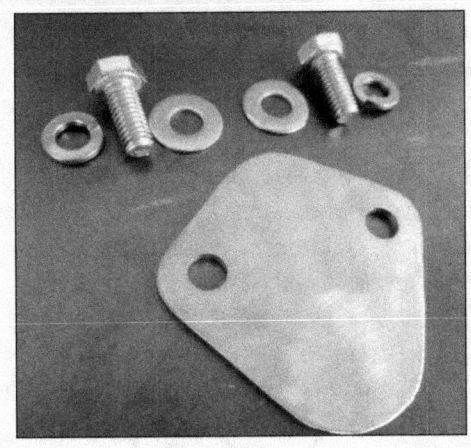

If you opt for the frame-mount electric pump without mechanical pump augmentation, you can make a stainless steel cover for the mechanical location.

Don't forget about the hole in the engine block that used to accommodate the mechanical fuel pump. This is important, of course, if you choose to remove the mechanical one. Trace around a mechanical fuel pump gasket on a piece of 14-gauge stainless steel. Drill the appropriate 5/16-inch holes, then add a few stainless bolts, hardware, and some gasket sealer.

You also may want to add a glass fuel filter before the pump. One of the primary reasons for any fuel pump failure is sediment from the gas tank fouling the pump. It is prudent to use a filter after the tank but before the pump.

For the bracket mounted on the engine, a simple 3/4-inch pipe clamp holds the filter in place. With the pump mounted on the frame rail, a 1½-inch stainless pipe nipple connects the filter to the pump. My preferred filter is the Spectre Performance 2369. It is glass with rubber seals and you can purchase new filter elements that come with new rubber seals. Summit Racing has them.

There is one thing about these filters that you should be aware of. The threads are supposed to be 1/8-inch NPT, but I have found the threads to be too tight and the 5/16-inch flare fitting does not go in far enough to prevent leaks. This is a simple problem to solve with a 1/8-inch NPT tap. Route out the threads with your 1/8-inch NPT tap and everything will be leak proof using a fuel-resistant Teflon tape.

Parts List and Comparisons

Finding the right electric fuel pump takes a little research, but I found the following good candidates.

- Airtech Model E8251: Puts out 30 gph and maximum PSI is 4½. Because the carb governs the fuel flow, 30 gallons is fine. This does not mean you use more fuel, it means the pump is capable of it. Because this is an OEM product, it is also manufactured by Carter (PN P74021) and Spectra Premium (PN SP1170); all three are identical.
- Holley Mitey Mite PN 12-426: Puts out 25 gph and maximum PSI is 4. It falls exactly within the target but is not OEM. You don't need to care much, but OEM means the pump is routinely used in the manufacturing of vehicles. This one is aftermarket only but still works fine.
- Facet/Purolator PRO87SV: Puts out 32 gph and a maximum of 5 psi. It has a built-in filter, which is a great thing, but so far I have only been able to source it through eBay, which is a red flag for me because it reduces its guarantee of future availability. Also, it's not OEM.

To build everything outlined in this sidebar yourself, some part numbers might come in handy. The following is a list of everything needed. Hardware is stainless steel wherever possible.

- Spectre Performance Products 2369: This inline gas fuel filter has 1/8-inch NPT threads on the ends. It is the best I could find that gives you the choice of screw-in flare fittings or hose barbs.
- Spectre Performance Products 2358: These are fuel filter replacement elements. If you can't swap out the elements, what good is a fancy glass filter?
- Standard Motor Products PS133: This oil pressure–actuated fuel safety switch is also an OEM product, so it is available from Delco D1834, Airtex/Wells 1S6555, or NAPA OP6626.
- Dorman 490-314.1: The 5/16-inch (tube) to 1/8-inch NPT flare fittings are the common fittings used on the carb and mechanical fuel pump.
- McMaster-Carr 4830K112: A 1½-inch stainless steel pipe nipple is needed for connection between the filter and the pump on a frame rail installation.
- McMaster-Carr 8897T12: This 3/4-inch stainless steel pipe clamp is used for clamping the glass filter to the engine-mounted electric pump assembly.
- McMaster-Carr 8897T23: A 1-inch stainless steel pipe clamp used for clamping the AutoPrime circuit to the frame rail.
- McMaster-Carr 50785K321: FMF 1/8-inch NPT tee

Beyond the Stock Stovebolt Fuel System (continued)

connector. This tee allows you to use your mechanical oil pressure gauge and add the PS133 electric switch to the oil system at the engine.

- Summit Racing SUM220446B: A –4AN to 1/8-inch NPT adapter is used to go from 1/8-inch NPT to –4AN for using a stainless braided hose for the soft line between the frame-rail-mounted electric pump and the mechanical one.
- Summit Racing SUM 220490B: –4AN hose fitting. This is the straight-in hose end for the soft line.
- Summit Racing ICB-9090-04B: –4AN 90-degree swivel hose fitting. This is the 90-degree fitting to make the transition to the frame rail a little nicer.
- Summit Racing SUM-230403: The 3 feet of stainless braided hose is bulk hose in –4AN (or 1/8 inch). Use the two fittings above for making this hose yourself.

All of the electric pumps and filters use a 1/8-inch NPT (1/8-27) thread size and allow you to use either barbs and flexible rubber hose or make it more permanent with hard lines using flare fittings. The common fuel line size is 5/16-inch tube.

The electric pump should be attached to your ignition switch and uses about 3 to 5 amps of current. A 10-amp fuse works great using 14-gauge hookup wire. Enjoy a reliable fuel system.

Of course, nothing is foolproof, but ask yourself why all car manufacturers went to electric years ago. The electric solution is considered more reliable and something you don't have to concern yourself with when you start your engine. I am not sure if engine performance is increased by removing the mechanical pump or not (due to no friction on the cam).

Fuel Pump Inertia Switch

A more modern solution to the oil pressure sensor available to stop the pump from working in case of a rollover/accident is a fuel pump inertia switch, such as the Airtech-Wells SW4177. This eliminates the need for the oil pressure sensor and the SW-1 switch because the pump activates on ignition startup. It sounds like a good idea, but the cost for a new one is about $60.

In addition to cost, a downside is that the carb's float valve is a wear item; maybe you do not want the electric pump running all the time that the ignition is turned on. This makes the original schematic more attractive. It would be nice, however, to have an automatic priming feature in the circuit.

You should not use the instructions that come with the pump because it shows the safety switch connected incorrectly. That is, the +12v line is used to make and break the switch. This puts excessive wear on the switch because making/breaking positive voltage is harder on the switch. A better and safer idea is to use ground to make/break the connection.

The pump's +12 positive is only used directly to the ignition switch. Ground is provided when the oil pressure safety switch in engaged. This is the only way an AutoPrime circuit is set up to work and the most logical method of connection.

To connect the oil pressure/fuel safety switch (PS133), add a 1/8-inch NPT tee connection at the oil pressure gauge line at the engine. One end of the tee is for the mechanical oil pressure gauge; the other is for the PS133 fuel safety switch. A short, black ground wire from a bolt on the engine block to the other side of the switch provides the ground needed for operation.

Introducing AutoPrime

So far, you have been able to perfectly emulate the mechanical fuel pump using an electric one. You have it mounted and delivering the same fuel volume. You have one major improvement to make, however. With the electric pump wired to the fuel safety switch (oil pressure), you still do not have fuel to fill the carburetor's depleted fuel bowl until after cranking. The easy way to solve this is to add a momentary pushbutton inside the vehicle. But why should you have to push a button when we are in the year 2018?

Why not incorporate a reliable circuit that starts the fuel pump upon hitting the ignition switch, runs the electric pump for 10 seconds, then shuts down, deferring control to the fuel safety switch? The system is cycled and ready for redeployment by turning the ignition switch off.

This circuit uses no moving parts, such as relays. I instead chose a power transistor (MOSFET) for triggering. With no parts to wear out and an intuitive, long-lasting design, you can be sure the little circuit will be long lasting and carefree. You need the circuit protected against the elements and an easy install, so encase this rascal in 3/4-inch (ID) PVC pipe. The LED is viewed through the end cap and the variable resistor to allow you to adjust the number of seconds (between 2 and 15) is on the end cap as well.

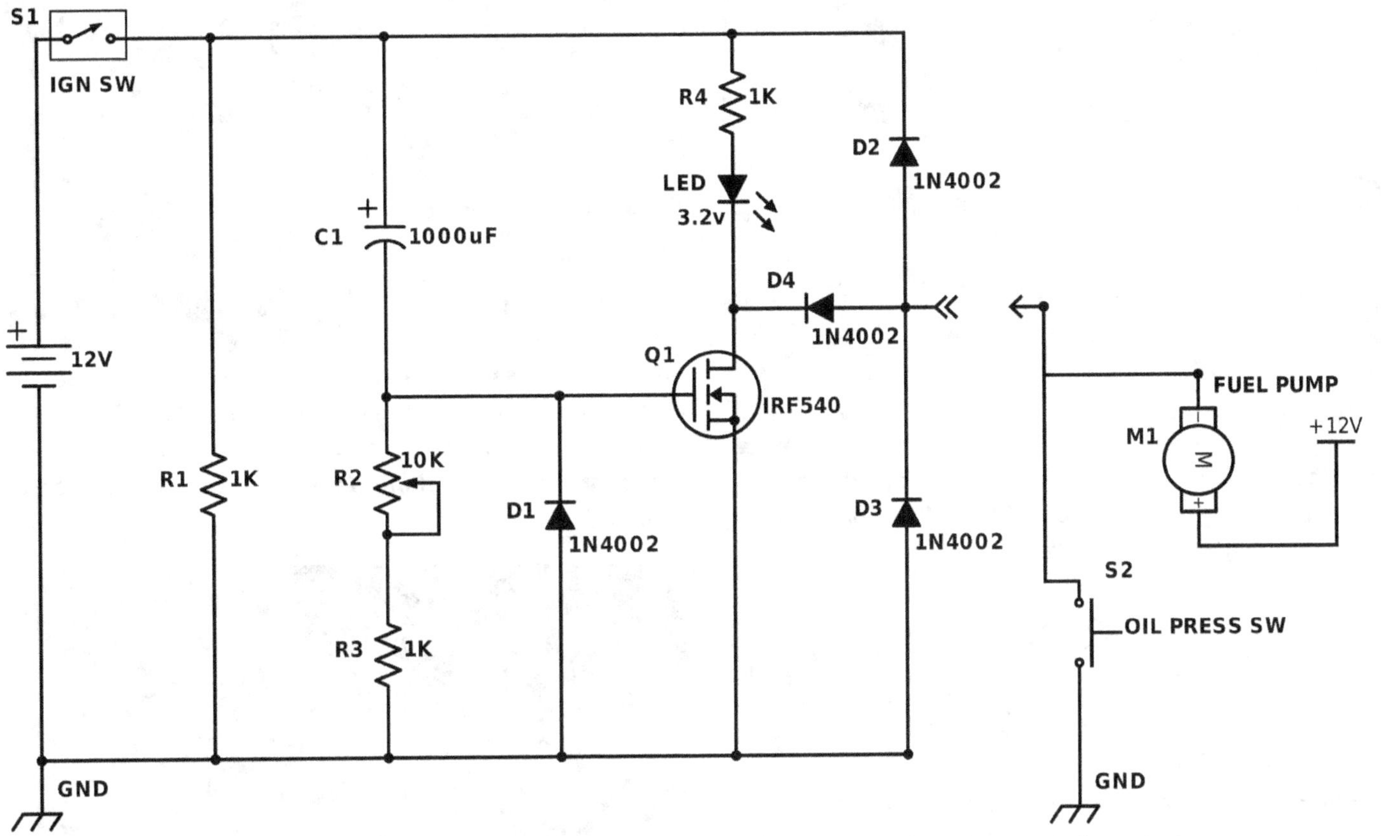

CARBURETOR

This is the complete schematic for the AutoPrime circuit.

This is the AutoPrime circuit ready for installation in its case. This is merely a piece of 7/8-inch PVC pipe with ends.

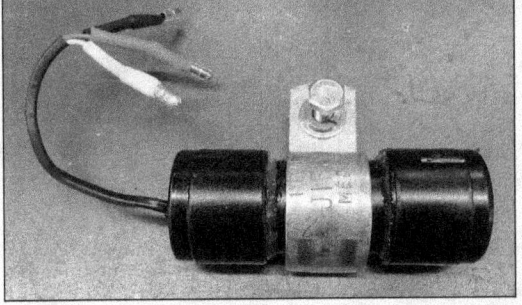

This AutoPrime circuit is ready to install. Using a 1-inch pipe bracket available in stainless steel, you can mount it using a 1/4-inch bolt to any existing hole in the frame that is free.

I use Digi-Key.com for all the parts listed below, except for the circuit board. For safety sake, get a professionally made one from devestechnet.com.

AutoPrime Parts List

Qty	Part
1	Deve's AutoPrime Bare Board
3	1K 1/4-watt resistor
1	1000uf aluminum capacitor
1	10K potentiometer
1	IRF 540 MOSFET
3	1N4002 diode
1	1N5401 diode
1	3.2v LED (green)
1	2-3/4-inch length of 1-inch PVC pipe
2	1-inch PVC end caps
1	1-inch pipe clamp (1/4-inch hole) for mounting

CHEVROLET INLINE-6 ENGINE 1929–1962: HOW TO REBUILD

Beyond the Stock Stovebolt Fuel System (continued)

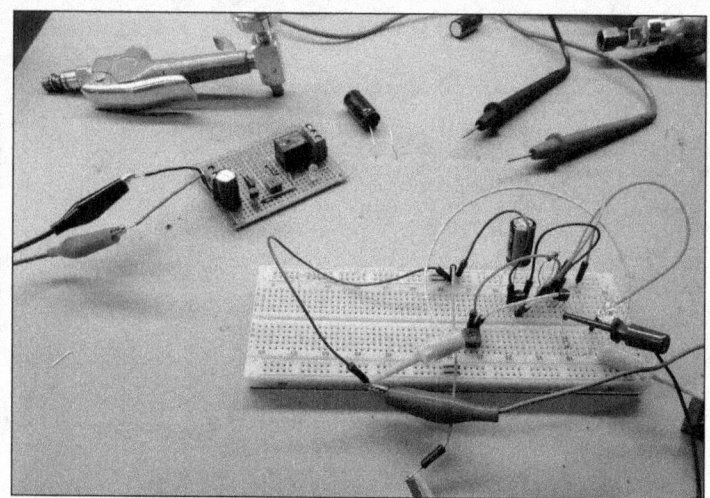

Part of the enjoyment of this endeavor is playing around with electronics to find just the right combination of parts to create a really elegant solution.

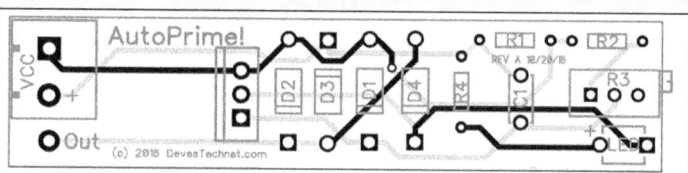

The AutoPrime circuit made via the computer program DipTrace. The program allows you to make printed circuit boards more efficiently using computer-aided design.

I use a fuel pressure gauge on the test engine to see how each solution behaves under real testing. I do not want to overpressure the carburetor's float valve, which is responsible for shutting down fuel flow when the carb bowl is full.

You can unscrew the tip from a regular air nozzle, and it turns out to be 1/8-inch NPT, or the exact size of the fuel safety switch. Air makes a wonderful substitute for testing oil pressure safety switches.

Augmenting an Existing Mechanical Pump

So far, you have replaced the mechanical pump with a more modern electrical pump, placed it in the location of your choice, and made it work as advertised. But what if you already have a perfectly good mechanical pump and wish to provide a redundant backup system? The word redundant often gets a bad name, but in the aircraft industry, it is a mainstay concept. Two of everything means a higher degree of safety. In this case it means twice the reliability of the fuel system. Electric one dies, fuel still gets there. Mechanical one dies, fuel still gets there.

During testing, I discovered that fuel flows from the tank to the carburetor without any restriction, even if the electrical pump is not connected or the mechanical one is not working. This makes it possible to put the electrical pump before (closer to the tank) the mechanical one on the frame rail, and everything works together perfectly. The pressure is not additive, so everything maintains its 3.5 to 4.5 psi window.

Simply install the electric pump on the frame rail and connect a soft line to the mechanical pump's inlet. To test the safety switch, you can use a standard air blower gun. Remove the safety end and screw in the switch. Then, using compressed air, you can test the switch.

I have one warning, however. In doing this, if the mechanical pumps diaphragm were to fail, fuel could be pumped into the oil pan. Although a rare occurrence, this has been known to happen. Even more reason to check your oil regularly. ∎

CHAPTER 10

MISCELLANEOUS IMPORTANT DETAILS

There are small but time-consuming details that need to be addressed before we get much further, including refurbishing the manifolds, determining flywheel tooth count, preparing and painting sheet metal parts, and choosing a water pump and a starter, and more. These details will matter a great deal. Just as precision in engine internals is so critical, so are the other details concerning your precious Stovebolt!

Intake/Exhaust Manifold Assembly

Because of the age of these components, some exhaust manifolds start to show their age. It may be because when people pull the engine, they put the chain around the exhaust manifold. Please do not do this! The walls of the manifold become thinner and thinner due to the constant heat cycles and now they are hard to find.

If you have a manifold with no cracks, does the butterfly valve rotate freely? In a lot of cases the answer is no. The exhaust manifold heat spring connects to a stud. Often it's broken off or rusted almost to nonexistence.

What about the exhaust pipe studs? If they are not perfect, you want to replace them. Once you have all of this addressed, let's hope you don't have a warped manifold and it bolts nicely to the intake and the engine.

On the project manifold, the heat spring stud is broken off, and the exhaust pipe studs need to be replaced. The butterfly is frozen solid. A lot of patience and prep work will be needed. Anytime you run across a vintage part, have the PB B'laster handy. In the case of this engine, the exhaust manifold is cracked and needs to be replaced. Not just a little crack but almost completely broken in two near the center of it.

On the replacement, I had to drill out the spring stud and tap and replace it with a long screw. The head of the screw keeps the spring from slipping off.

Loosen the Butterfly Valve

You can use PB B'laster over a few days to help loosen the butterfly valve. Although tight to begin with, it gets going again with a few taps of the hammer and more gentle prodding.

The exhaust pipe stud may not come out and you don't want to break the ear off so you end up with another junk manifold. If you know how to drill and tap into metal, you can grind off the stud so it's smooth with the surface, then with

The intake/exhaust system is one of the most important subassemblies on the engine. You want to start with good ones with no cracks or broken parts that can't be fixed. Procure other parts if necessary.

a center punch, punch in the center (that's the hard part). Making sure you are in the center, start drilling with a 1/8-inch bit then move to 5/16-inch, which is the correct size for the 3/8-16 tap. This isn't easy to get right, but you don't have much choice. Heat doesn't usually do the job, and if you try double nutting, you will probably strip out what was left. After you get the hang of the drill/tap procedure, it's really nice to have new studs on the fresh engine.

Once you chase and clean all the threads, it's time for paint. I use a 2,000-degree manifold paint. The color on the can from the vendor states stainless steel and is the correct color for a stock 1947–1955 engine. The intake manifold is the same color as the engine, Medium Gray. Once painted and ready for installation, the subsystem is complete. Gather up all the necessary bolts, nuts, washers, and fittings.

After replacing these two items, you may have an intake or exhaust leak that won't go away. To keep that from happening, set the assembly aside and refer to the prevention discussion in chapter 12.

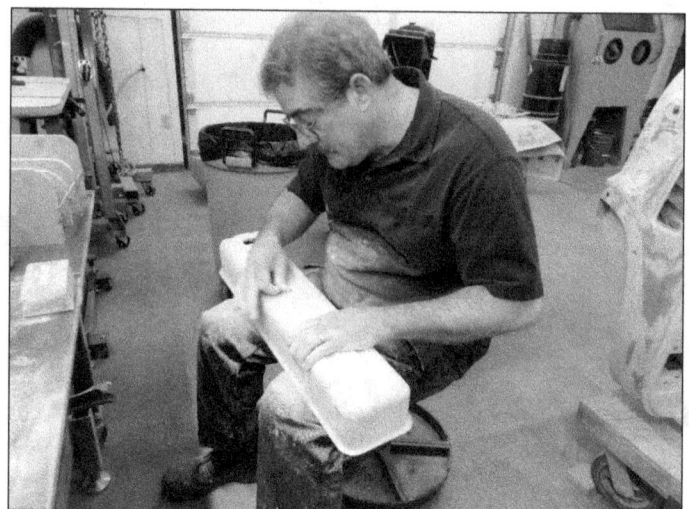

Sanding and metal prep is tedious work but very rewarding. Start with 80-grit, move to 180- or 220-grit, then 400-grit. When you are at 400, primer with epoxy primer, sandable primer, then hit it with topcoat. You can use this same procedure for all body work.

This is the result of many hours of sanding, primer, sanding primer again, etc., for an acceptable level of quality.

 **Prepping List**

You need to prep and repaint the following parts.

- Valve cover
- Oil pan
- Side lifter cover
- Timing gear cover
- Front timing gear/mounting plate
- Cooling fan
- Air cleaner
- Flywheel
- Bellhousing
- Oil dipstick handle

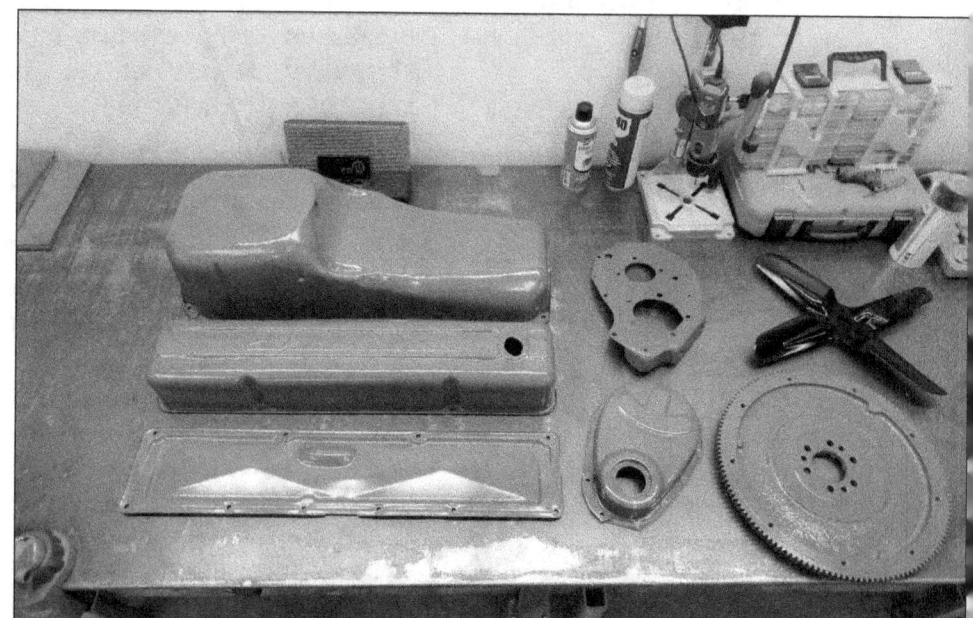

Be sure to use 500-degree primer and paint for these parts. You want the most durable paint products because these parts are exposed to many heat cycles and a lot of abuse.

MISCELLANEOUS IMPORTANT DETAILS

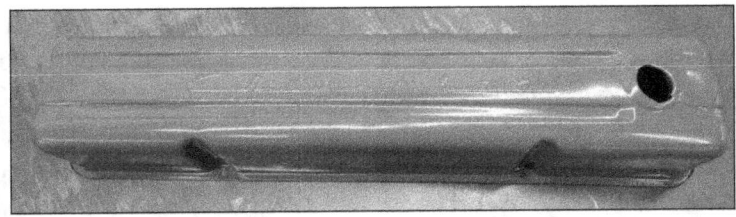

The goal is perfection, but in the end, you won't achieve it; but you can come real close!

Don't forget the oblong screw reinforcements for the valve cover.

Engine Sheet Metal Prep and Painting

After everything is sandblasted, use 400-grit sandpaper on all of the parts. That's the best way to notice any imperfections. Hammer out the blemishes and weld shut the damaged holes and rust-through areas. Thoroughly apply PPG DX330 metal prep. If you use paper towels, use clean, compressed air to remove any fibers or residue. Then proceed to apply PPG's DPLF epoxy primer on all the surfaces that do not encounter circulating engine oil.

DPLF epoxy primer is rated up to 500 degrees, the same as the engine paint. This provides a durable finish.

In the case of the valve cover and air cleaner, go the extra mile of adding urethane high-build primer (PPG K36) and sand with 400-grit sandpaper prior to the paint step. Then apply 500-degree engine paint in Medium Gray. This is to replicate the look of a Chevy 6-cylinder truck engine for the years 1947–1955. Paint everything but the cooling fan, air cleaner, and oil dipstick, which are painted a 500-degree Gloss Black. Taking a little time to add value to the engine by making it look as if it is going into a treasured vehicle is the least you can do for this venerable engine.

At the top is an imbedded ball bearing (BB) in the flywheel. Shine it up as much as possible. You use it every time you tune your engine.

Flywheel Tips

The flywheel then gets a bit of special attention. The ball bearing (BB) is

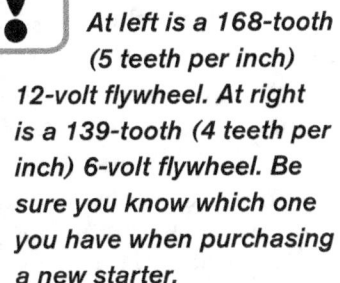

Important!
At left is a 168-tooth (5 teeth per inch) 12-volt flywheel. At right is a 139-tooth (4 teeth per inch) 6-volt flywheel. Be sure you know which one you have when purchasing a new starter.

shined up good using a Dremel then the flywheel is marked for clarifying the timing positions. This makes life so much easier when static timing the engine. Most vintage Chevy owners do not realize there are two different flywheels that are possible on your 1954–1962 235/261 engine. This matters a great deal, and you should be aware of which one you have.

216 and 235 Flywheels

Because the 1942–1953 216 engines have flywheels that are compatible with the newer 235, many folks opt to use the flywheel from an old 216. The reason has to do with the vehicle's system voltage and the starter.

The old flywheels have a 139-tooth ring gear and all starters until 1955 were 6-volt. They also have a 6-volt starter drive gear that only engages in a 139-tooth (4 teeth per inch) ring gear. This does not mean that if you have a 12-volt system, you have one or the other flywheel. That is because the 6-volt starter works fine in a 12-volt application. The reverse is not true, however, because a 12-volt starter has a starter drive gear that is only compatible with the 168-tooth (5 teeth per inch) ring gear of the newer-style 235/261 engine. And to make things more confusing, you can get the foot-controlled starter in either 6 or 12 volts.

Someday, you will need to purchase a new starter for your ride. It would be nice to know which one you need. So, while it's out of the vehicle for this project, shine up the ball bearing so it can be seen through the bellhousing's timing hole, then mark your flywheel as follows.

139-Tooth Ring Gear: On one side of the ball bearing, mark the number 1 and on the other, the number 6.

CHAPTER 10

This is how to properly mark a 139-tooth flywheel while it is out of the vehicle. Use a really good Sharpie. This will be important when adjusting valves and tuning the engine.

This is how to properly mark a 168-tooth flywheel. The engine works on a 720-degree cycle, so top dead center on each cylinder is shared with its counterpart.

have a much easier time with static timing and valve adjustments because you will know for certain which set of cylinders are at the top of their travel.

168-Tooth Ring Gear: If you have a 168-tooth ring gear on your flywheel, substitute the number 56 wherever you see a 46 in the 139-Tooth Ring Gear marking explanation.

Starter Engagement

This is a good time to look over the teeth to make sure the starter will engage properly. If you see excessive wear, it may be a good time to remove your ring gear and turn it over before reinstallation, or purchase a new one. Ring gears are pressed on and almost fall out by themselves when heated with a torch or with a brass hammer or brass punch. Slowly work your way around, being delicate so as not to warp or damage the ring gear.

To reinstall the ring gear, put it in the oven at 400°F until it's thoroughly hot, then quickly put it back on before it cools. Ring gears are not indexed in any way, so you do not need to worry about how it's placed.

The flywheel's ring gear can be worn quite a bit before it is unusable, but if you have dead spots when starting, it may be time to replace it. You can also turn the ring gear over and reinstall it on the flywheel if that hasn't been done before.

Mark every 10th tooth on your flywheel starting with the ball bearing, going counterclockwise. The final set has 9 teeth.

Count 46 teeth to the left of the ball bearing. Make a vertical mark from the top of that tooth toward the center of the flywheel about 1 inch long with a Sharpie. Mark a number 2 on the left side of the mark, and a 5 on the right side of the mark as you did for 1 and 6 above.

From the ball bearing, count 46 teeth clockwise and make a vertical mark from the top of that tooth toward the center of the flywheel about 1 inch long as before. Mark a number 3 on the left side of the mark, and a number 4 on the right side.

To check your counting skills, count from the 2/5 to the 3/4 marks. The total should be 46. Now you will

MISCELLANEOUS IMPORTANT DETAILS

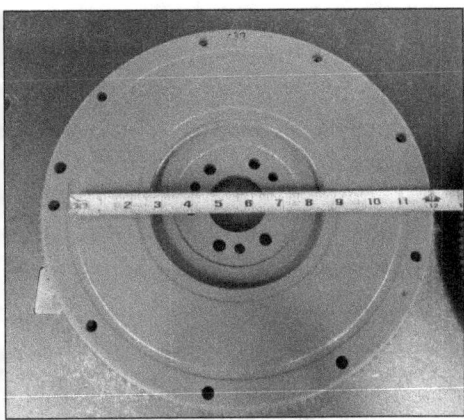

Measure across the clutch surface on the back of the flywheel to make sure your clutch is the proper unit. It is another machine shop function to resurface your flywheel when it becomes necessary.

The water pump adapter is used to return the fan to the center of the radiator for those vehicles that had a 216 engine previously. Otherwise, your fan is about 2½ inches lower than it should be. This also requires a specific water pump.

Clutch Choices

In addition to the ring gear considerations, it's also a good idea to know what clutch size is correct for your flywheel. On the back of the flywheel is the clutch plate mating surface. If the surface of your flywheel has a mating surface of 9½ inches, you can only install a 9-inch clutch. If your flywheel has a mating surface of 10½ inches, you can install a 9- or 10-inch clutch. If it measures 11 inches, you install an 11-inch clutch.

Clutch discs come in 9-, 10-, 10½-, and 10¾-inch-diameter sizes. Pressure plates come in 9½-, 10-, 10½-, and 11-inch diameters.

When purchasing new clutch parts, be sure you have the proper throw-out bearing for your clutch assembly. Tell the parts clerk the size of your flywheel mating surface to get the proper parts. Don't assume that you already have the correct parts. The previous owner could have installed whatever parts were available without knowing that most of these parts are interchangeable even if it's not a good idea. Taking the time to do these things will give you more information about your vehicle and take a lot of the guesswork out of it.

Water Pump Adapter

Some small things for my particular build may or may not pertain to your rebuild project. For example, there are differences in water pump installations. For my rebuild, I want this engine to fit into a 1947–1955 Advanced Design (AD) Chevy 1/2-ton. If you look at a 216-engine installed in this era vehicle, you notice that the fan blade is exactly in the center of the radiator. If you installed a newer-style 235/261, the fan is substantially lower, and the difference is enough that one could argue the cooling system is not as efficient.

To fix this problem, Dave Folsom created an adapter plate that allows the water pump to be installed higher and in the exact center of the radiator. This is about a $50 plate, but the water pump used must be short and of the proper V-Belt width. (Folsom's blog page, chev235guy.blogspot.com, is a must read.)

So, the perfect water pump for this upgrade is the 1953/1954 pump listed in the parts list. The formed radiator hoses work fine.

Another issue that isn't mentioned often is that you must install a 216 cooling fan on that water pump because the newer-style 235/261 fan is not compatible. They are slightly smaller, but they cool well. I used this setup on my 261 and am happy with it.

Do not over-torque the top bolts on the adapter plate. They are not backed by anything, so you could warp the plate.

Positive Crankcase Ventilation System

You also might want the PCV system to increase engine longevity. With a filtered breather-style oil filler cap, you can remove the old road tube and replace it with a more modern and much more efficient PCV system.

The PCV system was first introduced by Chevrolet in 1954 on its large trucks using 261 engines. All modern engines have PCV.

The Stovebolt era was the last not using PCV. After 1962, all engines had it. This mod is not expensive and helps keep the engine cleaner, longer. A good time to do this is now.

CHEVROLET INLINE-6 ENGINE 1929–1962: HOW TO REBUILD

It is necessary to reduce crankcase gases that mix with the oil, crud up engine internals, etc. This consists of a few fittings, a grommet, and tubing from the road tube to the intake manifold. You simply need to purchase a 1¼-inch cup-style freeze plug, drill a 3/4-inch hole in the center, install the freeze plug with the cup facing upward 1/32 inch from flush with the engine block, then use gasket sealer to glue the grommet into the cup. Place the PCV valve and plumb it to your intake manifold with 3/8-inch hose. Be sure to use a filtered breather-style oil filler cap, such as the Stant 10064.

Spin-On Oil Filter Adapter

Another modification you might consider is a spin-on oil filter adapter in addition to the machine shop modifying the engine block for full-flow oil filtration.

I found a cool place to put the adapter. The newer 235 engines have a triangular side-engine mounting boss. Three 3/8-inch bolts are used to hold the engine in place on a newer-style vehicle. Because this engine will go in a 1947–1955 pickup it is mounted at the front on the timing plate. This leaves three holes to mount the spin-on adapter directly to the engine.

This is the best way because any torquing or engine movement will not cause stress on the adapter or hoses. It would be nice if someone

Installing a PCV System

The road draft tube survived many years as Chevrolet's way of eliminating crankcase gases, so most of us don't consider changing it, but it has its drawbacks. It's dirty, it leaks small amounts of oil, and it's difficult to clean properly. The PCV system simply pulls the unwanted and unclean gases out of your crankcase using the engine's vacuum pressure. This same system is used today. Because the 216/235/261 engines were the last without PCV from the factory, it is not hard to adapt them. In fact, a stock PCV system was available on some AD models in 1954, but good luck finding one!

With 216, 235, and 261 engines, you remove the road draft tube, which is a press fit, and the bracket holding it in place. Then install a 1¼-inch cup-style freeze plug (such as the Dorman 555-024) with a 3/4-inch hole in the center big enough to accommodate the PCV valve. The plug fits snuggly, so it's perfect. Install the plug with the cup up so the grommet can be set inside of it.

Do your best to align the hole in the center and without distorting the freeze plug. If you use a step drill bit, or step up slowly to 3/4 inch you can be pretty exact. Install this freeze plug about 1/32 inch below the surface of the block.

Tap it in with a 3/4-inch socket, which fits the application perfectly. You then install the grommet (such as the Mr. Gasket No. MRG-6379), which is available at your local automotive parts store, inside the cup of the freeze plug. You can use Permatex high-temperature copper gasket sealer on the inside of the freeze plug (using your little finger, you should be able to access it) and around the grommet to better hold it in place. It's the perfect fit, so it's not going anywhere anyway. Finally, you simply push in the PCV valve.

Removing the road draft tube and installing PCV at this location proves to be the most convenient and provides for great PCV performance.

Tap the 1¼-inch freeze plug into the road draft tube location using a hardened impact socket so that the lip of the freeze plug is 1/32 inch below the edge of the block.

made a spin-on oil filter adapter that had that bolt pattern, but no, you must make an adapter for the adapter. It's not a big problem if you have rudimentary metalworking tools. This is only if you are putting this engine in an earlier pickup.

If you have changed the oil with a canister filter on the intake manifold, you know there has to be a better way. There is. You can use a regular spin-on filter with a 1/16-inch reducer inside the filter adapter for standard bypass systems. If you opt for a full-flow modification, you can run larger lines with no reduction.

This valve is a Standard Motor Products V-237. Through extensive testing, I found that this is the perfect unit for these Stovebolt engines.

The grommet sits into the freeze plug and is held in place with gasket sealer. The valve is then pushed into the 3/4-inch hole in the freeze plug.

The valve is a Standard brand V-237 and the PCV/fuel line hose is 3/8 inch. You need about 4 feet. You connect the PCV valve via the hose to the intake manifold's vacuum inlet on the other side of the engine. How you go about doing this is up to you.

I prefer making a hard line from the intake port to about 3 inches from the PCV inlet and then run a 5-inch-long 3/8-inch soft line to connect them together. It works just as well to run soft line the whole way.

If you are using the line for windshield wipers, you have a problem that can be solved by installing a fuel pump that comes equipped with a vacuum outlet. Those are available, or you can install electric wipers in your ride. The truth is, there is enough vacuum to run both. This valve does not suck excessive oil into the intake manifold because it is designed for the vacuum properties of this engine.

Because the airflow is from top to bottom, you need to install a filtered and vented cap on the valve cover. These are readily available at any auto parts store. Ask for the twist-on type, such as the Stant 10064.

Air moves from the vented and filtered cap, through the engine, and out to the intake manifold. For a clean installation, purchase new fittings to accommodate the 3/8-inch hose. Simply hook up the PCV valve via the hose to the intake manifold, and you have just installed your own PCV system.

This is much better for your engine and will extend its life. You also need to lean out the fuel mixture a little during setup. I have tested this system and am pleased with the results. This modification is cheap and doesn't hack up your engine in any way, so there is no harm in trying it.

You can read more about the testing information and how I arrived at the V-237 valve at: devestechnet.com/Home/PCVInstall. ∎

CHAPTER 10

If you are putting it in a car or you have an engine that does not have that engine mount pattern, you must use an alternate method of mounting the adapter such as clamping it to the frame. (Devestechnet.com has several solutions.)

High-Energy Ignition

If your vehicle is a 12-volt, you can add a nice upgrade to the ignition system. HEI came out in the mid-1970s and revolutionized the ignition system. It provides several advantages. The GM HEI module gives the system its ability to self-adjust the dwell based on engine RPM. Its secondary function is to speed up dramatically the ramp and fire circuit to 3.6 milliseconds, which enables much faster coil response.

This means that you can use hotter coils because you are no longer limited to 12,000 volts, which is about the maximum a points system has time for in one complete cycle. This also means a more complete burn of leaner fuel mixtures. It also has a current control circuit that keeps the amperage of the entire ignition system to 5.5 amps.

The problem for vintage vehicle enthusiasts has always been more cosmetic. Who wants a big, honking HEI distributor sticking out of their precious Stovebolt? Not me. So, you need a modification for your stock distributor. This can only be done on a tall-cap (1954–1962) distributor, but there is plenty of room to do it.

Thermostat and Housing

When assembling the thermostat housing, use high-temperature gasket sealer on almost everything. It's just added insurance. A gasket comes with the rebuild kit. The important thing is to install the thermostat in the right direction. The spring is down when installed on the engine.

I use plumber's Teflon wrap around the heater-hose barb. You need rubberized clamps for the fuel line and all the proper bolts for installation. When the engine returns, you will be ready. The pitting around the hose connection is unavoidable I'm afraid. If you have the fitted upper radiator hose, you can install that to the top of the housing now, too. This is a chore because the hose diameter is too tight, so it takes some real work to install it. Use grease to make it easier.

An old farmer's trick for the thermostat used to be to drill a 1/8-inch hole in the thermostat before installation. This relieved the trapped air in the engine and allowed for better cooling. Nowadays, the jiggle valve thermostat does the same thing. It has a 1/8-inch valve that opens to let air escape.

This completed thermostat housing assembly has a jiggle-valve thermostat.

You can see which way the thermostat is oriented in the housing.

The jiggle-valve thermostat ends the issue of trapped air inside the engine side of the thermostat and allows the thermostat to work more reliably. ACDelco and MotoRad make them for this vintage.

This is my test engine, so the install could be cleaned up a bit, but as you can see, no permanent modifications to the stock distributor means no problem going back to points and no ruining vintage parts.

Oil System Upgrades

The last year for cars and light trucks to have a bypass-style oil filtering system was 1962. It was also the last year for Chevrolet dealers to install any oil filter on the engine at all. That's right, GM engines, back in the day, did not come with oil filtering from the factory.

Engine designers didn't have much concern about keeping the oil clean in all pre-1953 engines. You find slits in the valve cover exposing the engine's top end to whatever road grime was swirling around under the hood. We now know that it is a good idea for engines to have full-flow oil filtering found on modern cars today. This contributes to the several hundred thousand miles an engine can go nowadays between engine overhauls.

All 235 engines had only bypass filtering. This means that only approximately 12 percent of the oil in the engine goes through the filter. Which 12 percent? you might ask. The answer is the 12 percent that is closest to the oil pump's pickup screen at any given time.

This is where the required hole is. The one you want has a stamp "4" beside it.

Although it is better than nothing by far, it is not comforting to the customer of the engine machine shop during an engine rebuild as described in this book when the national average bill for this kind of work is about $3,500 as of this writing. This is why I encourage you to have the machine shop modify your 1954–1962 235 or pre-1958 261 for full-flow oil filtering. Then, 100 percent of the oil in your engine goes through the filter before oiling the vital engine parts.

In full-flow filtering, oil is picked up and pumped directly out of the engine from the front oil port through the outside filter assembly, then back into the engine via the rear port and on to oil vital engine parts. This system has one downside. The hoses must be in good condition, and the front port must be connected (even if through a filter) to the back port at all times. Very important! That is why you don't see modern vehicles with outside oil lines.

The oil pump's internal line is connected in the center of the block. With a 1/8-inch NPT tap, create threads for a 1/8-inch NPT pipe plug at the 1.375-inch point in the hole. Do not damage the threads for the pump fittings. This plugs the passage to the mains.

The Full-Flow Modification

This modification should only be done during a rebuild at the machine shop step. This way, you can clean all the metal shards out of the oil passages that were created. You can also have the professionals at the machine shop do it.

Step One: In the hole stamped with a "4," use a 1/8-inch NPT tap to create threads about 1.375 inches. Insert a 1/8-inch NPT Allen-head pipe plug using Loctite Red. This caps off the oil going directly to the mains.

Step Two: Use a 1/8-inch drill bit to drill at a slight downward angle into the main oil gallery. Stop when you are through, then go to a 3/16-inch bit, then final drill it to 37/64 inch. Tap this hole with a 3/8-inch NPT tap, being careful to maintain the downward angle you drilled it at.

Step Three: The next hole that requires attention is the rear oil inlet that was used for the bypass system. This one needs to be enlarged. Drill this one out to 37/64 inch and use a 3/8-inch NPT tap.

Oil System Upgrades (continued)

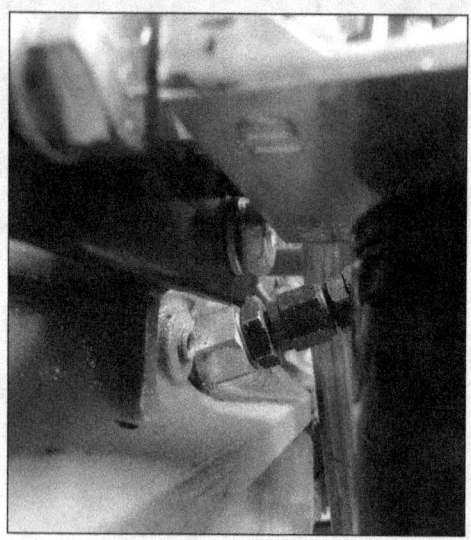

This hole must be drilled at a slight downward angle to meet the center of the inside gallery. Start with a 1/8-inch drill, then 3/16-inch, then final drill it to 37/64-inch for a 3/8-inch NPT tap.

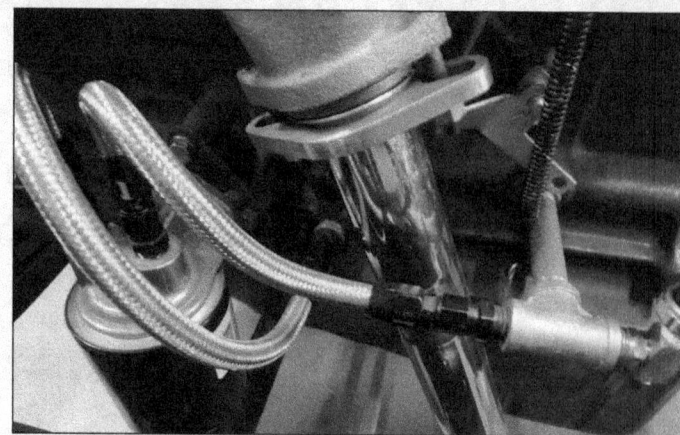

With this design, the tee connection connects to your oil pressure gauge.

You may need to clear a little metal so the brass 3/8 x 3/8-inch adapter can seat properly.

The machine shop drilled the holes and tapped for our full-flow modification.

Once this modification is complete, it is essential that the outside ports are joined together at all times. It can be through a filter or one hose from the front port to the rear port, but there must be full oil flow through them. With the inside journal capped off, oil now flows from the oil pump, out of the front port, in to the rear port before any engine parts get oiled. Don't forget!

Once completed, use 3/8-inch outside lines instead of 1/8-inch and change your oil filter system to allow for faster and more-efficient oil flow.

This is the rear oil port that was already there. Drill to 37/64-inch for a 3/8-inch NPT tap.

Step Four: Install 3/8-inch male to -6AN adapters in both of the new 3/8-inch NPT holes. Use an air rasp to clear some of the engine block's metal away for the front adapter to seat flatly.

Tech Tip

The complete instruction for the machine shop to make this full-flow modification is available at devestechnet.com/Home/FullFlowOil. This can be verified by perusing the article at inliners.org/tech/fullflow2.html.

Canister Modification

The old canister that is normally mounted to the intake has its problems. Oil changes are made more difficult than they need to be and messy too. Let's offer some ideas on how to change all that.

For a stock 216, 235, or pre-1958 261, the first consideration is the design must include a 1/16-inch restrictor somewhere in the oil flow. In the canister, restriction is in the standpipe. Any solution we engineer must have that. Without it, we can cause a drop in oil pressure that is not good for the engine.

The next consideration is where to put the restrictor. An unmodified engine will do better with the oil not having to travel upward against gravity any more than necessary, so we should mount this solution lower. Another consideration is the ease of changing the filter. Personally, I like how the modern system works. The spin-on filter with the necessary bracketry allows you to mount it a few different ways.

Bypass filtering uses a much tighter filtration mesh that cleans better. But it only cleans 12 percent of the oil. In addition, the most harmful shards of metal, sand, and whatever happens to end up in the oil stream are easily handled by a good modern spin-on filter. Remember in the day Chevrolet didn't send any engine out of the factory with a filter on them at all.

I chose the Trans-Dapt 1028 spin-on filter adapter for my project. In the out port, add a 1/16-inch reducer so that the filter will trap any crud before that reducer. It can be mounted low on the engine or on the upper frame rail across from the alternator or generator so the filter is hanging down low but protected by the frame. This provides a relatively easy place to remove and replace the filter.

Use stainless steel braided rubber hose (size is -4AN or 1/8 inch) for a bypass system and -6AN or 3/8-inch hose for a full-flow system. If the engine is mounted on the very front timing cover plate, then you can use the engine side mount boss for mounting the filter. This is preferable since the oil lines move with the engine and are not compensating for engine movement versus the frame.

If your Stovebolt has dual exhaust, the soft oil lines are only rated for 300 degrees, and there is no decent route to keep these lines sufficiently away from the exhaust. In that case, we must make hard lines to get around the exhaust.

The Trans-Dapt 1028 uses the tried-and-true FRAM PH8A or WIX 51515 oil filter with the 3/4 x 16-inch thread. The ports use 1/2-inch threads.

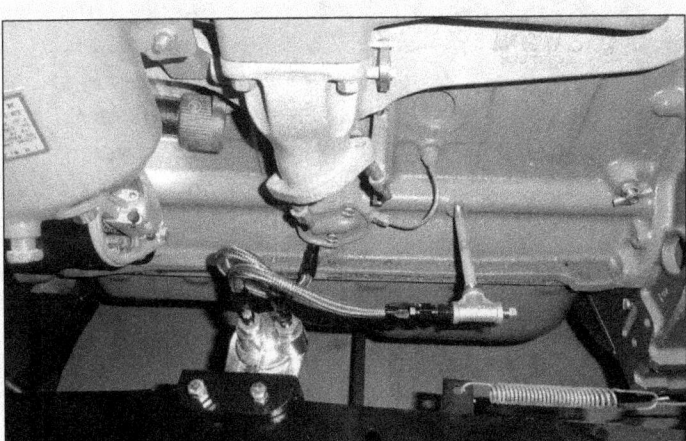

Here is a 1950 216 engine with the bypass filtration and frame-style clamp-on setup.

This is our 1959 235 with full-flow modification mounted to the triangular mounting boss.

This is a 261 full-flow motor with dual exhaust. The soft hoses are not rated for the intensive heat, so we must get around that with stainless plumbing.

Oil System Upgrades (continued)

The Trans-Dapt 1028

This adapter is solidly made and provides additional plumbing, allowing you to add a second bypass canister to the system if desired. It uses the FRAM PH8A, or WIX 51515, standard spin-on filter. The reducer is a fitting that is drilled and tapped on the inside with a length of threaded rod screwed into it with a 1/16-inch hole drilled through it.

Here is the Tran-Dapt 1028 from another angle.

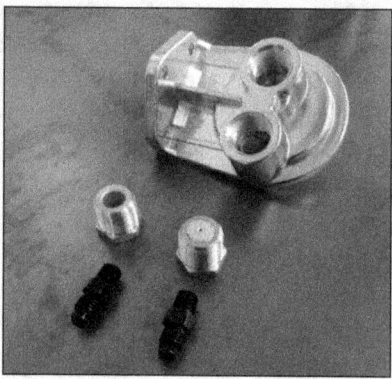

The Trans-Dapt 1028 with the necessary fittings for the bypass system including the reducer.

The reducer that screws inside the out port of the Trans-Dapt 1028.

Drill the inside of this adapter using a 29/64-inch drill bit. This is to accommodate a 1/2 x 20-inch tap.

Tap to 1/2 x 20 inches to accommodate the aluminum insert for the reducer.

The WIX 51515 oil filter that goes with the system.

The Reducer

I prefer McMaster-Carr for all my automotive and hardware needs. In this case we need two 1/2-inch straight reducing adapters that screw into the Trans-Dapt. Since we are talking about a bypass system, we need the reducing adapter to reduce to 1/8 inch NPT. On one of the reducer adapters, drill the inside out using a 29/64 drill bit to open it up for a 1/2 x 20 tap. Then thread the inside of this reducer with 1/2 x 20 fine threads.

Get a 1/2 x 20 fine thread aluminum rod from McMaster. Slice a screwdriver slot in the top of it, then screw it into the adapter. Once the rod is tight and bottomed out, cut the rod flush with the bottom of the adapter. Now we have

The aluminum rod used to make the insert is available at McMaster-Carr. Slice a screwdriver slot into the end for easy tightening.

As best we can show, here is the insert with the screwdriver slot and 1/16-inch hole drilled in the center.

MISCELLANEOUS IMPORTANT DETAILS

a removable aluminum insert in this adapter. Use a center punch to punch it in the center of the rod (thus the center of the adapter). Go to the drill press and drill a 1/16-inch hole in the center. Remove the insert using a screwdriver from the top. Using a high-pressure air nozzle, blow out all metal shards and dirt from everywhere, then use Loctite Red on the aluminum threads and screw it back in to the adapter. Wipe it down, and it is ready for installation in the out port of the Trans-Dapt.

Connect the Trans-Dapt out port to the rear engine connection and the in port to the front engine connection.

Mounting Options

There were three types of side motor mounts on the Stovebolt engines: triangular boss, upside-down L, and none.

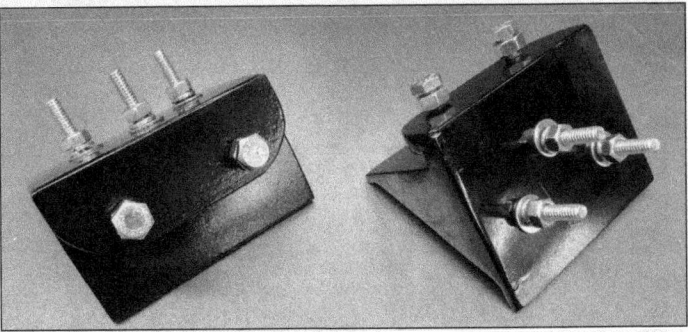

The clamp-on adapter is made from heavier-gauge steel using 5/16-inch clamp screws.

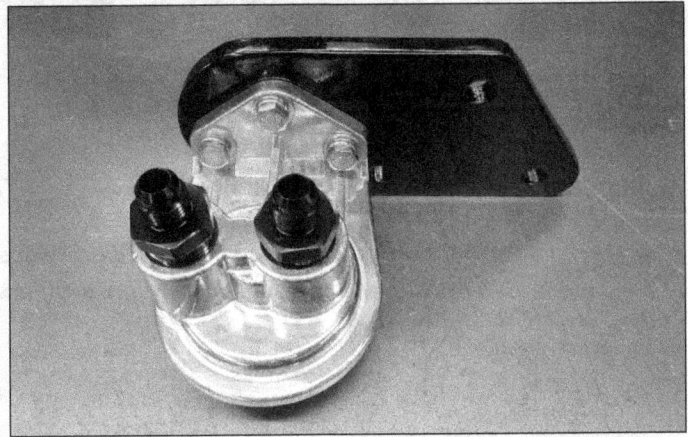

This is the version of the triangular-mounting boss that works best with dual exhaust. The farther away those soft hoses are, the better!

A few standoffs and an 11-gauge plate and you have your mount. These days I just use old lug nuts for the standoffs.

A few 235s had this sort of motor-mounting boss on them. We try to have a solution for everyone!

The triangular boss with one hole on top and two on the bottom in a perfect triangle is the most common. The upside down L has two holes on top, and another on the bottom that is offset toward the rear of the engine slightly. If you have one of those and are not using them to mount your engine, you have the perfect place to mount your new oil filter system.

Pre-1952 engines did not have any side-mounting bosses. For those, you will need to go with a frame mount or design your own solution.

Dual Exhaust Options

Those with dual exhaust must make sure to keep hoses away from the hot exhaust. Since that is not possible, I used stainless steel plumbing pipe to route the system around the exhaust in such a way as to keep the soft lines as short as possible.

Oil System Upgrades (continued)

Full-Flow Differences

If your engine is a full-flow engine, rather than -4AN fittings and hose, you can use -6AN (3/8-inch) fittings and hose with no reducer. To make your own system, create a template out of cardboard by holding it up and tapping around the motor mount bosses enough to make indentions for drawing out your metal for cutting.

For the triangle mounts, I use old lug nuts for the spacers. I drill them out to 1/2 inch then use stainless steel hardware to finish off the look. ∎

The 1/8-inch NPT stainless steel pipes are for the bypass system, and the 3/8-inch NPT stainless pipes are for the full-flow systems of either a modified 235 or a native full-flow 261.

Although this mod is too low in the engine compartment to be easily seen, I feel it adds character to the engine bay and performs much better. It makes oil changes easier too!

CHAPTER 11

POST-ENGINE SHOP PREPARATION

With the engine back from the machine shop, you can prepare for your part of the rebuild. Two things you need right away are a proper engine stand and an engine hoist. While you are at it, get folding ones so they don't consume all your shop's floor space. You need the hoist to lift the engine out of your vehicle and ready it for the engine stand. Do not cheap out on the engine stand. These 6-cylinders are long and top-heavy, and it's unsafe to assemble an engine on an unstable platform. Take seriously all safety precautions.

Building an Inline-6 Engine Stand Adapter

I'm taking the opportunity to end the misery of trying to make a generic engine stand work properly with an inline-6. The problem is in connecting the engine to a generic stand. In this case it's the Harbor Freight 2,000-pound engine stand. It has six wheels, foldable for easy storage, and is quite stout. The plan is to reengineer the head so that it bolts perfectly to the Stovebolt engine.

Start by using the bellhousing for the template. Use a small ball-peen hammer and some 11 x 17-inch chipboard and lightly tap around the indentions and holes until it falls away. Then add to the outside of the template 1/4 inch to the wings to give that thin area more strength and rigidity. To do this, you can move the template 1/4 inch and trace the 1/2-inch plate to accommodate the new size. A piece of 10 x 12 x 1/2-inch plate steel works well.

Use a piece of round drawn-over-mandrel (DOM) steel tubing for the pivot piece. My stand

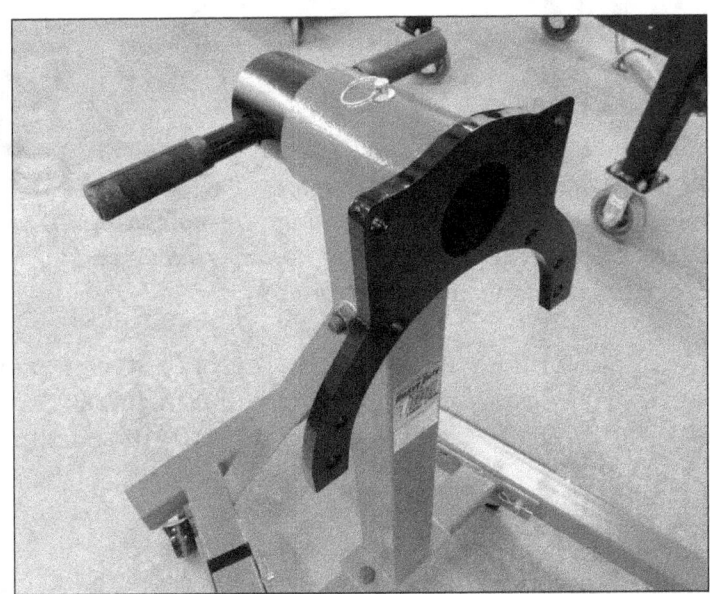

A 2,000-pound engine stand with a special 6-cylinder adapter plate is the safest way to go.

The first step in engineering a proper mount for this engine is to make a template of the mating surface. No better template opportunity than to use the bellhousing.

CHAPTER 11

This is the rough main plate. Use at least 1/2-inch plate steel for this.

Running a hole saw through 1/2-inch plate steel is pretty time consuming, but it is possible. It takes patience.

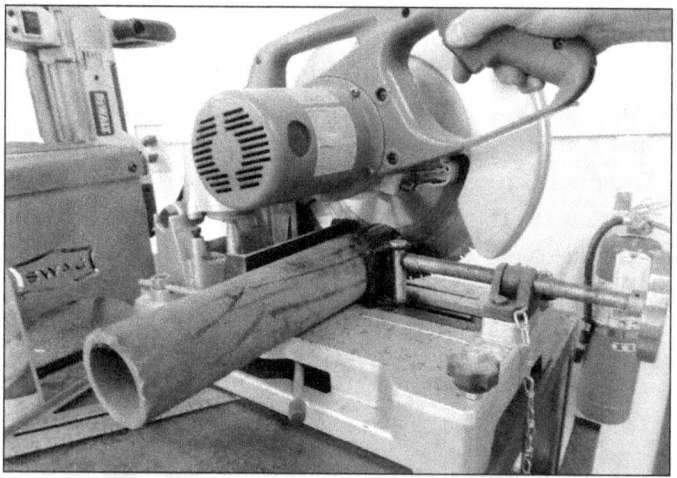

Thick DOM tubing is necessary for stability. Also run your welder up to hot. Measure the old receiver that came with the Harbor Freight stand and make the cut the same length.

After beveling the edges for a stronger weld, these parts fit together nicely. The next step is to grind the outside edge of the DOM for a bevel that is filled in with weld. Use a 220 welder on maximum penetration for this job.

uses a 3-inch pipe, so I cut it out of a 3-inch DOM with 5/16-inch walls. This is much stouter than the original one supplied with the stand.

The drilling process is standard. The six mounting holes in the flat plate are 1/2 inch. The two that are used to get around the mounting pegs are 7/16 inch. You drill the round stock evenly around it for the stop pin, also 1/2 inch. The holes adjacent to each other for the handle are 7/8 inch.

The eight stop pin holes are placed 2¾ inches from the plate end. Cut a 3-inch hole out of 1/2-inch plate steel with a bi-metal hole saw. You want the tubing to go all the way through the plate so you can get a good weld on the front and the back. Can't have this thing falling off!

Before welding them together, bevel the edge all the way around the tubing to give good room for the weld. This is important! You can bevel a little over half of the

POST-ENGINE SHOP PREPARATION

The 6-cylinder Stovebolt is heavy in a bad place so you should use thicker DOM than the original for safety. You can keep the old mount for other-style engines.

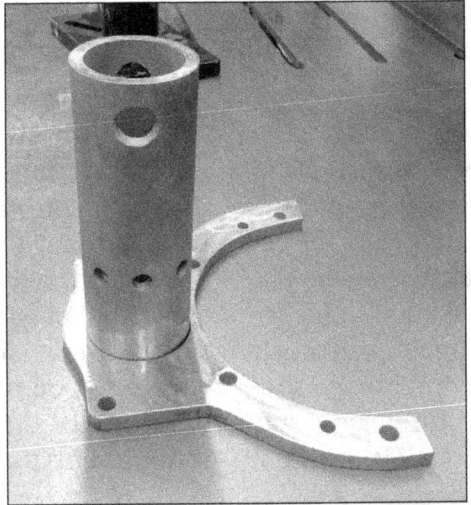

Set these two pieces on a perfectly flat surface, then check the tube with a level. If the DOM was cut perfectly flat, the level will show it. Now it's ready for welding. You want your handles to be across left to right when assembled, so take care in aligning the holes before welding.

Side view of the new engine stand head. With this plate bolted to the bellhousing holes on the engine block, you have a stout solution.

I like this particular engine stand because not only is it foldable, but the legs extend beyond the end of the engine. This makes the platform stable.

thickness of the tube, then sandblast everything. Clean both pieces with metal-prep cleaner.

You want these welds to be strong; use a 220 welder on its hottest setting and increase the wire speed. This gives you good penetration. Finally, test fit and then give it a nice, shiny coat of paint.

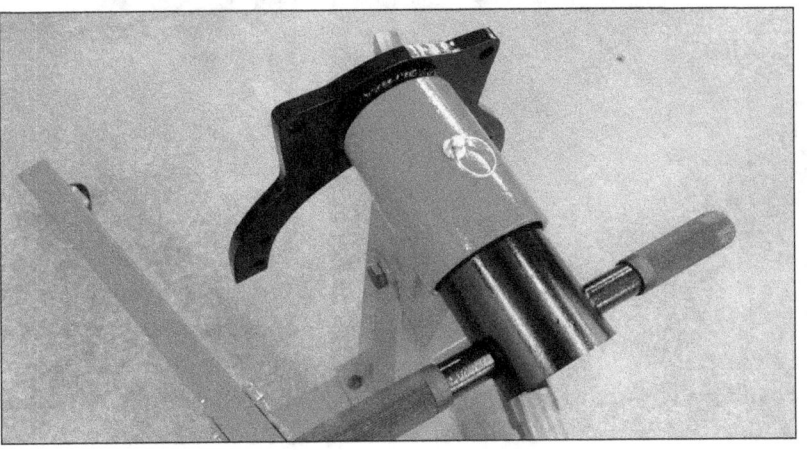

After a little paint, nobody will know it's homemade. Dupli-Color engine enamel in Gloss Black gives it that "Right off the Harbor Freight showroom floor" look.

CHAPTER 11

Cleaning and Prepping for Paint

The engine is mostly clean when it comes back because it has been boiled out. However, machine shops are inherently dirty places, and you must clean the entire outside surface of the block and the head so that the engine paint sticks properly. Use a wire brush, shop rag, and lacquer thinner to start with, then switch to PPG DX-330 metal-prep cleaner.

It's time consuming but you may find a few places that needed extra attention. You can use a rotary grinder to grind off any sand casting that looks as if it could come off in the wrong place. Some of those places are the fuel pump cutout and along the oil gallery areas.

The next step is to tape the engine so you don't have overspray in unwanted areas. I realize you can walk around with a piece of cardboard in your hand while painting and shield the areas you do not want overspray, but I prefer to do it this way. After two good coats of Dupli-Color 7272 Gray you want to spray a few coats of 500-degree clear coat as well. Both products are 500-degree paint, so it should work nicely.

You also want to paint the harmonic balancer. I like to paint the pulley part black and the rest of it the engine color.

After the engine shop has done their thing, you need to clean and prep for paint. Lots of time and attention to detail keeps the paint from peeling off at the first startup.

Cleaning is tedious but so necessary. I use a wire brush and Simple Green on my second pass. It's critical to remove all grime prior to paint. Because the shop boiled and cleaned the engine, you just have to remove any oil residue.

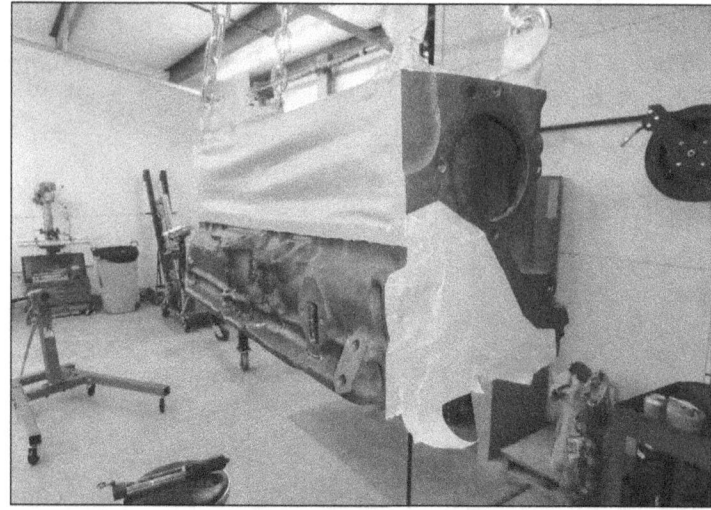
Tape the areas you do not want paint to penetrate. It's worth the extra time.

The head receives the same treatment: super cleaning and epoxy primer (because it is rated at 500 degrees) prior to painting with 500-degree engine enamel. If you choose inferior primer (not rated at 500 degrees), the paint chips off quickly.

POST-ENGINE SHOP PREPARATION

Final Machining Prior to Assembly

Any machine work that is still left to do, or any process that could introduce metal shavings or contaminants should be done now, prior to assembly. Using Dave Folsom's water pump adapter plate raises the water pump to the center of the radiator. Most people do not realize that the original 216 had its fan directly in the center of the radiator, but the newer-style 235 has it considerably lower. This fixes that issue.

Following Folsom's instructions carefully, drill two 5/16-inch holes 3/4 inch deep, which is the correct hole size to then tap for 3/8-16. Use a flat-bottom tap to take full advantage of the 3/4-inch-deep hole. Do not drill any deeper, and especially be careful on the side where the head bolt is close.

Blow out all the metal with air and clean the area thoroughly. (There is much more to this modification, but this is the machining part. I discuss that upgrade in chapter 12.)

Now is a good time to put the PCV freeze plug in place. It is a 1¼-inch cup-style freeze plug with a 3/4-inch hole in it. Tap it down below the lip by about 1/32 inch. Use copper gasket sealer to hold the Mr. Gasket No. MRG-6379 grommet in place. The road tube hole is the perfect place for this mod. It even has a splash guard on the inside of the block to keep raw oil from being sucked into the intake.

I have performed testing on which PCV valve is best for this vintage; the Standard Motor Products V-237 fits nicely. It uses 2 inches of mercury out of the engine's available 20 and is not enough to suck oil, but enough to evacuate the gases perfectly.

Finally, don't forget to install the splash guard on the inside of the block. It is held in place with two sheet-metal screws with thin, flat washers.

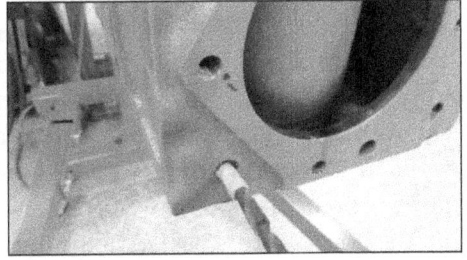
Now is the time to address the water pump adapter issue. Drilling two 5/16-inch x 3/4-inch deep holes in the block (using Dave Folsom's instructions) works really well. Be sure to not allow the drill bit to wander.

Tapping the new holes is pretty straightforward. Just take your time and use a bottoming tap.

This is the 1¼-inch freeze plug with a 3/4-inch hole drilled in the center that replaces the road draft tube for the PCV system. Sealer goes around the hole, and the grommet sits right in place.

The PCV valve slides right into place. I've done extensive testing to make sure no oil is sucked into the intake. It's a solid solution.

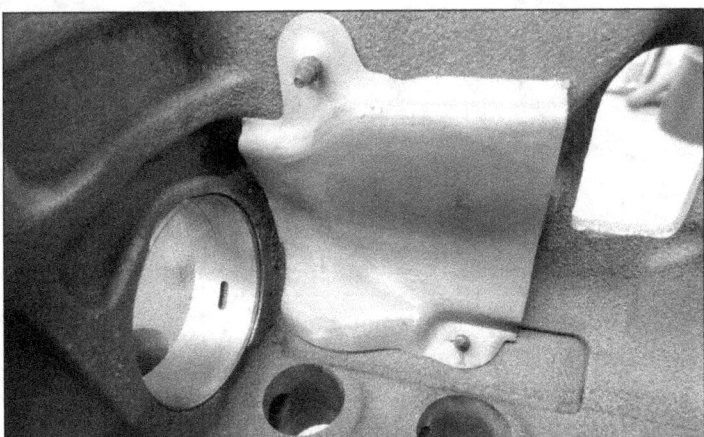
This is the splash guard for the road draft tube/PCV hole so oil doesn't splash. The road draft tube leaks badly enough as it is.

CHAPTER 12

ENGINE ASSEMBLY

The Chevrolet shop manual for the year engine you are working on is an indispensable tool and provides answers to almost any question. You can buy one from several sources.

This front view has the timing cover installed. This harmonic balancer bolt allows you to turn the engine from the front using a breaker bar and socket but only with the spark plugs removed. You do not want to overstress the bolt.

They are specific on methods and tolerances, and I recommend that you read the assembly section prior to this chapter so that you can verify that the sources match.

In addition to engine assembly tools, you also need assembly lube, assembly grease, and nondetergent engine break-in oil.

Crankshaft

The first real step in engine assembly is to install the crankshaft. When you examine the crank bearings, you see that they install in one

A good assembly lube is essential in protecting your new engine components. Slather it on everything with the exception of the cylinder walls and pistons/rings.

way only. Do not block any oil holes. You can do that easily if you observe the journals and caps carefully.

Use assembly lube (such as Royal Purple's Max-Tuff) liberally throughout this process. Everything you do in the engine assembly process needs assembly lube except for the cylinder walls and pistons/rings. Use regular nondetergent oil or castor oil for those components. This helps better seat the pistons and rings in the cylinders, causing less initial engine wear.

The crankshaft has four caps. The rear one is the thickest; continuing up the block, the saddle one is thinner; then the thinnest one; then the front cap, which has the flush surface. Be sure the bearings are properly marked with the correct clearance.

For example, this build is .010 under, so each bearing should have .010 stamped on it somewhere (if your machine shop made them all uniform). The writing on the intermediate caps reads left to right from the back of the block.

Once each crank bearing is properly installed in the block and you apply a liberal amount of assembly lube on the block's bearing surfaces, install the rear main seal.

108   CHEVROLET INLINE-6 ENGINE 1929–1962: HOW TO REBUILD

ENGINE ASSEMBLY

The rear main seal installs into the outside channel. Use plenty of assembly lube.

This is the rear main bearing cap showing the rear main seal in its place. Be sure to read the Professional Mechanic Tip "Neoprene Seal Installation" on how to best install this seal.

One type of rear main seal is a (usually orange) Fel-Pro rubber one that slides through the track. The other (which came with my kit) is the rope type. The latter is impregnated cloth with a Kevlar outer cover. It works fine if you can cut it per the shop manual.

I asked several enthusiasts which type of rear main seal is better and if there are ways to make sure the rear main doesn't leak prematurely. The consensus was to use the rubber-type seal that slides in the track. The Best Gasket 4519S is the best choice for the two-piece rubber type.

Some years do not have the machined channel for the Best Gasket rubber seal. Also, if your crankshaft is badly pitted, that seal may not be appropriate. In that case you should go to the trusty old rope seal.

Now, making sure that you have a liberal amount of assembly lube, carefully install the crankshaft. With

 **Neoprene Seal Installation**

A trick for installing the neoprene seal is to install it with a bit of offset in the block, which matches the offset in the cap. That way the joint line between the halves doesn't match up with the seam line on the block and bearing cap. A drop of Permatex on the ends of the neoprene seal works wonders. Take your time on these steps and read the shop manual for that year engine to verify. ■

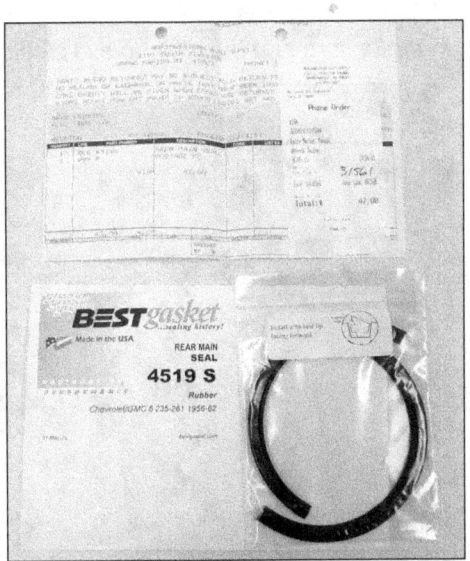

Fel-Pro no longer makes the rubber-type rear main gasket, but Best Gasket does. Truthfully, the Best Gasket version was better anyway, with just a little more rubber used.

With upper bearings installed carefully, set the crankshaft in the block. Be sure to use lots of assembly lube, but then wipe it off the face (shown). Set a piece of the correct Plastigauge on the top (shown), then torque down the bearing cap per the instruction.

CHEVROLET INLINE-6 ENGINE 1929–1962: HOW TO REBUILD

CHAPTER 12

Plastigauge works great for an accurate measurement. If you are not certain of the measurement, Plastigauge is cheap, so you can repeat it.

With all four bearing caps torqued down, you can move on to the piston rods. So far the machine shop's work is exemplary.

the bearings installed, put the caps on and torque down all of them to 110 ft-lbs. Everything must be properly torqued for the Plastigauge test. You only need to check the bearing tolerances in one place, the top of each bearing journal. Test one bearing at a time. Remove the rear main cap and cut off enough Plastigauge to reach across the surface.

Clean off both surfaces of the assembly lube and insert the Plastigauge. Evenly crank the bolts to 110 ft-lbs. Remove the bolts and the cap. The smashed Plastigauge will likely be on the journal. Use the repeating .001- to .003-inch gauge on the side of the Plastigauge wrapper see your bearing tolerances. If the number falls between .004 and .005 inch, the bearing insert is satisfactory. If you have any question, consult your machine shop to resolve it.

Follow the same procedure for all bearing caps and journals. Remove the Plastigauge without scarring the journal (fingernail works well), reapply assembly lube, and tighten to 110 ft-lbs. When you get to the front main cap, hand tighten it for the time being.

Tech Tip: Crank Specs

This is how the project 1959 235 crank came out:

Rear main	.002
Rear intermediate	.0025
Front intermediate	.002
Front main	.002

Timing Plate

After installing the crankshaft, the timing plate is next. Use the gasket supplied with the kit. Use gasket sealer on all surfaces that require a gasket. Extra attention to detail during assembly pays high dividends in longevity and a quality build. Once the gasket is gooped up, use the three countersunk screws that attach it.

Put the two front engine-mount bolts through the holes. You do not want to install the timing cover and then decide you should have put the bolts in first because one of them

The timing plate gasket installs as shown here. This is the final opportunity to make sure that the oiler hole is clear.

The timing plate slips right over the crankshaft gear and is secured with three flat-head screws. If applicable, be sure to install the engine mounting bolts.

110   CHEVROLET INLINE-6 ENGINE 1929–1962: HOW TO REBUILD

ENGINE ASSEMBLY

(especially) does not go in the hole after the cover is installed.

Be sure the three countersunk screws are torqued down tight. A wide, thick screwdriver must be used for this. A crescent wrench on the shaft of a screwdriver allows you to get another 1/3 turn without damaging the slots. For engine parts you cannot access easily, you should do this as a routine.

Camshaft

With the timing plate installed, it is now safe to install the camshaft. You can have the machine shop install the cam gear and thrust plate or do it yourself. Verify proper clearance depth by using a feeler gauge between the back of the thrust plate and the front of the first bearing journal. You should have less than .004 inch. This one was .0015.

Check the measurement in several places around the shaft to detect any imbalance. If it is consistent all the way around, the shop did a great job.

It is important that the cam gear runs perfectly true. If it isn't installed correctly, it makes lots of noise.

If the new cam that you purchased for this build does not have the gear installed; you must press it on using a shop press. But before you do that, install the thrust plate. Be sure to orient the thrust plate in the appropriate direction, lay it in place, then put the crescent key in the slot and press in the cam gear until it is flush on the outside.

To install the cam, liberally apply assembly grease. You don't use assembly lube because grease is longer lasting on the cam lobes, which is what you need! Grease the lobes and all bearing surfaces well.

The cam is the most finicky during the initial break-in process, so you want to carefully install it in the engine assembly. Use both hands and make sure not to nick any of the bearings. When you meet the crankshaft gear, mate them together with the timing marks of both gears

With the thrust plate installed on the camshaft first, then the cam gear, use a liberal amount of assembly lube and carefully slide the cam into place. Guide it straight in to prevent damage to the cam bearings.

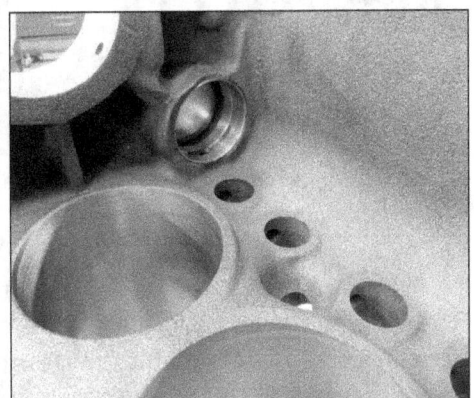

Because the machine shop pressed in the cam bearings, taking care when installing the cam is crucial. You do not want to ruin a cam bearing when sliding the cam in place.

Use a hardened impact socket (1 5/8 inches) and a hammer to carefully tap the front main seal into the timing gear cover.

Installed front main seal. Be sure to use a large socket or similar for an even push into the fragile tin. Some use a 4x4 piece of wood. Whatever you use, it needs to end up nice and flat at the bottom.

exactly together, then push it in all the way.

Use the two camshaft retainer screws that go through the holes in the gear to tighten down the cam. Make them good and tight. I have heard horror stories about them loosening. If you do not have the torque you used to (these are Phillip's head screws), use a vise-grip on the shaft of the screwdriver to get more torque. You can turn it about 1/4 inch farther that way. Also use medium-strength Loctite on the threads to prevent the camshaft from going anywhere.

If you are not installing new gears and didn't have the shop machine everything, you may want other measurements to ensure you have everything correct. Consult the shop manual for backlash, runout, etc.

Oil Seal

Once you are sure everything is properly torqued and ready, install the oil seal in the timing cover with the open end toward the inside of the cover. Do not overtighten this seal. You can easily ruin the seal and the timing cover. Use a 3/4-inch drive with a 1⅝-inch socket. It covers the entire surface. Tap on it as straight as possible until it begins to seat, then tap it the rest of the way in. You can use a block of wood with the same result. Be gentle.

Timing Cover and Harmonic Balancer

Installing the timing cover is straightforward except for the two hex bolts that go through from the engine inside. Be sure your front crankshaft bearing cap is loose, and then install the two hex-head bolts loosely. Install the rest of the screws for the timing cover with lock washers less than hand-tight.

With everything loose, install the harmonic balancer. Use a very large ball-peen hammer and a block of wood. Line up the keyway and key so it starts itself.

It isn't an exact science, so you hammer until the balancer no longer moves. With the balancer installed press-fit around the crankshaft, install the harmonic balancer retaining bolt. (This is one of the improvements you can have the machine shop do. If you do not like fitted balancers, you will feel much better with a 7/16-20 bolt holding it in.) Use an air impact wrench and torque it down well. If the harmonic balancer doesn't continue to move, you are probably good to go.

With the cam properly installed and the timing cover installed loosely, slide the harmonic balancer into place. This allows the timing cover to self-center on the crankshaft and seal. Then, tighten the timing cover screws. Also notice the 7/16 x 20 x 1½-inch bolt that now keeps the harmonic balancer from sliding off. It's cheap insurance!

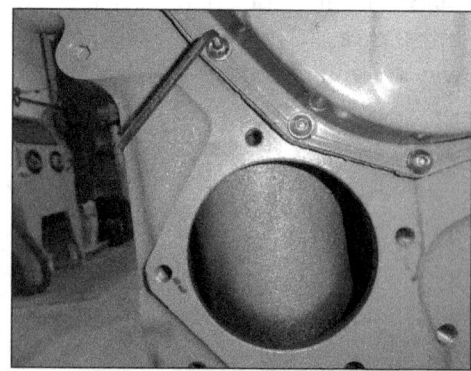

The hanging Allen wrench indicates the extra-long screw on the timing cover.

Now tighten all the bolts for the timing cover. Do not forget the two hex head bolts inside the front bearing cap. Use the retainer plate to secure them. When the hex bolts are tight, torque down the front crankshaft bearing cap to 110 ft-lbs like all the rest. Do not forget to torque down the front bearing cap.

ENGINE ASSEMBLY

The torque spec for the small screws is 6 to 7½ ft-lbs. Be sure to position the extra-long screw correctly.

By making the timing cover screws loose all the way around and inside, you gave the timing cover the opportunity to center itself on the front seal. This decreases the likelihood of a front main seal leak.

Oil Pump and Pickup

The oil pump assembly is next. To reconnect everything properly, you need to follow the proper sequence or the fittings will be impossible to line up correctly.

Screw on the pickup screen assembly so that it is tight but sticking up. Use a high-temperature copper gasket sealer on the threads of this entire assembly. Set the oil pump in place, and hand tighten the oil pump retaining screw. Use medium Loctite on it.

One problem is that the hard line to the other side of the block does not flex enough to install it last. The solution is to install both adapters, one in the oil pump and one in the block across from it.

Tighten the oil pump retainer screw and lock it in place.

Remove the top of the oil pump with four screws. Now you can install the hard line. Tighten the fittings, then put the screws back in the oil pump using medium Loctite. With a screwdriver, rotate the oil pump to make sure it rotates freely. Tighten the retaining screw one last time and lock it down with the lock-down nut.

Pistons and Piston Rods

To install the pistons on the piston rods, orient the rod so the clamp part of the rod is on the cam side of the block. The cylinder number also faces the cam side. The cylinder number should be stamped near the piston rod bearings. The piston has an arrow on its top edge. Face it toward the front of the engine.

Once oriented properly, remove the piston pin, slide the piston over the rod, and install the pin. Do your best to center the rod inside the piston, then tighten it.

Installing piston rings correctly is important. The .080-inch overbore of this particular engine means that the rings have to be matched to the pistons and cylinders. If the machine shop took care of ordering the set, make sure you have the right ones. Use the piston to place each ring in

For the oil pump and pickup assembly, be sure everything is tight, and the screen is sitting straight so it doesn't conflict with the oil pan.

Put the oil pump retainer nut on the screw first, then screw it in place, tighten it down, and lock it in place with the nut.

Clamp a long punch into the vise and slide the piston on the rod through the piston wrist-pin hole. Be sure to center the piston rod on the piston before tightening. Doing it this way ensures you do not twist the piston rod when tightening.

CHEVROLET INLINE-6 ENGINE 1929–1962: HOW TO REBUILD

CHAPTER 12

The new piston rings are separated in the box to help you install the right ring in the correct groove.

Correct gap thickness is imperative to prevent blow-by and poor engine performance. Place the ring inside the cylinder about 2 inches, then use a feeler gauge to check this gap. If you purchased the correct rings for the bore size, this gap should be within tolerance.

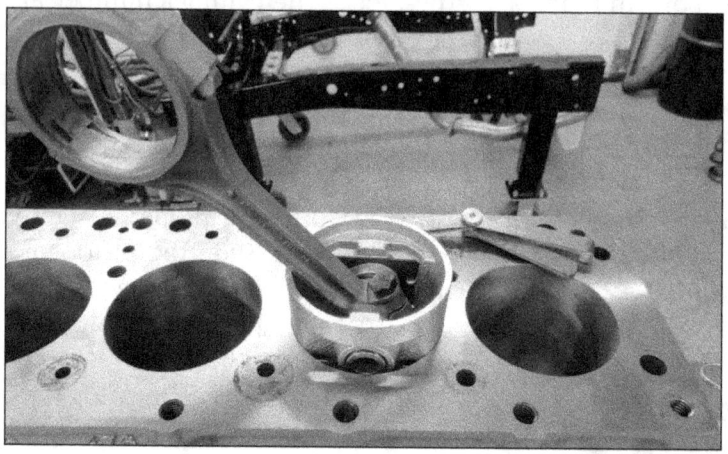

Use the piston to push the ring down the 2 inches for checking the gap. This ensures that the ring is installed flat.

Clamping Piston Rods

The shop manual is specific about not using a bench vise to clamp the piston rods. You do not want to twist the rods. To do this safely, use a long punch or a piece of rod. Place this punch or rod sticking outward in the vise. Slide the piston on the rod through the piston pin hole. Tighten the clamp to 35 ft-lbs.

the cylinder bore about 2 inches from the top, which is far enough to stabilize the piston in the cylinder to give you a flat measuring surface. With a standard gap gauge in the proper range, check the gap thickness.

Piston Ring Tolerances

The tolerance specifications in the shop manual are the following.

Compression ring gap	.007 to .017
Oil ring	.015 to .055

The actual tolerances for this project engine were nicely within the ranges specified by the shop manual.

Cylinder Number-1

Compression ring number-1 (top)	.015
Compression ring number-2 (center)	.014
Oil ring number-1 (top)	.024
Oil ring number-2 (bottom)	.022

Cylinder Number-2

Compression ring number-1 (top)	.012
Compression ring number-1 (center)	.015
Oil ring number-1 (top)	.025
Oil ring number-2 (bottom)	.024

Cylinder Number-3

Compression ring number-1 (top)	.015
Compression ring number-1 (center)	.015
Oil ring number-1 (top)	.024
Oil ring number-2 (bottom)	.022

Cylinder Number-4

Compression ring number-1 (top)	.013
Compression ring number-1 (center)	.014
Oil ring number-1 (top)	.024
Oil ring number-2 (bottom)	.025

Cylinder Number-5

Compression ring number-1 (top)	.014
Compression ring number-1 (center)	.015
Oil ring number-1 (top)	.025
Oil ring number-2 (bottom)	.024

Cylinder Number-6

Compression ring number-1 (top)	.015
Compression ring number-1 (center)	.014
Oil ring number-1 (top)	.025
Oil ring number-2 (bottom)	.024

ENGINE ASSEMBLY

Rings

Installing the rings can be done in various ways depending on the YouTube video you watch. The shop manual suggests rolling on the rings without tools. Other sources suggest that can cause deformities and you should use piston ring pliers to put equal pressure on the entire circumference. I follow the shop manual and carefully use the roll method on the oil rings. It's basically starting one end in the groove and carefully rolling the ring into place. Use your finger on the end to prevent the sharp edge of the ring from scarring the piston.

For installation of compression rings, I use piston ring pliers. It's so much easier and you do not run the risk of scarring the piston. If you are unsure as to which compression ring goes where, the top piston ring has no chamfer or markings on it, the second compression ring has a chamfer on it and has a dot on the top. Yes, the dot faces upward (the chamfer downward). When installing the oil rings, the center expander goes in first.

Positioning, or "clocking," the rings is a crucial step. If all the gaps were lined up, it would allow oil to travel where it's not wanted, and because of the gap, compression would suffer. You want to make sure the rings are 120 degrees from each other (three sets of rings divided by 360 degrees). This is only slightly complicated by the oil ring set because the shop manual specifies that you place the top oil ring no less than 1 inch to the right of the center (spacer) and the bottom oil ring no less than 1 inch to the left.

The idea is to be certain that your gaps do not even come close to lining up. You can use the sidewall of the piston as the gauge for the oil rings: one on the left, one on the right, spacer centered on the piston pin.

Even though this is a time-consuming and painstaking process, it's worth the time to check the gaps and get the clocking right. Before you install the pistons into the cylinder, check the clocking again.

The third ring groove looks like this when all three pieces are in the groove. Be sure to observe proper piston ring clocking.

Install the center expander first, then the bottom and top rings, observing proper clocking.

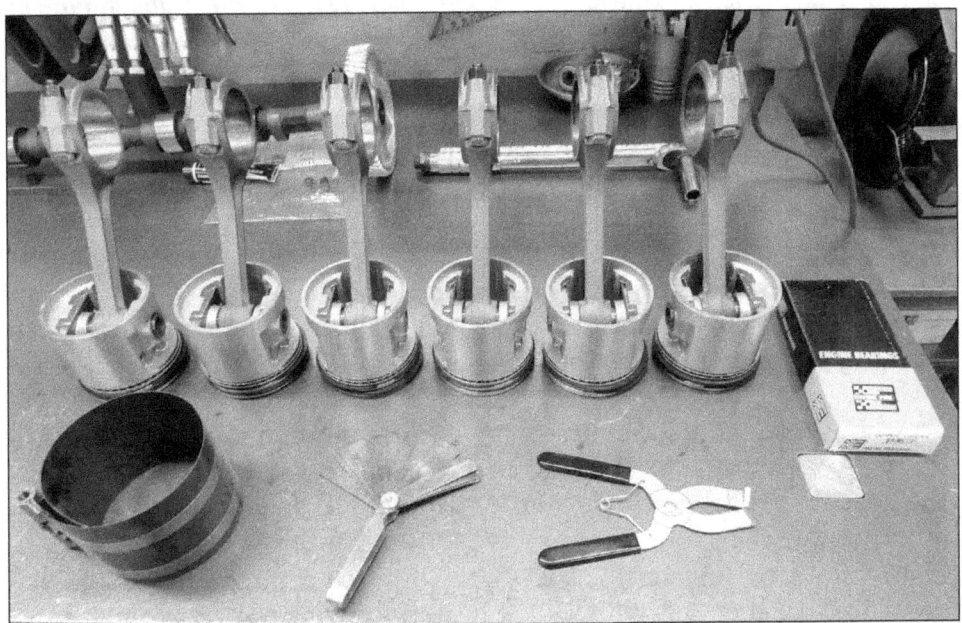
With all of the piston rings properly clocked, the next step is installation. Be sure to recheck the clocking before setting the rings inside the piston ring compressor/cylinder. The ends of the rings must not be near each other.

Pistons

Install pistons slowly, flipping the engine over at each set so you do not inadvertently mess something up. Rotate the engine stand so you have the top of the engine facing upward. It's important to install the pistons in the correct way.

The piston rod bearing housings have the cylinder number on each

CHAPTER 12

With lots of 10W30 oil slathered all over everything, insert one half of the piston into the ring compressor with the band loose. This allows you to carefully get over the rings without disturbing their clocking. Then tighten the band.

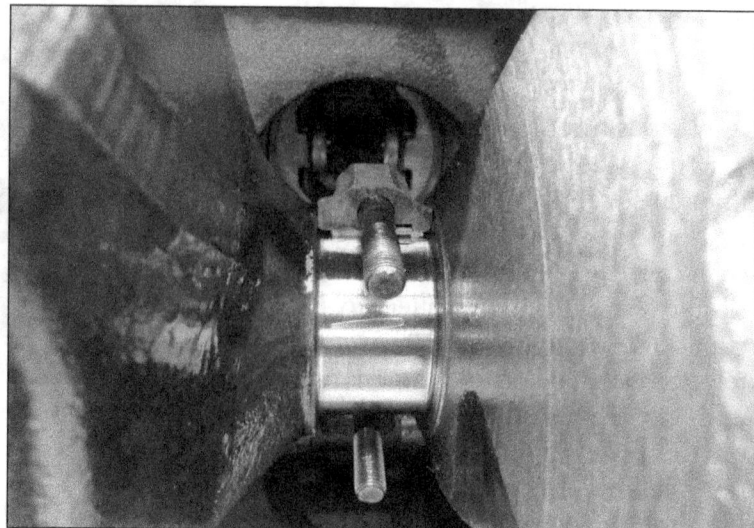

When guiding the piston rod, you do not scar the crankshaft or cylinder walls. Reach in from the bottom and use your hand to guide it properly.

one. That number goes on the cam side. Using a piston ring compressor, oil the inside of the compressor tool, the cylinder walls, and the pistons themselves. Do not use assembly lube here. Use a good SAE30 nondetergent engine oil to slather everything involved.

The cylinders are numbered 1 through 6 with number-1 being in the front. Starting with number-1, check the clocking on the rings to make sure each ring opening is far away from another one.

Install the piston ring compressor so that about half of the piston is in the compressor, the other half in the cylinder. Do not mix up your parts or get the orientation of the pistons wrong.

The rings are sloppy in their correct positions, so you have a little wresting to do when clocking. It's important that your rings do not move. The most efficient way to do this is to clock the two that are in the same place at the same time. This means installing number-1 piston and number-6 piston at the same time because the crankshaft is in the same place for both.

Next, rotate the crank so it is on its bottom-most point for number-2 and number-5. Finally, do the same for number-3 and number-4. Make sure you don't mar the bearing surfaces with the rod bolts.

If you don't trust yourself to avoid marring them, you can tape the ends of the bolts with masking tape. Or you can simply turn the crank so that the bearing surface is the farthest away from the top of the cylinder and in the center of the piston hole. With the latter method, the rod drops in the perfect place. Of course, you still need to guide it with your fingers to prevent scarring.

Install the piston rod bearings on the rod side and use lots of assembly lube. All the rod bearings are exactly the same. Be sure to put a bearing on each one.

Install the number-1 piston in the cylinder with the rod's piston clamp toward the cam. This positions the number "1" stamped on the side of the rod near the bottom on the cam side. Hold the piston from underneath so that the rod doesn't scar the cylinder walls or the crank bearing surfaces. You can use a shop rag stuffed in such a way to keep it where you want it (maybe a few shop rags). Use whatever works to protect the surfaces. Keep about half of the piston sticking out the top for now.

Oil the inside of the ring compressor. Once again check the clocking, then install the compressor and ratchet it down tightly. Check underneath to make sure the bearing cap screws will go down smoothly and the bearing will stay put.

Then, with the wooden end of a hammer tap the piston into the cylinder. Continue tapping until the bearing is tight on the crank.

So, just to confirm: When you are finished with the number-1 cylinder, the arrow at the top of the piston should be facing front, the piston rod clamp nut/bolt should be on the cam side, the rod number should be on the cam side, and the piston rod caps should have the bearing locator tangs together.

ENGINE ASSEMBLY

To check bearing clearances, use Plastigauge on the rod bearings in much the same way you did on the crankshaft's main bearings. Cut off a small piece of Plastigauge and put across a clean bearing surface (wipe off any assembly lube), then place the bearing cap with the bearing in the rod end, bolt it down, and torque to 45 ft-lbs. Remove the cap and read the Plastigauge.

My machine shop did such a thorough job making sure to resurface the rods and caps, all six of the piston rod bearings are .002. This is within the spec of .001 to .003 for new bearings. Remove the Plastigauge, put assembly lube on the bearings, and retighten the caps to 45 ft-lbs.

There is a lot to think about and a lot to do concerning pistons. Take your time. You will sleep better knowing you did it right. With the proper ring clocking, ring gaps, and bearing clearances, you will be successful!

Oil Pan

Install the rubber end pieces over the end caps using high-temperature copper gasket sealer on all surfaces. Lay out the correct gasket pieces, left and right, and make sure you are using the correct ones. Place gasket sealer on both sides once again, but this time, concentrate on where the rubber meets the cork.

Once you have everything sealed, bolt down the oil pan starting with the four 1/4-inch bolts in the corners, then add the number-10 screws one by one. Tighten from the center outward. Wipe off any excess sealer that is bothering you, and you have just successfully finished the bottom end of your engine.

With everything buttoned up, properly torqued, and addressed, it's time to install the oil pan.

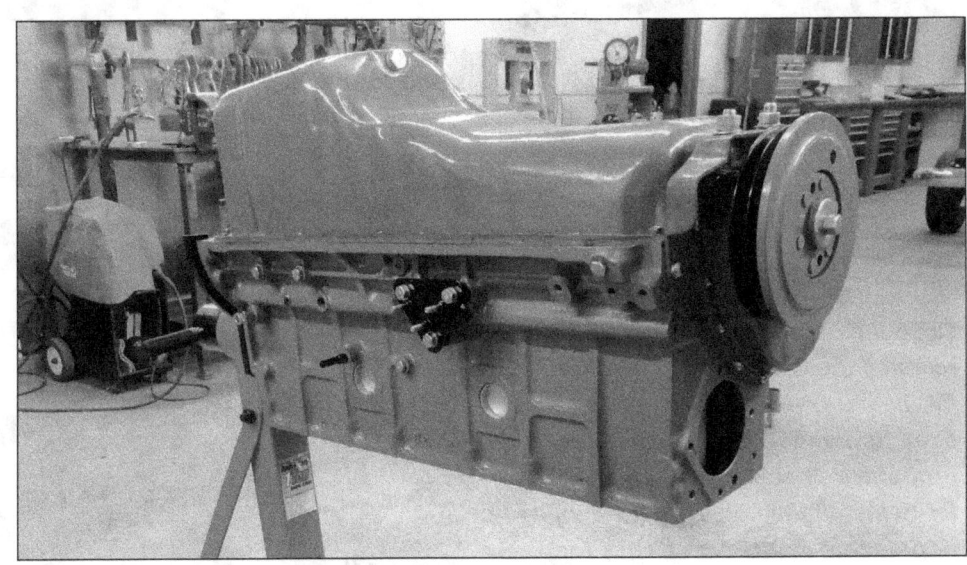
With the oil pan installed properly, that concludes the bottom end rebuild. Congratulations!

Head

For installing the head and finishing, you hear of many different methods. My preferred method is to remove the engine from the engine stand and put it on a test stand. I use the front end of a 1954 truck that was badly burned out. If you do not have such a stand, you can place it directly into the vehicle. Sure, it's difficult to wrestle with that heavy head, but this way you have the corner head bolts available for grabbing the engine for installation.

I put wheels on it, painted it, and now it acts exactly as if it were going in an actual frame-up restoration. I use a Harbor Freight 880-pound 120-volt electric winch that I installed on a support beam to move the engine around. Makes things a whole lot easier. After you install the head, remove the radiator so you can better access the front of the engine.

You can run into all sorts of

CHAPTER 12

Once the oil pan is installed, you can reinstall the bellhousing, then the flywheel using flywheel retainers. Even though the engine stand could probably withstand the weight, I prefer to install the engine in the vehicle or on a test stand such as this for completion.

I use the front end of a badly burned out 1954 Chevy pickup to make a test stand for this process.

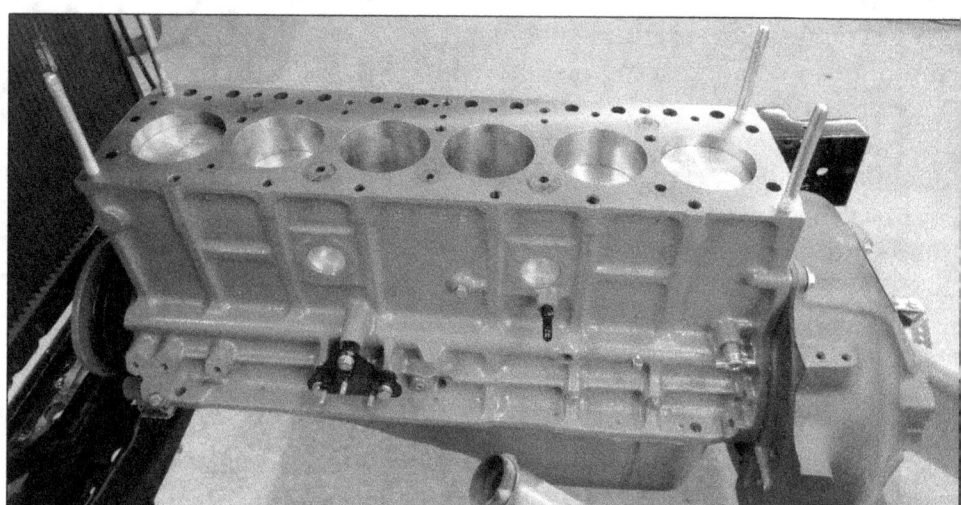

To install the head properly, you need to make new tools. Four head bolts with the heads ground off make perfect guide pins. This prevents the head gasket from damage during installation.

problems installing a head if you don't take the time to make at least two guide pins (I prefer to use four). These ensure that the gasket stays perfectly centered and in its place when you place the head on it. You can make them from an old set of head bolts. Do not cut off the heads. One corner will be too short for you to get in there to pull it out. You want to grind down the heads, leaving that extra length.

Using guide pins is essential, and you will be much happier with the

Install the head gasket, making sure you do not block any holes in the engine block. If you see some holes covered, do some research into why. It is not normal for any hole to be covered on this engine.

ENGINE ASSEMBLY

Tech Tip: Hollow Bolts versus Solid Bolts

Some year models of this engine came with a single hollow head bolt. This hollow bolt is what allows oil from the bottom end to get to the top end. Be sure all your bolts are solid, and if you find that you have one hollow bolt, be sure to put it in the center of the head where the rocker assembly tube goes down into the head.

The special bolt that installs in the center of the head nearest the oil inlet has a hole in the center at the bottom and a smaller hole just at the thread line to allow oil to pass to the rocker assembly, as in the left example. On the right are two homemade solutions to the problem of losing it or using the wrong bolt.

Be sure to use copper gasket sealer spray or equivalent. Wear gloves and do not spray into the cylinders, rather, hold the gasket up and out of the way when you spray. When you position the head, be sure to keep your fingers out of the way!

result. Test set the head gasket in place and notice the orientation. A Fel-Pro copper gasket has "THIS SIDE DOWN" stamped on it. Also notice if the gasket is covering any holes. If it does, ask the machine shop for clarification. In my case, there were no holes covered by the gasket.

The copper gasket in a Fel-Pro kit requires copper gasket sealer spray. Available at most auto parts stores, it sprays on sticky, much like rattle-can paint. You need an even coat on both sides. Spray it away from the engine.

Lay the gasket back down, observing the proper orientation, over the guide pins. Place the head in its proper position and install the head bolts to hand tight.

Head Bolt Tightening

Use the diagram and tighten according to the pattern shown. Set a 1/2-inch-drive torque wrench to 30 ft-lbs and tighten. Then set the wrench to 60 ft-lbs and tighten. Finally set to 95 ft-lbs and tighten. This is a critical three-part step, so take your time.

I know the shop manual wants a warm engine to do the final torque, but in this case, I don't have one, and I want the gasket sealer to set with it at 95 cold. I will re-torque with a warm engine later.

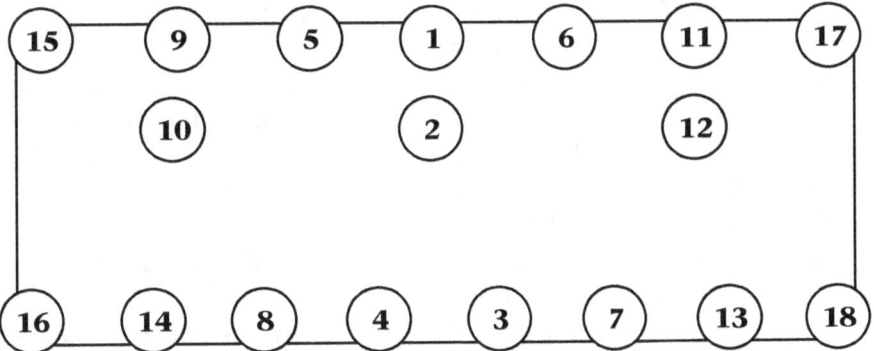

Use this diagram to select the proper pattern to tighten the head bolts. Be sure to tighten in three steps, making sure the head is flat to the block at each step.

CHAPTER 12

Some head bolts are longer than others, so your disassembly notes will come in handy. If you didn't write down where each one goes, hand tighten each one loosely, making sure they hold properly.

It's important that the intake and exhaust are put together correctly. The three alignment rings are critical to keeping this assembly straight. The foil side of the gasket goes to the manifold side.

Intake and Exhaust Assembly

The intake and exhaust manifold installation can be a real bummer or it can be easy. You must have three guide rings for the intake manifold to set correctly. They are an integral part of the assembly, so don't continue until you have them! If you do not have them, our vendors sell them so please wait until you do! Slide the three guide rings into the manifold until they stop.

Using high-temperature copper gasket sealer, place the three sections of gasket onto the manifold assembly with the metal (foil) side toward the manifold, not the engine. If you think you have exhaust or intake leaks, don't use gasket sealer until you verify that you have no leaks.

If you have already bolted the intake and exhaust together, remove the bolts and nuts and install the gasket included in the kit, foil side toward the exhaust. Put the two manifold parts back together using the proper bolts and nuts, but leave them loose. This is essential!

Place high-temp gasket sealer on the exposed side of the gaskets as well. The two guide pins that go on the outside-most part are also the two short hold-downs. Place the assembly on these guide pins and, with a rubber mallet, tap the three guide rings and assembly into place. Bolt it down using the rest of the hardware.

Tighten the intake to the exhaust at the same time you perform the final torque on the manifold-to-head bolts. (At this point, you could take the intake properly mated with the exhaust back to the machine shop to have the mating surface decked to the head.) Leave them torqued together with the gasket installed.

You can now install the exhaust flap spring and place the carb riser and gasket. If you damage the gaskets and need a replacement set, the Fel-Pro part number is MS-9193B.

Water Pump

As I mentioned earlier, 1954–1962 235/261 engines do not have the water pump in the center of the radiator as did the older 1947–1953 216/235 engines. This can lead to poor cooling and more unwanted heat stress on the engine. To avoid that, use a water pump adapter with the specific 1953 water pump.

Earlier I described how to locate, drill, and tap the two extra holes needed for this adaptation. Remove the old plate from the water pump, keeping the gasket for comparison. Use gasket sealer between the new gasket and the new plate. Use the two inset Phillips screws that came with the plate to secure the plate near the bottom of the water pump.

Keep the nuts facing the outside just below the crescent-shaped opening. Use lock washers on the nut side and tighten them securely. Add sealer to the outside of the gasket that is on the block; then, using four bolts, tighten to 35 ft-lbs. Do not overtighten the two that you tapped; just snug them to the block. You do not want to warp the plate, so do not overtighten them.

The adapter plate comes with detailed instructions and photos. Follow them, and you won't go wrong.

ENGINE ASSEMBLY

Place the water pump gasket on the block, then install the pump. In this case, a water pump adapter plate is used.

Here is a pic showing the actual location of the water pump on the newer 235/261 engines. Notice the space between the thermostat housing and the water pump.

Having the fan in the center of the radiator is essential to proper cooling. Older 216/235 engines had it this high already.

Carburetor

Install the carb using the black riser block and the gasket on top of the spacer. A vacuum orifice on the mounting face of the carb corresponds to a notch in the gasket. The riser block itself notches but in the wrong place.

It is imperative that the vacuum orifice is clear and able to do its job, so you need to notch out the riser to match the gasket with a Dremel tool. You want to also be sure to use the correct gasket so you do not block that notch or the hole on the bottom of the carb.

The intake/exhaust install as a unit is pictured and is assembled first. That nicely redone carburetor is ready for installation too.

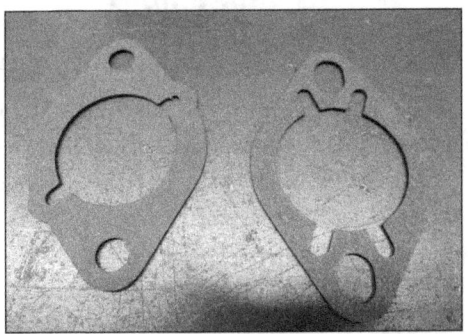

Two carb-to-spacer gaskets are available. When installing a gasket on the carb studs on the manifold, be sure it does not block the air hole in the carb spacer.

Miscellaneous Attention to Detail

In addition to installing a spin-on oil filter adapter and the alternator brackets, now is the time to work with the thermostat housing assembly, dipstick tube, and, while you are at it, you can slip a 3/8-inch rubber grommet on your dipstick to help seal the opening during use.

You may have to cut some mounting bolts to length to install some items. For example, I had to modify the alternator bracket to accommodate the 3/8-inch bolts, etc.

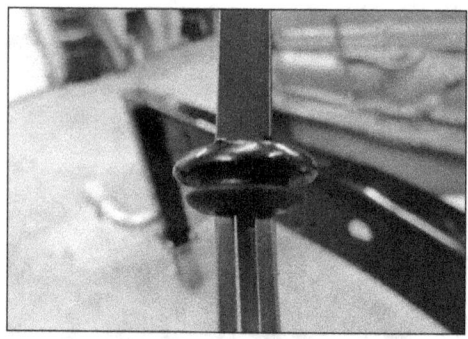

The dipstick originally came with a cork gasket that is probably long gone. Use a rubber grommet for this. Because if you are going to PCV, you want the engine sealed as well as possible.

Fuel Pump

Install the fuel pump using the gasket that came with the kit. Don't forget to put some assembly grease on the pusher arm first. This keeps the cam from galling right away.

At this point, I like to look the engine over carefully and add bolts wherever there are unused threads. So, if there is a threaded hole in the block that is unused, cut bolts to fit snugly to add more attention to detail. I use stainless bolts for this with some medium Loctite.

Valves

Valve adjustment procedures can be intimidating. I hope to change all of that here for hydraulics. If you have solid lifters, devestechnet.com/Home/ValveAdjust provides a good understanding of how to adjust that type.

Use assembly lube liberally inside the lifter bores and install the new lifters. As you put them in, make sure they are loose and easily slide up and down.

Install the pushrods with the cups facing upward, making sure to add assembly lube on the tops of the lifters beforehand.

Installation

So, for hydraulics, the first thing to do is to use assembly lube liberally inside the lifter bores and the lifters, including the bottom of them. Then install all 12 lifters. With the rocker assembly removed, position all 12 lifter rods in place through the appropriate holes. Rotate the lifters a

ENGINE ASSEMBLY

With the new pushrods installed correctly and the lifters not binding in their holes, you are ready to install the rocker assembly.

bit in their new home.

My machine shop checked my old lifters and decided new ones would cost the same as grinding the old ones. If you have the same situation, there is no need to take them apart and put oil in them. They pump up almost right away during operation, and it is not needed for a proper initial adjustment anyway. In fact, I haven't even put oil in this engine yet. The idea of an initial adjustment is to get you close so you aren't so hard on the engine. Once you have it initially adjusted, you can follow these same steps with oil in the warm engine.

Loosen all the adjustment screws on the rockers and back off the rockers most of the way so that there is plenty of adjustment room available. Keep them loose for now.

Install the rocker assembly on the head. Install it as a unit, making sure the center oil tube goes down into the head. Be sure to have it all pre-assembled correctly using the appropriate rockers, springs, washers, etc., as described in chapter 3. Tighten down the six assembly bolts, making sure everything lines up. Don't force anything.

Do not bend the pushrods, and make sure to set each rocker assembly ball into the top of the rod before tightening. Lots happening here, so take it slow and easy. (Review the instructions on how to mark your flywheel in chapter 10.) Each marking set is 120 degrees from the other. The flywheel installs only one way, so you can use this to your advantage.

With the head on the engine block, there are several ways to determine when the pistons are at the top of their cycle. One way is to insert a plastic straw into the spark plug hole and try to gauge where the top is.

Another method is to mark the flywheel.

Yet another way is to install the distributor properly, then notice where the rotor is pointing.

I am not ready to install the distributor yet, so I am going to rely on the more precise flywheel method. Because I had the machine shop drill my crankshaft for a 7/16-inch bolt to hold the harmonic balancer, I needed an easy way to turn the engine. A 1/2-inch-drive ratchet and 5/8-inch socket is all I need to easily turn the

Hold the two pieces of the rocker assembly together and set it down straight on the head using the four hold-down bolts to secure its location. This isn't easy because the rockers tend to get in the way of the rods, but it can be done.

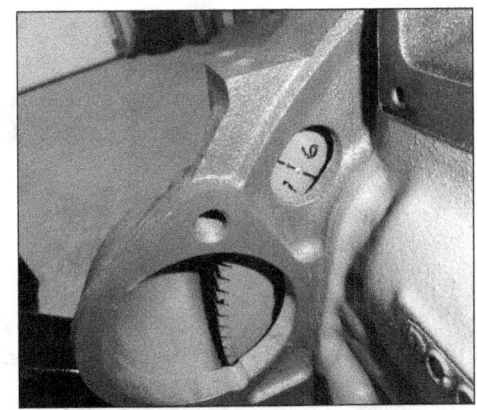

These old Stovebolts do not use markings on the harmonic balancer; they use flywheel markings. This example shows the ball bearing at 5 degrees before top dead center and pistons number-1 and number-6 at the top of their stroke.

CHAPTER 12

engine with the spark plugs out. It is even below the radiator.

Timing Theory

Before I get to the adjustment part, I'd like to discuss some of the theory behind the timing of these engines. When you turn the engine so that the ball bearing is visible in the window and 1/6 are also visible because you marked it that way, both the number-1 and number-6 cylinders are at the top of their cycle. (Actually, the upper center really is, but this is close enough for the initial adjustment of hydraulics). The system works on a 720-degree cycle.

So, the first full 360 degrees of rotation fulfills the intake/exhaust and firing cycles of half of the cylinders. The next full 360 degrees of rotation fulfills the intake/exhaust and firing cycles of the other half of the cylinders. So, it is not true that one rotation of your engine gets the job done. It takes two.

To understand how intake/exhaust and then firing take place, you need to know that the cam has lobes, and on the back of the lobes is the base circle. This base circle is where firing occurs.

So, how do you tell if the number-1 cylinder is at the top because it's firing or because it is on the intake/exhaust stroke? The lifters are not moving on the firing stroke. The lobe is 180 out, and the cam is on the base circle, or firing position.

So, to test this, for number-1 you rotate the engine off the ball bearing about 20 degrees clockwise and then rotate it counterclockwise the same amount while observing the number-1 rockers. If they move, you are at the firing stroke for number-6. If they do not move, you are at the firing stroke for number-1.

This is called "rocking" because one set of rockers for those two cylinders are rocking back and forth.

Adjustment

The biggest problem you are going to have in doing this is rotating your engine if you didn't opt for the bolt. You adjust the valves by using the slotted screw/lockdown on each rocker.

You start by adjusting the number-1 cylinder. Rotate the engine to the ball bearing and 1/6 marking.

Move the flywheel back and forth 20 degrees to determine which set of lifters is rocking. If number-1 is rocking, go another full 360 degrees. Now the number-1 lifters are not rocking, but number-6 is. This is the number-1 firing position and where you need to adjust both intake and exhaust valves. The pushrods should be relaxed and not touching the rocker assembly ball.

With your fingers, spin the number-1 pushrod while screwing down the adjustment. It becomes tighter when the ball of the rocker is up against the rod and the rocker is up against the valve stem. Now turn the screw another half turn tighter and lock it down. Keep the screwdriver oriented when you tighten so it doesn't move.

Perform this procedure for the other valve for the number-1 cylinder, and you have adjusted the hydraulic lifters for the number-1 cylinder. Next, queue up number-2 with number-5 and so on.

When you have all the valves adjusted properly, you can button up the side cover. This initial adjustment is necessary to get to initial startup.

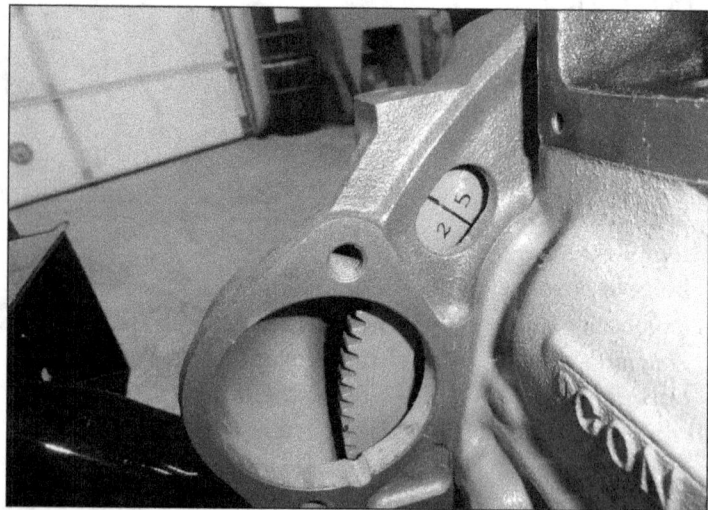

Here, pistons number-2 and number-5 are at the top of their stroke.

Here, pistons number-3 and number-4 are at the top of their stroke. Marking the flywheel in this way allows you to easily time the engine and adjust the valves.

ENGINE ASSEMBLY

Making a Balancer tool

If you did not opt for the 7/16-inch bolt to hold the harmonic balancer on the engine, you will be happier if you take the time to make a special tool for turning your engine.

With these engines, one of the first things you notice is that there is no good way to turn it over without the starter. This tool fits inside the hole in the balancer and allows you to use a socket with a breaker bar to turn the engine over. It's also great for vehicles that have the hand crank hole in the grill. ∎

This unique harmonic balancer tool allows you to use a socket and breaker bar to turn the engine from the front. This is the harmonic balancer end.

This is the socket end of the tool. I machined it with a Sharpie and a Makita grinder so it isn't perfect, but a 3/4 socket will turn the engine nicely.

Here is the tool in action. The radiator has to be higher than the center of the balancer because the original engine has a hand crank. Now you even have clearance (on a 1947–1955 GM truck) after all of the sheet metal is assembled.

Spinning the pushrod with your fingers to gauge the resistance is a good way to determine if you are on top dead center or 180 degrees out.

TECH TIP: Valve Adjustments

The following list helps you figure out which valves to adjust.

- 1/6 with number-6 rocking, adjust number-1
- 2/5 with number-2 rocking, adjust number-5 (1st clockwise rotation of 360 degrees)
- 3/4 with number-4 rocking, adjust number-3
- 1/6 with number-1 rocking, adjust number-6
- 2/5 with number-5 rocking, adjust number-2 (2nd clockwise rotation of 360 degrees)
- 3/4 with number-3 rocking, adjust number-4 ∎

CHAPTER 12

Hard Lines

At this point, you have about 90 percent of the engine rebuild done, but there is more to do. You need to bend up some hardlines for PCV, oil, fuel, and vacuum advance. I recommend using stainless steel for the lines. It's the last time you will ever have to service those lines.

Stainless comes with two challenges: It's hard to bend it, and it's hard to straighten it. A BrakeQuip tube straightener and a BrakeQuip tubing bender is fully adjustable for all sizes in one tool. The hardest part is deciding where you need to cut, bend, shape, etc.

With the water pump adapter in place, you have about 3/8 inch of space for the PCV hard line. Of course, you don't have to use hard lines, but it's not good that the rubber breathes. (Because I am testing PCV valves to determine which one is best suited for the engine, I didn't want any anomalies.) The placement of the fuel line is different with a newer-style Rochester B, so you need the correct-profile 5/16-inch fuel line. The vacuum advance line should be bent to follow the fuel line as much as possible.

A tubing bender is really handy. This BrakeQuip version has a tab to insert in the vise to hold it and an Allen set screw for adjusting the thickness of the tubing. The only downside is that it doesn't have an index or any way to tell how far to bend, which takes some getting used to.

The fuel pump I purchased for this project is the correct one, but I do not like that the inlet and outlet are not across from each other. So, I changed to a glass-bowl type. It has connections across from each other and enables me to see the fuel.

Straightening stainless steel tube is not easy. This tool makes it a breeze.

This flaring tool eliminates the problem of slippage while making these flares. It is essential for stainless steel.

This is an example of the PCV hard line that goes from the PCV valve on the other side of the engine to the intake manifold's vacuum port.

ENGINE ASSEMBLY

Notice the stainless steel fuel line to the carb and the PCV line. These tools also work great for fuel, brake, and vacuum advance lines.

This is a really intelligently designed bender. It is fully adjustable through all of the normal-diameter tubing and has a tab for clamping into a vise.

You can see the differences between the in and out ports on pre-1953 glass-type pumps and post-1953 mechanical ones. If you replace a fuel pump with the wrong one, it still works, but the hard lines need to be tweaked to fit properly.

A spin-on oil filter with the machine shop's full-flow oil modification ensures that 100 percent of the oil is filtered 100 percent of the time.

When you order from an auto parts store these days, you never know which style of inlet/outlet you will get. I suggest making a few extra adapter lines so that if you order a fuel pump for your 235 engine and you receive the wrong style, you can still use it by substituting your two adapter lines.

After researching this annoyance, it turns out that the 1942–1953 fuel pumps have the lines across from each other and the newer 1954–1962s have them offset. Get an older fuel pump if you want them straight across.

This engine is special in that it is a sealed system. The road draft tube is replaced with PCV, the valve cover cap is replaced with a filtered and vented cap, and a full-flow modification is used for the oil. These engines were notorious for gumming up the rocker assembly and causing no flow to the rockers or valves. This can be avoided by filtering 100 percent of the oil and closing it to outside dirt.

The oil lines that come out of the block are now (after the machine shop modification) 3/8-inch NPT. Add a brass 3/8-inch NPT extension on the oil pump outlet to keep it away from the engine block, then add a 4-inch 3/8-inch NPT stainless pipe with a stainless 3/8-inch NPT tee connection. This moves the rubber/stainless lines away from the hot exhaust and has a good oil pressure gauge connection. That is done with a 3/8-inch-NPT to 1/8-inch-NPT adapter on the gauge end of the tee.

Go with stainless braided rubber hose made for this purpose. You can buy it from Summit Racing and other suppliers in any length. The best connectors for this purpose are –6ANs. You simply purchase adapters for the Trans-Dapt spin-on filter to go from the original 1/2-inch NPT to –6AN. You use the –6AN for 3/8-inch NPT adaptations. These connectors eliminate the worry about the adapters coming loose

CHAPTER 12

The full-flow oil modification allows use of 3/8-inch lines for a constant flow of oil to all engine parts.

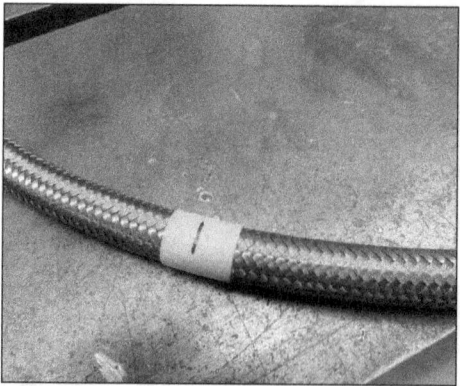

Cutting this braided stainless rubber hose is difficult because the hose ends require a crisp hose end. By using tape and a Makita grinder with a thin cutoff disc, you can cut through the middle of the tape easily.

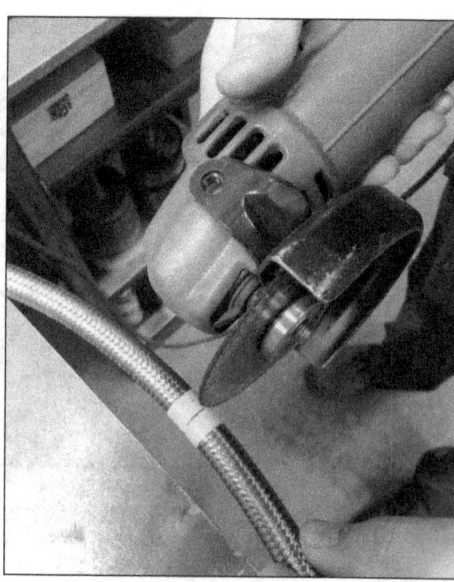

Cut around the hose, removing the stainless steel braiding first.

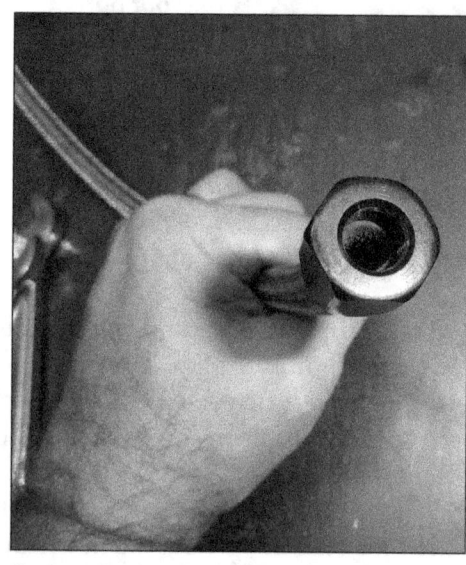

Screw the hose into the hose end until the hose is bottomed out as shown here.

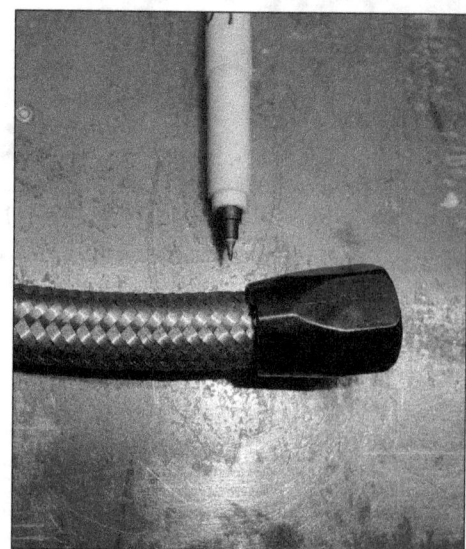

Mark at the junction so you can tell if the hose backs back out while installing the rest of the hose end.

while driving. The first tip to success is knowing that they come apart.

Next, you need to know how to cut this braided rubber hose and have an edge smooth enough to install the connector. Oh, trust me, this is the hard part!

Measure the length of hose you need and then apply two or three tight rounds of masking tape around the center of the mark. This keeps both sides of the tape tight so the stainless doesn't unravel.

Next, with a thin cutoff disk on your Makita grinder, make the cut. Go slow and easy, turning it as you cut through to the rubber so there are no loose ends. Once the cut is finished, you can remove the tape and screw on the connector.

After the connector is screwed on all the way so you can see that the rubber is right up against the threads, make a mark at the end of the connector, then screw the other part of the connector into the hose assembly. The mark verifies that the hose does not back out when you screw the connector together. That is a very secure connection. AN connectors are used heavily in automotive applications today because they do not leak and are easily removed.

Those outside oil lines are crucial, so no skimping on quality here! The stainless braiding provides a finished appearance, and you don't have to invest in any special tools or have special hydraulic lines made for this purpose.

Remember that the path of the oil has dramatically changed with the full-flow modification. Oil comes directly from the pickup in the bottom of the oil pan, through the oil pump, and directly out of the block into the filter. After it exits the filter, the oil then does its job on vital engine parts, and then the flow is the same.

Spark Plugs and Plug Wires

The plugs I chose for this project are new ACDelco R45 plugs. I gapped them to the spec of .040. I later discovered, during extensive performance testing, that E3-52 spark plugs with a fixed .040 gap provide better fuel economy and better oxygen stats, so they are now my preferred plugs.

Whichever plugs you decide are better for your application, be sure to use the washers that come with them, and tighten to 25 ft-lbs, which is the spec.

For plug wires, you can use an Accel kit to shorten them yourself. You can get a little less than 2 ohms per wire if you shorten them properly. These kits are fine, but they require a special tool that you may not have.

I decided to use an Accel crimper/cutter tool. It comes with the plug wire dies and crimp-on wire connector dies in two different types. It works well.

I never really understood the need for plug wire kits where you had to put the ends on by yourself. All these years I have purchased plug wires already made. Go figure! These wires are suitable for both stock ignition systems and HEI.

It is important that you do not nick the center conductor while stripping, so the tool really helps. Put the boot on first with dielectric grease. That allows you to slide the boot up and down as needed. Cut 5/8 inch off the end to expose the center conductor, then install the metal end per the instruction sheet, leaving 1/16-inch gap between the top and bottom of the barrel. You may have to tweak the metal barrel so that it inserts into the crimper properly, but take it slow and don't get in a hurry.

This tool made by Accel allows you to cut and crimp your own plug wires. You have better performance and lower ohm values when the wires are shorter. This allows you to customize the length.

This crimper does a great job in crimping around the pliable silicone wire.

Use dielectric grease to make sure you can install the boots after the crimping.

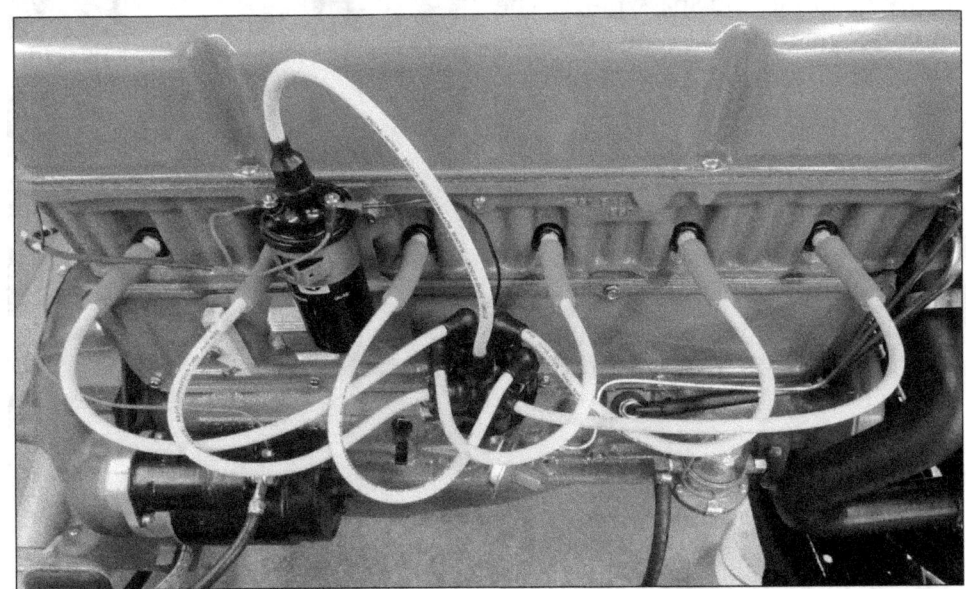

Here is the result of customizing the spark plug wire lengths.

CHAPTER 12

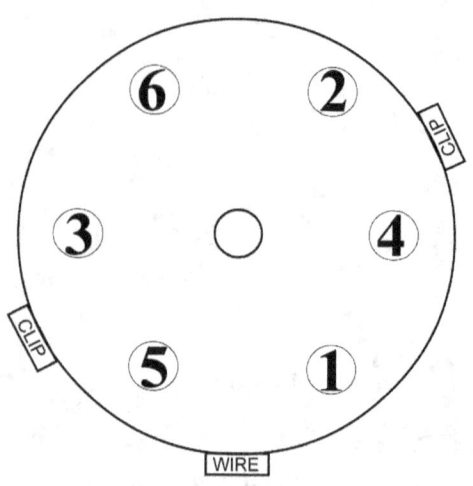

This is the correct orientation when installing plug wires and installing the distributor properly.

on to filling the engine with fluids. It's one of the last things on the list.

First, verify that you have no water leaks anywhere in your system before you put the oil in. Two places that give you the ability to bypass the thermostat and add water to the engine are the water temp sensor at the top of the head and the heater inlet to the water pump. The water pump connection is probably the easiest to access, but whichever location you choose, open the drain cock on the driver's side back of the block, and fill your engine with water. No anti-freeze yet.

Once you have added about 2 quarts of water, it should begin coming out of the drain cock. Use a pan to catch it. It is important to open the drain cock to be sure it is open. The last two engines that came back from two separate machine shops, had a plug in the drain-cock hole, and no water came out.

If you have this problem, twist a length of .040-gauge safety wire to root around through the hole. Eventu-

With an ohm meter, measure each one; it should read less than 2 ohms or so. The longer the wire is, the higher ohm value, but they should each measure close to the same. In this example, short ones were 1.80 ohms; long ones were 1.94 ohms. It's good to test each one so you are not surprised when one of your cylinders isn't receiving spark.

If you do not plan on turning over the engine by hand, you are ready to install the spark plugs. The engine can turn by hand with the spark plugs out, but with them in, compression is taking place, making it harder to turn over. If your engine is at the number-1 top dead center firing position, you may be close enough to the initial run-up to install them.

You are also not ready to put the distributor in yet permanently. This is because you have some oil priming to do.

Water and Oil

Once you have set up the fuel, water, and oil lines, you can move

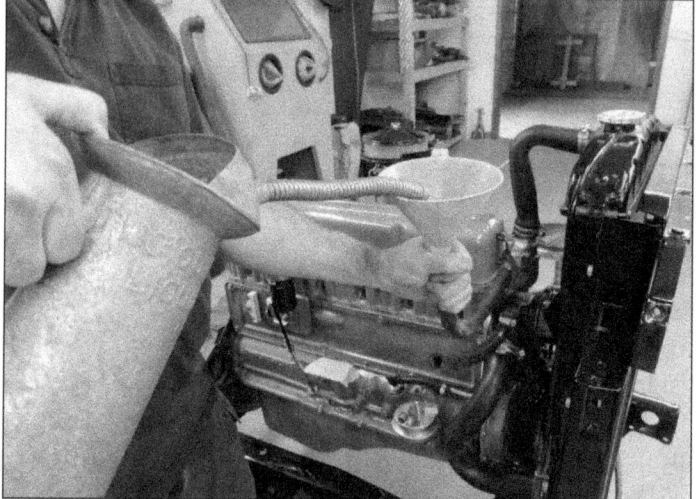

One method for filling the engine with water is to keep the heat sensor plug out of the head and watch until water flows over the top of that plug hole. Then tighten the heat sensor plug and put the hoses back together.

A good engine break-in oil is essential for the first engine run. This engine takes 6 quarts with the filter installed.

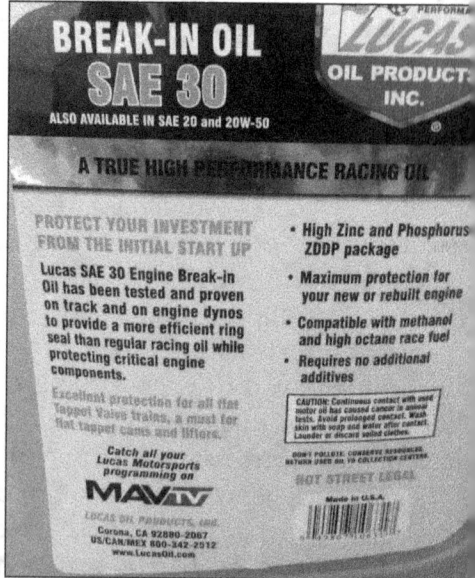

Here are the specifications for the break-in oil.

ENGINE ASSEMBLY

ally (it took me an hour this time) the water flows, and black crud comes out.

To be fair, machine shops work on all kinds of engines and may not necessarily understand a particular anomaly associated with a Chevy 235 engine. Be sure your instructions are clear and, even then, have some safety wire handy.

The good reason you are putting water in the engine first is so that you can be sure there is no water in the oil, no leaks on the floor from anywhere, etc. After the engine is full of water, wait a day to pull the oil pan plug, inspect the floor for water, etc. You should be good to go. If not, you need to address any problem right away.

If the water jackets are holding, now on first run-up there is water in your engine. If you want to add anti-freeze, use the drain cock on the back of the engine for draining.

With a full-flow oil system such as this, make sure all the hoses are connected properly. You need 6 quarts of oil for this configuration. One in the filter, 5 in the engine or until the dipstick tells you to stop. When you put in the oil, pour it over the entire valve and rocker assembly without the valve cover (it needs to be off for the next procedure anyway). Check for leaks or anything that could mess up a full-engine run. You want to do whatever preventative maintenance is required before the initial engine break-in.

Engine Break-In

I prefer to do the initial break-in (also called run-up) procedure with Lucas SAE 30 break-in oil. Brad Penn is good for this too. Both meet all the break-in requirements. They have extra zinc and other additives

Set up the choke and throttle cables prior to the run-up. Install them on a test stand if you have one. If the engine is on the chassis, be sure you can access the choke linkage for manual control. Also be sure to have the accelerator spring on the throttle control, so it doesn't go to maximum RPM upon starting.

This is the correct orientation for the distributor cap. The rotor points to number-1 and the flywheel reveals the ball bearing in the center of the display window.

Hold the electric drill straight and wait for the top rocker holes on each cylinder to weep a little oil. They do not spurt; they just weep.

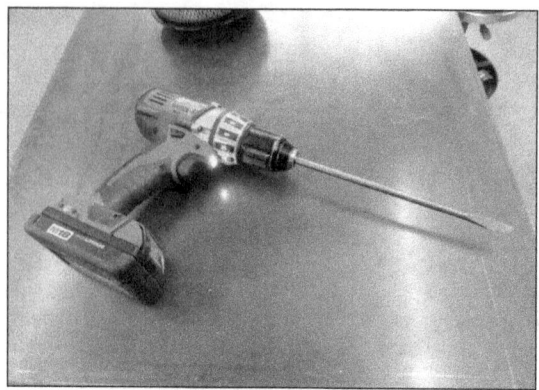

Break the handle off a large screwdriver. You use it to make sure that oil is circulating properly to vital engine parts. The slot at the bottom of the distributor hole is where you manually prime the oil system. You can also use this to test oil pressure; if you run the drill at maximum RPM, the gauge reads maximum oil pressure.

A vacuum gauge is a quick way to assess timing on the fly. You can look at the gauge and turn the distributor if necessary to achieve the highest vacuum.

I made a Start Kart that has the gauges, battery, and fuel tank on it. That way I can push it up to any non-running vehicle and run tests. I use it for the initial run-up.

to help with seating the rings, cams, lifters, etc. You pre-fill the oil filter, then add enough for a good reading on the dipstick. Check the oil often throughout this process and add more when needed. Of course, before initial run-up, make sure the valves are adjusted cold (with engine off) so they are in the ballpark.

Also run the oil pump using a screwdriver without the handle in an electric drill to get all the oil flowing where needed. The last place oil is sent is to the rocker assembly, so if you have oil at all the rockers, you can be sure oil flow is good throughout the system.

You use the drill by chucking in the screwdriver and placing it inside the distributor hole all the way, which engages the oil pump slot. Rotating this slot clockwise pumps the oil at about the same rate as the engine does by itself. In fact, you can attach a pressure gauge and see an accurate reading. This test is important! You need to see oil weeping from each rocker arm oil hole. If you do not, there is something wrong. Be patient, it takes about a minute for the oil to start weeping from those holes.

Ensure that your distributor is installed so that it is in the number-1 firing position. (I prefer the five o'clock position on the distributor with the distributor wire connection facing directly away from the block.) You install the distributor with the rotor facing at about six o'clock because the cam gear will move it back. Set the oil pump drive at the bottom with a screwdriver, so this is allowed to happen. Remember, with the valves of number-6 rocking, number-1 is in firing position, thus where you install the distributor.

Prior to starting the engine,

Fire-Up Checklist

You are almost ready to fire up the engine. You want to be prepared. The following are a few things to think about.

- Prior to the run, have a known good carburetor full of gas with a fuel system supplying fresh gas.
- Have the water level full in both the block and the radiator with no air pockets in the engine.
- Have the timing as close to optimal as you can. Once started, raise the RPM and do not play with the timing during this initial run if the timing is okay. If you hook up a vacuum gauge to the intake, you can keep the distributor slightly loose and simply turn it a little to have it timed closer on the fly. Maximum vacuum pressure is a close indicator. Do not make changes during these first 20 minutes. This break-in procedure is not for that purpose.
- Prime the oil system with a drill and have the valve cover off to be sure oil is circulating to the top of the engine. If you have hydraulic lifters, rotate the engine two full revolutions while running the oil pump to get them pumped up. Two turns get you back to the point where you removed the distributor.
- Have the rockers adjusted. Loose is better than tight if you err on the safe side.
- Create some exhaust with a muffler, even if temporary. You need to hear the engine and what's going on with it.
- Mount some temporary gauges under the hood or on the engine. They keep you from running back to the cab to check. It's also a good way to double-check the factory gauges.
- Have a charged battery, heavy cables, clean grounds, and a quick way to disable the battery if needed.
- Have a garden hose handy to cool the radiator if needed. It's best to keep it running and not turn it off and on.
- Have a fire extinguisher handy.
- Keep your work area clear and do not try this in a garage without the necessary ventilation equipment.
- Get a good oil made specifically for break-in procedures. They have additives that help with the break-in.
- Do not walk away from the engine while it's running. Stay alert! ∎

Break-in Compression Numbers

The post–break-in compression numbers for this engine were:

- Number-1   117 psi
- Number-2   117 psi
- Number-3   123 psi
- Number-4   117 psi
- Number-5   120 psi
- Number-6   117 psi

Of course, the post–break-in compression numbers change (increase) once the break-in oil has been replaced with regular 10W30.

The oil pressure remained at a constant 30 psi during the entire test. ∎

CHAPTER 12

Tech Tip

Much has been written on how to properly time these engines to get the best performance. The truth is, these are wonderfully simple engines and my favorite way to time them is by ear. Here is the procedure:

1. With the engine at idle, loosen the sideways screw in the back of the distributor just enough to be able to move it with some effort.
2. Listen to the engine and its RPM. Rotate the distributor slightly both ways until you get the fastest RPM possible. Once you have it running at its highest RPM, turn the distributor counterclockwise about 5 degrees (about the width of a spark plug wire).
3. Tighten the distributor screw again and call it a day! I find this every bit as accurate as timing lights or vacuum gauge methods once you get the hang of how much 5 degrees is. ∎

set up a vacuum gauge. This is a quick way to get your timing in the ballpark. Also, when you are shooting for a flawless 20-minute run, this helps stabilize the engine as soon as possible. The procedure is to hook the vacuum gauge to the intake manifold. The PCV valve has a second unused port on it so you initially plug the PCV valve; it's essentially directly to the intake.

Engine Break-In Review

During this initial break-in, I could have done a few things better. So, in the interest of helping you do it right the first time, here are a few tips:

A freshly rebuilt carb that you have never seen run before could present a few issues. In my case, I forgot to screw the jet all the way in and found it on the bottom of the carb bowl. Even so, adjustments in the floats and needle valve were necessary to get it running decent. It's a good idea to use a known good carb.

The distributor had a rubber O-ring on the shaft. NAPA sells rebuilt ones with this O-ring. If you try to install the distributor with the O-ring, it can fool you into thinking the distributor is all the way down and seated in the oil pump, when in fact it is not. The rotor even turns properly. If you do not have less than about 3/8 inch of distributor shaft showing from the top of the shaft to the top of the vacuum advance bracket, it is not in far enough. Therefore, you want to watch the oil pressure carefully throughout the procedure. If your distributor has a big O-ring anywhere on the shaft, remove it. It doesn't belong there.

Be sure the flywheel is torqued down, and the retainer tabs are bent properly. Always do a double-check of all bolts, etc., prior to the run-up. In my case, no damage was done, but it started making noise, and I was pleased that it was just the loose flywheel.

Even with proper exhaust-venting hose and other precautions, a lot of smoke is generated from oil on hot surfaces, such as the exhaust-venting hose becoming hot and clouding up your shop. It is best to perform this 20-minute run outside. If you can't, be sure that the ventilation fans are running, and wear proper safety gear.

At 2,000 rpm, with the valve cover removed, oil spews everywhere, but you should keep it off until you see good oil flow to the rockers. Then carefully place the valve cover back on. I set it in place, but I didn't bolt it down. I got away with this because of a secret: Fel-Pro makes two thicknesses of gaskets for the valve cover. One is 5/32 inch and one is 7/32 inch (part number VS-50190C). Use high-temperature gasket sealer and seal the 7/32-inch gasket to the head. This creates a dam for the oil, so it stays within the boundaries of the gasket. I don't put gasket sealer on the valve cover, just on the head for this purpose.

The break-in run was 20 minutes at 2,000 rpm with the last 5 minutes slowly raised to 2,250 rpm. Everything aside, it went rather well, and I did not have to do anything during the run except keep an eye on things. In the end, the exhaust fumes were clear, no smoke, and there was no blow-by apparent at the valve cover cap. The spark plugs had a little soot on them, which I attribute to it being a vintage engine with a one-size-fits-all carb jet.

To see this initial runup, check out the YouTube video named 235 Initial Break-in Run. For more information on how to properly install the distributor, check out the YouTube video named HEI Kit Installation. There are even more videos found on these engines when you search YouTube for Deves Technet. For discussions on all aspects of these engines and restoration topics, join the conversation at forums.devestechnet.com.

APPENDIX

The following information is by no means a complete document, and there is much more to learn. If you suspect your engine to be original, the GM Heritage Center can provide you with an online package pertaining to your specific vehicle complete with letter/number combinations.

1942–1962 GM Engine Casting Numbers

The chart below lists the engine casting numbers and should help you arrive at the make, year, and displacement of your engine.

Number	Make	Year	Displacement (ci)
839910	Chevrolet	1942–1951	216
389770	Chevrolet	1942–1951	216
839770	Chevrolet	1942–1953	216
3835253	Chevrolet	1942–1953	216
3835794	Chevrolet	1942–1953	216
3835497	Chevrolet	1942–1953	216
3835849	Chevrolet	1942–1953	216
3897702	Chevrolet	1942–1953	216
3835527	Chevrolet	1951	216
3835353	Chevrolet	1948–1952	216
3835894	Chevrolet	1953	216
837751	Chevrolet	1942–1949	235
839931	Chevrolet	1942–1949	235
3693374	Chevrolet	1942–1949	235
3835309	Chevrolet	1942–1949	235
3835335	Chevrolet	1942–1949	235
3835374	Chevrolet	1942–1949	235
8397715	Chevrolet	1942–1949	235
3629703	Chevrolet	1950–1952	235
3692703	Chevrolet	1950–1952	235
3692708	Chevrolet	1950–1952	235
3692713	Chevrolet	1950–1952	235
3835692	Chevrolet	1950–1952	235
3701946	Chevrolet	1953	235
3835846	Chevrolet	1953	235
3835946	Chevrolet	1953	235
3783949	Chevrolet	1953–1954	235
3701481	Chevrolet	1954	235
3702436	Chevrolet	1954	235
3733949	Chevrolet	1955	235
3835911	Chevrolet	1955	235
3843363	Chevrolet	1953–1955	235
3773949	Chevrolet	1954	235
3835363	Chevrolet	1954	235
3835491	Chevrolet	1954	235
3835949	Chevrolet	1954	235
3733946	Chevrolet	1954–1955	235
3835917	Chevrolet	1954–1955	235
3858190	Chevrolet	1954–1955	235
3837004	Chevrolet	1955–1957	235
3856233	Chevrolet	1955	235
3836223	Chevrolet	1955–1957	235
3836233	Chevrolet	1955–1957	235
3836386	Chevrolet	1955–1957	235
3738307	Chevrolet	1958–1962	235
3738476	Chevrolet	1958–1962	235
3739716	Chevrolet	1958–1962	235
3764476	Chevrolet	1958–1962	235
3769716	Chevrolet	1958–1962	235
378307	Chevrolet	1960–1962	235
3702436	Chevrolet	1954	261
3703414	Chevrolet	1954–1956	261
3738813	Chevrolet	1956	261
3733950	Chevrolet	1955–1957	261
3837012	Chevrolet	1955–1957	261
3836340	Chevrolet	1955–1962	261
3769925	Chevrolet	1959–1962	261
3739365	Chevrolet	1958–1962	261
3759365	Chevrolet	1958–1962	261
3769717	Chevrolet	1958–1962	261

APPENDIX

1954–1962 Chevrolet Serial Numbers

The following information deciphers the serial number by listing the last letters in the engine serial number on the flat of the distributor deck.

Passenger Car

A	Regular production with standard 3-speed or overdrive
AE	Regular production with heavy-duty clutch (1119-1519 taxi cab)
B	Regular production with Powerglide (hydraulic lifters)
Z	Regular production engine
ZC	Regular production engine with heavy-duty clutch
ZH	Fleet engine with aluminum cam gear
ZJ	Fleet engine with aluminum cam gear and heavy-duty clutch
Y	Automatic transmission

Truck*

J	3100-3200-3800/CK 10-20, C30 regular production
JA	CK 10-20, C30 with RPO 311
JB	C10-20 with RPO 311
JC	4000 (31-32-36-3800 RPO 227)/C40 CK 10-20, C30 RPO 223
JD	CK10-20, C30-40 with RPO 225 (heavy-duty clutch)
JE	C1402 with RPO 232
JF	31-32-36-38-41-4400 with RPO 314 and 321
JG	P10 base engine
JH	P10 with RPO 311
JK	P10 with RPO 223
K	34-35-3700/P20-30
KA	34-35-3700 with RPO 321/P20-30 with RPO 321
L	6000/CLS50
LA	CS50 with RPO 225
LB	CLS60
LC	6000 with RPO 309/CS60 with RPO 225
LD	6000 with RPO 413/CL60 with RPO 413 and 585
LE	6000 with RPO 413 and 309/CLS60 with RPO 350
LF	T60 base engine
LG	T60 with RPO 350
LJ	CLS60 with RPO 309
LK	CLS60 with RPO 350 and Powermatic
LM	C60 with RPO 413 and 585 and Powermatic
LU	CLS60 with RPO 223
LV	CS60 with RPO 225 and heavy-duty clutch
LW	CLS60 with RPO 223 and power steering
LX	CL60 with RPO 223 and air brakes
LY	T60 with RPO 223
LZ	T60 with RPO 223 and power steering
M	31-32-36-3800-4000/CK10-20, C30-40 with RPO 408
MA	31-32-36-38-41-4400 with RPO 314, 321, and 408
MB	31-32-36-38-4000 with RPO 227 and 408/CK10-20, C30-40(RPO 409)
N	5000 regular production/L50 with RPO 408
NA	5000 with RPO 309/L60 with RPO 408
NC	5000 with RPO 413
ND	5000 with RPO 309 and 413/T60 with RPO 408
P	6000 with RPO 408/C50-S50 with RPO 408
PA	6000 with RPO 309 and 408/C60-S60 with RPO 408
PB	C50-S50 with RPO 409
PC	6000 with RPO 408 and 413/C60-S60 with RPO 409
PD	6000 with RPO 309, 408, and 413
PJ	C60 with RPO 223 and 418
PK	C60 with RPO 223, 408, 413-585
PL	C60 with RPO 223, 408, 413-585
PM	L60 with RPO 223 and 408
PN	L60 with RPO 223 and 418
PQ	L60 with RPO 223, 408 and 413-585
PR	L60 with RPO 223, 408 and 413-585
PS	T60 with RPO 223 and 408
R	7000 regular production (5000 with RPO 418)
RA	7000 with RPO 309 (5000 with RPOs 309 and 418)
RC	5-7000 with RPO 413 and 585
RD	5-7000 with RPO 309, 413, and 585
S	8000 regular production (6000 with RPO 418)
SA	8000 with RPO 309 (6000 with RPOs 309 and 418)
SC	6-8000 with RPO 309, 413, and 585
SD	6-8000 with RPO 413 and 585
T	9000 regular production (7000 with RPO 385)
TA	9000 with RPO 309
TB	M70-C70-S70-C80 with RPO 409
TC	T70-T80
TD	C-L-70-80-M-S-70 with RPO 309
TE	T70-80 with RPO 309
TF	CL70-80, MS70, S67 with RPO 385
U	10000 regular production (excludes 10800)
UA	10000 (excludes 8800-10800) with RPO 309
V	R10 base engine
VA	R10 with RPO 225
WR	10 with RPO 667
WA	R10 with RPO 225 and automatic transmission

* All solid-lifter engines

APPENDIX

235 & 261 Torque Specifications

Location	Size	Ft-Lbs Minimum	Ft-Lbs Maximum
Camshaft Thrust Plate Screws	1/4-20	6	7.5
Connecting Rod Bolts	3/8-24	35	45
Cylinder Head Bolts (oiled)	1/2-13	90	95
Exhaust Manifold to Cylinder Head (center)	3/8-16	25	30
Exhaust Manifold to Cylinder Head (ends)	3/8-16	15	20
Fan Blade Assembly to Flange	5/16-24	15	20
Flywheel to Crankshaft	7/16-20	55	65
Flywheel Housing Plate Cover	1/4-20	10	12
Flywheel Housing to Crankcase	7/35-14	45	55
Intake Manifold to Cylinder Head	3/8-16	25	35
Main Bearing Cap Bolts (oiled)	1/2-13	100	110
Oil Pan to Crankcase Screw	5/16-18	12.5	15
	1/4-20	6	7.5
Oil Pan Drain Plug	Special	25	30
Oil Pump Cover to Body	1/4-20	6	9
Pulley to Balancer Hub	3/8-16	15	20
Rocker Arm Cover to Cylinder Head	1/4-20	20 inch-pounds	25 inch-pounds
Temperature Indicator Thermal Unit	1/2-Pipe	15	20
Spark Plugs	14 mm	25	25
Carburetor Nuts	3/8-24	15	20
Water Pump Bolts	3/8-16	25	35
Thermostat Housing	3/8-16	25	35
Oil Filter Bolt	7/16-20	50	60
Starter Bolts	1/2-13	20	30
Generator Bolts	5/16-24	15	20
Fuel Pump Bolts	5/16-18	10	15

Head Torque Pattern

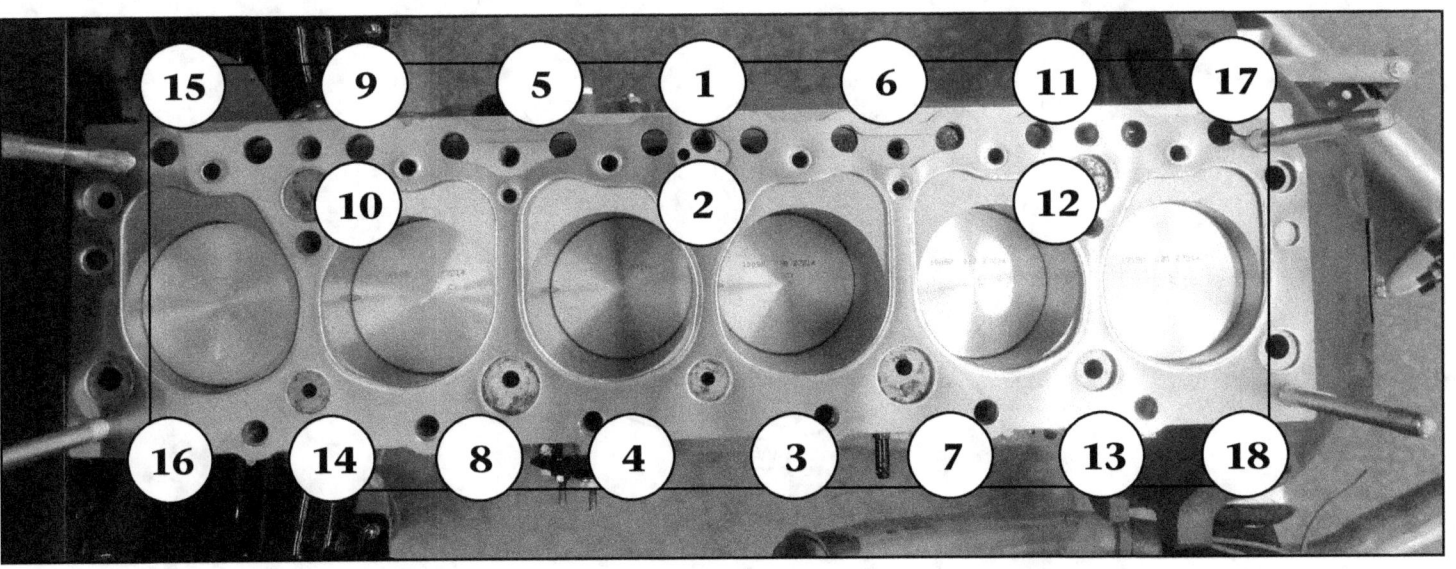

CHEVROLET INLINE-6 ENGINE 1929–1962: HOW TO REBUILD

APPENDIX

1960 Tune-Up Specifications

Note 1: Ignition Timing—4° BTDC with spark vacuum line disconnected (cover opening on manifold)

Note 1A: Ignition Timing—5° BTDC with first short radial mark clockwise from top dead center timing ball

Engine	Compression Pressure (Cranking)	Spark Plugs Make and Number	Ignition Distributor Point Gap	Ignition Distributor Spark Plug Gap	Ignition Distributor Tappet Clearance	Ignition Timing	Oil Pressure	Engine Idle RPM
Thriftmaster L-6 Engine–235	130 psi (min.)	AC-44 E3.52	.018	AC-44=.035 E3.52=.040	Intake=.006 Exhaust=.018	5°BTDC (see note 1A)	30 to 35 psi at 2,000 rpm	475
Thriftmaster Special (Updraft)	130 psi (min.)	AC-44 E3.52	.018	AC-44=.035 E3.52=.040	Intake=.006 Exhaust=.018	5°BTDC (see note 1A)	30 to 35 psi at 2,000 rpm	475
Jobmaster L-6 Engine–261	130 psi (min.)	AC-44 E3.52	.018	AC-44=.035 E3.52=.040	Intake=.006 Exhaust=.020	Top Dead Center	30 to 35 psi at 2,000 rpm	475

Distributor Orientation and Firing Order

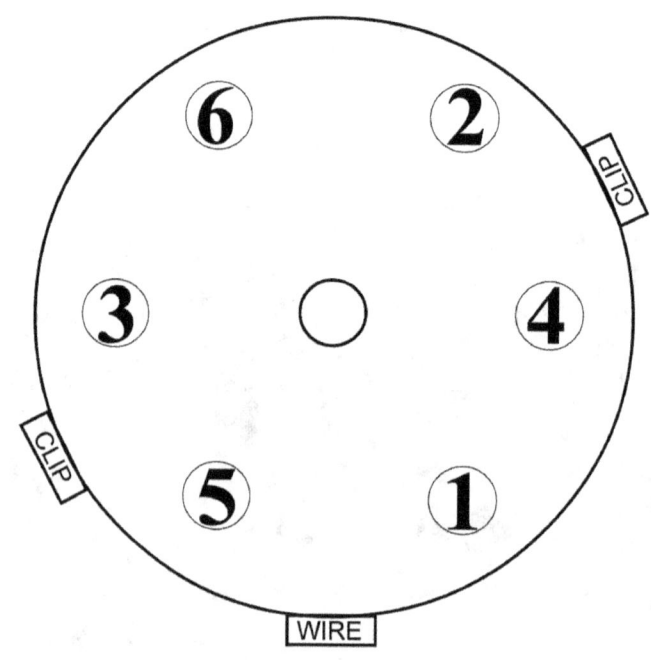

APPENDIX

Solid Lifter Adjustments

So you just laid down a lot of cash to get your precious StoveBolt ready for the road. You followed all the procedures in the text and want to get this engine tuned as perfectly as possible. Let's get started!

Valve Cover Gaskets

Fel-Pro makes two different thicknesses of valve cover gaskets: 5/32 inch and 7/32 inch. Get the thicker one for these engines. Use gasket sealer to seal the gasket to the head. This creates an oil dam and keeps the oil in. Do not put sealer at all on the top of the gasket. This way you can remove it when you need to without purchasing a new one if you are careful. Since these engines are installed in the vehicle at a 3-degree back slant, often people mistake a rear valve cover leak for a rear main oil leak because of incorrectly installing this gasket. ∎

Let's decide if you have hydraulic or solid lifters. If you haven't done the rebuild yet, we need to know for sure which one you have. To find out which you have, you can either: get another side cover gasket and remove the side cover or get another valve cover gasket and remove the valve cover.

The difference between hydraulic and solid lifters is easy to spot. If the top of the lifter has a clip, like a keeper to keep the hydraulic parts inside, it's hydraulic. If the top of the lifter is cone-shaped and has no clips at the very top, it's solid.

With the side cover removed, it will be obvious. With only the valve cover removed, shine a flashlight down a push rod hole and see if you can see any clips on the top of your lifters. That is the physical way to tell. And it's best because people have been known to put hydraulic lifters in a solid lifter engine block. The other way is through the casting number database in appendix 1.

Procedure for Adjusting Solid Lifters

The steps for adjusting the hydraulic lifter is documented in the body of the book. Here we will do the same for solid lifters. This should be done with a warm engine, but to ballpark it very close it's okay to do cold.

Turn the engine until you see the steel ball bearing (like a BB) in the flywheel line up with the pointer. Carefully remove the distributor cap by holding it in place and gently prying the two spring clips off with a screwdriver. Lift the cap away and see if the outer tip of the rotor is pointing in the same position as the number-1 plug wire occupied in the distributor cap. It may well be 1/2 turn away (180 degrees). If that is the case, turn the engine one full revolution until

APPENDIX

the steel ball is again lined up in the window with the pointer and the rotor tip is pointing toward where the number-1 plug wire goes.

The first two rockers should be slightly loose. If they are very loose, take your feeler gauge and unfold the .006- and .018-inch blades, fold up the rest, and tighten the nut so they're not sliding all over. See if the .018-inch blade will fit between the tip of the rocker and the first valve, then see if the .006-inch blade will fit between the number-2 valve; if not, take a box-end wrench and loosen the locknut on the far end of the adjuster, fit your screwdriver into the slotted screw, and adjust until the feeler gauge blade just lightly fits with a slight drag. Be aware that the angle you hold it at has a great affect on how accurate the adjustment is. Once you have it where you feel it's good, hold the screw from turning and tighten the locknut again with the box wrench, then recheck the adjustment. Use a close-end wrench for this to keep from sliding off when tightening. Snug is fine.

Once you've set the two front valves, count down the valves from front to back. There are 12 of them and the next one to adjust is number-3 to .006 inch (this is an intake valve) then on to number-5 to .018 inch (this is the number-3 cylinder exhaust valve). Next is number-7 to .006 inch (this is the number-4 intake valve) then on to number-9 set to .018 inch (this is the number-5 cylinder exhaust valve).

Do all of the above without turning the engine. You are halfway through. Now turn the engine one complete revolution until the steel ball lines up on the pointer in the window again; you're now on top dead center (TDC) of cylinder number-6, so let's do the other six valves in this order, working from front to back: valve number-12 to .018 inch, valve number-11 to .006 inch, then valve number-10 to .006 inch, then valve number-8 to .018 inch, next is number-6 to .006 inch, and lastly number-4 to .018 inch.

General Motors has varied the exhaust valve clearance for different engines over the years: 216s used .013 to .015 inch and 235s used .018 to .020 inch. It is always recommended to use the larger gap if the engine was to be run in severe service. That's what we do today with our higher road speeds and freeway driving. You're miles ahead if you set the intakes to .008 inch and the exhaust valves to .020 inch; they're supposed to clatter a bit!

This is information that is not obvious. It is easy to get confused as to which is intake and which is exhaust since they alternate. Per the diagram on page 139:

Cylinder 1

1–2: Exhaust then intake

Cylinder 2

3–4: Intake then exhaust

Cylinder 3

5–6: Exhaust then intake

Cylinder 4

7–8: Intake then exhaust

Cylinder 5

9–10: Exhaust then intake

Cylinder 6

11–12: Intake then exhaust

APPENDIX

S-A Design Work-A-Long Sheet©

DISASSEMBLY

Project Statistics

Your Name _____
Today's Date _____ Vehicle Engine Removed From _____
Engine Year _____ CI _____ Block Casting _____ ☐ 1 barrel

Accessories Attached to Used Engine

- ☐ A/C Pump
- ☐ Flywheel
- ☐ Starter
- ☐ Alternator
- ☐ Motor Mounts
- ☐ _____
- ☐ AIR Pump
- ☐ Clutch
- ☐ Fuel Pump
- ☐ Distributor
- ☐ Motor Mount Attaching Brackets
- ☐ Dipstick Tube
- ☐ AIR Distributor Lines and Hoses
- ☐ Flywheel
- ☐ Exhaust Manifold
- ☐ Coil
- ☐ All Bolts; except _____
- ☐ Water Pump
- ☐ Transmission
- ☐ All Pulleys; Except _____
- ☐ Carburetor

Operational Notes

Oil consumption _____ Compression check pressure variation _____ psi
Leak-down percent _____ Other observations _____

Disassembly Notations

Crank uses centerbolt	☐ Yes	☐ No
Heat riser restricted on	☐ Yes	☐ No
Head gaskets	☐ Copper	☐ Composition
Worn/damaged lifers	☐ No	☐ Yes; where _____

Vibration damper pulley screws ☐ 5/16
Location of timing-pointer attaching points: _____

Oil filter adapter type:
- ☐ Spin-on
- ☐ Long cartridge (late)
- ☐ Short cartridge (early)

Type of rear main seal:
- ☐ Rubber-two piece
- ☐ Rope (early)

INSPECTION

Initial Parts Inspection Observations

Block OK	☐ Yes	☐ No; describe problem _____
Heads OK	☐ Yes	☐ No; describe problem _____
Crank OK	☐ Yes	☐ No; describe problem _____
Bearings OK	☐ Yes	☐ No; describe problem _____
Pistons OK	☐ Yes	☐ No; describe problem _____
Cam/lifters OK	☐ Yes	☐ No; describe problem _____
Damper OK	☐ Yes	☐ No; describe problem _____
Intake manifold OK	☐ Yes	☐ No; describe problem _____
Exhaust manifold OK	☐ Yes	☐ No; describe problem _____
Oil pump OK	☐ Yes	☐ No; describe problem _____

APPENDIX

Oil pump/rear main cap mating surfaces damage/abnormalities ☐ No ☐ Yes
Identifying mark you placed on all part: _____

AT THE MACHINE SHOP
Parts Delivered to the Machine Shop

☐ Block   ☐ Main Caps   ☐ Crankshaft   ☐ Oil Pump   ☐ Oil Pump Pickup
☐ Connecting Rods   ☐ Pistons   ☐ Piston Rings   ☐ Camshaft   ☐ Lifters
☐ Vibration Damper   ☐ Main Bearings   ☐ Rod Bearings   ☐ Cam Bearings   ☐ Rod Bolts
☐ Gasket Set   ☐ Push Rods   ☐ Rockerarms   ☐ Head Bolts   ☐ Main Bolts/Studs
☐ Miscellaneous Nuts/Bolts/Brackets for Cleaning
☐ Water Pump   ☐ Timing Cover   ☐ Oil Pan   ☐ Flywheel
☐ Clutch   ☐ Exhaust Manifold   ☐ Motor Mounts   ☐ Motor Mount Attaching Brackets
☐ Assembled Head   ☐ Disassembled Head with: ☐ Valves   ☐ Springs ☐ Retainers   ☐ Keepers
                                                                ☐ Rocker Balls and Nuts
☐ Intake Manifold   ☐ With Heat Riser Shield ☐ Installed   ☐ Not Installed
☐ _____   ☐ _____   ☐ _____   ☐ _____
☐ _____   ☐ _____   ☐ _____   ☐ _____
☐ _____   ☐ _____   ☐ _____   ☐ _____
☐ Other Accessories _____

Special Instructions for Machine Shop

☐ Bore black   ☐ Use torque plates   ☐ Desired piston-to-wall clearance: 0._____-inch
☐ Grind crank   ☐ Rod bearing clearance: 0._____-inch   ☐ Main bearing clearance: 0._____-inch
☐ Deck to clean   ☐ Surface heads   ☐ Install cam bearings   ☐ _____
☐ _____   ☐ _____
☐ _____   ☐ _____

Is pilot bushing to be installed in crankshaft (required for manual transmission)? ☐ Yes ☐ No

After You Pick Up Your Parts

☐ Yes ☐ No   Threaded holes reconditioned/chased ☐ Yes ☐ No   Drilled holes and edges chamfered
☐ Yes ☐ No   Galleries tapped for screw-in plugs ☐ Yes ☐ No   Add 0.030-inch hole in gallery plug

PRE-ASSEMBLY FITTING
Measured and Recorded During Pre-Assembly Fitting

☐ Yes ☐ No   Do all valveguides have proper clearnce? If no, which are correct_____
☐ Yes ☐ No   Do all valveseats meet dimensional specs? If no, which are faulty_____
☐ Yes ☐ No   Do all valveseats hold solvent? If no, which leak_____
☐ Yes ☐ No   Have all valveguides been machined concentric for press-on seals?

Retainer to Valveguide clearance 0. _____-inch; adequate on all vales? ☐ Yes ☐ No   If no, which valves have insufficient clearance?_____

Recommended valvespring set pressure _____psi at_____-inch installed height.

Measured valvespring installed height:
1_____   3_____   5_____   7_____
2_____   4_____   6_____   8_____

CHEVROLET INLINE-6 ENGINE 1929–1962: HOW TO REBUILD

APPENDIX

Spring shims used to obtain correct installed height:

1_____ 3_____ 5_____ 7_____
2_____ 4_____ 6_____ 8_____

Measured valvespring solid height _____ -inches

Calculated compressed spring clearance:

1_____ 3_____ 5_____ 7_____
2_____ 4_____ 6_____ 8_____

Connecting rod bore OK?	☐ Yes ☐ No;	Which rods are defective _____	
Crank straightness OK?	☐ Yes ☐ No	Runout on center main of 0. _____ -inch	
Main bearing clearance OK?	☐ Yes ☐ No	Measured clearance 0. _____ -inch	
Crank thrust OK?	☐ Yes ☐ No	Measured clearance 0. _____ -inch	
Main bearing clearance OK?	☐ Yes ☐ No	Measured clearance 0. _____ -inch	
Camshaft bearing fit OK?	☐ Yes ☐ No;	Describe problem _____	
Block required clearance grinding for upper sprocket?	☐ ☐		
Pin end clearance OK?	☐ Yes ☐ No	Measured clearance 0. _____ -inch	
Piston-to-wall clearance OK?	☐ Yes ☐ No	Measured clearance 0. _____ -inch	
	Pistons with incorrect clearance _____		

Measured ring end gap:

1 Top_____ 2nd_____ **3** Top_____ 2nd_____ **5** Top_____ 2nd_____ **7** Top_____ 2nd_____

2 Top_____ 2nd_____ **4** Top_____ 2nd_____ **6** Top_____ 2nd_____ **8** Top_____ 2nd_____

Rod bearing clearance OK?	☐ Yes ☐ No	Measured clearance 0. _____ -inch
Rod side clearance OK?	☐ Yes ☐ No	Measured clearance 0. _____ -inch
Piston-to-head clearance OK?	☐ Yes ☐ No	Measured clearance 0. _____ -inch
	Cylinders with incorrect clearance _____	
Rotating assembly clearance OK?	Yes No	Cause of interference _____
Crank index OK?	Yes No	Maximum _____ ° out of index on journal no. _____
Cylinder-to-cylinder deck height accurate?	Yes No	Maximum 0. _____ -inch variation.
Rocker geometry OK?	Yes No;	Describe problem _____
Rocker-to-stud clearance OK?	Yes No	Maximum 0. _____ -inch (Intake); 0. _____ -inch (Exhaust);
Piston-to-valve clearance OK?	Yes No	Maximum 0. _____ -inch (Intake); 0. _____ -inch (Exhaust);
Oil pump drive clearance OK?	Yes No	Maximum clearance 0. _____ -inch
Intake manifold end-rail clearance OK?	Yes No	Maximum clearance 0. _____ -inch
Mainfold surface parallel with head?	Yes No	Describe problem _____
Pulleys/accessories aligned?	Yes No	Describe problem _____

_____
_____

Resources

Besides devestechnet.com, there are a few resources worth mentioning that help cover this subject.

To get a very nice package concerning your vintage Chevy, go to the GM Heritage Center:
https://www.gmheritagecenter.com/gm-heritage-archive/vehicle-information-kits.html

It takes some fishing, but the following sites have a lot of manuals that pertain to these vintage engines. There is great and sometimes obscure information that could prove to be very informative:
http://chevy.oldcarmanualproject.com/#year
http://www.oldirononline.com/

This site has been around forever and has some amazing articles and a great Bulletin Board (Forum) for discussion of these old Stovebolt engines:
http://inliners.org/

If you are looking for a very complete casting number database for all years of Stovebolts, here is a good resource:
http://www.1954advance-design.com/Stovebolt-engine/casting-numbers.html

My friend and mentor Dave Folsom has a blog concerning these engines that has a very important read here:
http://chev235guy.blogspot.com/

Interestingly, this is the only place I have seen actual torque specifications for just about every bolt on these engines. Well worth the read! My shop manual isn't this precise!
http://www.canadianmilitarypattern.com/1960%20235-261%20Engine%20Manual.htm

www.ingramcontent.com/pod-product-compliance
Lightning Source LLC
Chambersburg PA
CBHW081450070526
44586CB00019B/2298